THE  MONEY COULD BUY

THE COLLAPSE OF THE NEW YORK METS

Bob Klapisch and John Harper

RANDOM HOUSE • NEW YORK

Library of Congress Cataloging-in-Publication Data

Klapisch, Bob.

    The worst team money could buy : the collapse of the New York Mets / Bob Klapisch and John Harper.

      p. cm.

    ISBN 0-679-41975-6

    1. New York Mets (Baseball team)—History. I. Harper, John.

II. Title.

GV875.N45K56 1993

796.357'64'097471—dc20   92-56825

Design by ROBERT BULL DESIGN

Manufactured in the United States of America

9 8 7 6 5 4 3 2

First Edition

HARPER:
To Liz, Matt, and Christopher. Thanks for understanding.

KLAPISCH:
For you, Stephanie.

ACKNOWLEDGMENTS

To Random House editor David Rosenthal, copy editor Amy Edelman, and assistant Rebecca Beuchler, whose ideas, editing skills, and tireless effort were responsible for turning a couple of wise-guy baseball writers into authors.

To Esther Newberg of International Creative Management, whose style and business savvy helped find the right home for this project.

INTRODUCTION

The worst part about sportswriting is that it kills the fan in you. Baseball writing, especially. The thrill of a ninth-inning comeback becomes the agony of rewriting the lead to a game story sometimes before the winning run has even crossed the plate; the drama of extra innings becomes the torture of deadlines fast approaching. Rain delays become excuses for another god-awful press-room hot dog.

The games and stories become a blur. Interviews with the likes of Eddie Murray, only slightly less painful than a tax audit, take the mystique out of getting to know big leaguers. Inevitably, cynicism, the great press-box disease, claims another victim. Maybe it's always been this way, but surely the staggering rise in salaries and egos in recent years has stolen more of the allure from the writing end of it than ever.

All of which is a long-winded way of saying that the two of us, baseball romanticists turned tabloid reptiles, have written a book to get even.

It was either that or hours of therapy, and we didn't think the Mets would be willing to foot the bill. Never mind innocence lost; we're convinced that covering a team that, in recent years, qualifies as the most overpaid and underachieving—not to mention grumpiest—in baseball has left us in serious need of emotional repair.

We thought of suing the ball club. We considered trying to hold the franchise responsible for taking the fun out of baseball,

•

for ruining the dynasty that never was by dismantling the raunchy, rowdy, rollicking Mets of the eighties before the championship rings ever made it onto the players' fingers.

But we figured a book would be more fun. And it was.

There were so many stories to tell, stories we couldn't write for our newspapers—some because of their off-the-record nature at the time; some because we didn't have all the details until the news value had passed; some because of the day-to-day space limitations on the beat; and some because they didn't belong in a newspaper.

And then there was a story to tell as well: a season that symbolized all that is wrong with baseball in the nineties, from the outrageous salaries to the attitudes the money has created, to a manager and management consumed with image. It wasn't just one season, but the punctuation to an astonishing skid from the top for a ball club whose future once had seemed so bright.

So much has happened since the Mets won that World Series in '86, most of it wonderful material for a soap opera . . . or a book. From rape and rehab to firings and flops, we've had the pleasure, and we use the word loosely, of being there every misstep of the way. This was our chance to dig in and take our hacks. Our only hope is that we made better contact than The Worst Team Money Could Buy.

—JOHN HARPER
BOB KLAPISCH
January 1993

CAST OF CHARACTERS

Here are thumbnail sketches of the leading "players" on the 1992 Mets—the worst team money could buy.

BOBBY BONILLA

The $29 million man. Came home to New York as the local boy made good, but probably wishes he'd stayed in Pittsburgh after fans fingered him as a scapegoat and the press saw through his image-conscious posturing. Definitely wishes he never had flashed his famous smile at the media upon signing as a Met and said: "I know you all are gonna try, but you're not gonna be able to wipe the smile off my face. I grew up in New York. I know what it's all about."

VINCE COLEMAN

Qualifies as one of the worst free-agent signings ever, having missed 180 games in two years, and that's one of the nicer things the media has to say about him. On a good day he's merely indifferent toward the press; on others he's as cantankerous and downright nasty as anyone making $3 million a year can possibly be. But his agent loves him.

HOWARD JOHNSON

A prisoner of his own talent, HoJo remains forever in search of a 2-and-0 fastball as well as everlasting peace of mind. Haunted

•

by off-speed pitches and his own insecurities, he turned to Christianity in 1991 for inner tranquillity. Hit thirty-eight homers in '91, seven during a miserable '92. Time to renew his faith.

EDDIE MURRAY

The question isn't which cap he'll wear to his Hall of Fame induction some day, but whether he'll show up with that chip on his shoulder. Gave the Mets everything they hoped for in '92 except a better image. Why does Eddie hate the press so thoroughly? Apparently the world will have to wait for the autobiography to find out.

WILLIE RANDOLPH

He wanted one last lap around the track in New York, but the legs just weren't there at age thirty-eight. Too bad, because he brought quiet class and the status of a champion to a locker room badly in need of both. Jeff Torborg convinced Al Harazin to sign Randolph as the Mets' everyday second baseman, and it was one of his worst judgments.

DAVE MAGADAN

A poor man's Keith Hernandez, Magadan was a fish out of water in '92—a solid, if one-dimensional, hitter whose contributions were minimized by the total lack of offense around him. Nice guy with a wry sense of humor, one of the few stand-up Mets in recent years, ever willing to take responsibility for failure as well as success.

KEVIN ELSTER

The All-Star who never was. Had the look of another Cal Ripken, Jr., when he arrived in the bigs, but never came close to realizing his potential. Sidetracked by his own nonchalance, not to mention his affection for blondes and beers, Elster hit more like Billy Ripken, and then his shoulder gave out on him in '92.

•

TODD HUNDLEY

Catcher of the nineties. At least the Mets are still hoping so. Suffered through long bouts of insecurity that kept his average under .200 most of the season, finally finishing at .209. Kept properly quiet and low-key all summer, as rookies are expected to, but has the savvy to eventually emerge as a force in the clubhouse.

MACKEY SASSER

Jeff Torborg's personal whipping boy, the target of the manager's utter neglect in the second half of the season. Why did Torborg hate Sasser so much? No one—not even Mackey— knew for sure. Sasser, a dangerous line-drive hitter, simply dropped out of the Mets' consciousness by August, not even asked to attend daily pitchers-and-catchers meetings anymore. By then Torborg decided the less he saw of Sasser, the better.

CHARLIE O'BRIEN

So good defensively that Dwight Gooden adopted him as his personal catcher, but he can't hit a lick. A country boy from Oklahoma, he's a perfect Met for the nineties: quiet, invisible to the press, not about to cause trouble. Distrustful of reporters, though not hostile.

DARYL BOSTON

For a platoon outfielder with a .250 career average, Boston has the style and grace of a star—at least after the final out. No Met ran a smoother nightlife. Well dressed, surrounded by beautiful women, nicknamed the Mayor for the way he appropriated the P.M. hours. A terrific athlete, Boston might've enjoyed real star status in the big leagues if he'd ever solved the mystery of the slider . . . and maybe seen a little less of the other side of midnight.

•

DAVE GALLAGHER

An American League transplant, acquired from the California Angels for Hubie Brooks. Served as an outfield defensive replacement, losing almost two months of his season after suffering a broken hand. Finished with only 175 at-bats. A quiet, but witty player, best known for inventing what he called A Hitter's Aid, a device that prevents overstriding while swinging the bat.

DICK SCHOFIELD

The April replacement for Kevin Elster, acquired by the Mets from the Angels for Julio Valera. Quiet and shy, quickly established himself as Elster's alter-ego. Had a fabulous year defensively, but the Mets couldn't afford his .205 batting average and cut him loose when former Met exec Joe McIlvaine, cutting costs as GM of the Padres, dropped Tony Fernandez in their laps last October.

DWIGHT GOODEN

The spiritual ace of the staff, the Mets' most marketable player since Tom Seaver. Injuries to his shoulder have diminished his fastball in recent years, but nothing—not even a rape scandal in spring training—has loosened the bond Gooden enjoys with New York and its baseball media. Easygoing and polite, Doc has never blown up at a reporter, even in his most stressful times last March, during the Florida rape investigation.

DAVE CONE

The loose cannon who was too dangerous for the Mets to handle. A pitcher with an explosive fastball and equally volatile personal life, Cone was named in a lawsuit by three New York women in 1992, charged with exposing himself in the Shea Stadium bullpen. Also linked peripherally to the alleged rape victim in the spring-training scandal, Cone was eventually traded by the Mets in August. The club claimed it had no hope of re-signing the free-agent-to-be, but privately the front office was also glad it was free of screaming tabloid headlines about Cone.

SID FERNANDEZ
On the receiving end of years of fat jokes after allowing himself to swell to over 260 pounds at one point. Question: What does Sid think the Eat to Win diet is? Answer: The more he eats, the more he wins. Finally checking into a diet center before the '92 season, Fernandez dropped forty-five pounds, and with them, many of his insecurities. Married and finally maturing, Fernandez had perhaps his best all-around year in '92, though he's yet to reach the twenty-win potential the Mets were once sure he had.

PETE SCHOUREK
Would've fit in nicely with the eighties Mets: not afraid of the nightlife, not afraid of the press, not afraid to throw his curveball when behind in the count. Has the stuff to be a big winner, but it's too early to tell if he'll blossom in the National League.

BRET SABERHAGEN
One of the hardest throwers in the National League and, when he's on, perhaps the most untouchable righty in the game. Reaches ninety-four miles per hour on the radar gun, and can spot his fastball on either corner. Was the Met closest to Dave Cone, having been teammates with him in Kansas City a decade ago. His lively presence rejuvenated the inner-circle Mets, and, with Cone gone, has become one of its few holdovers.

JOHN FRANCO
A street-smart lefty from Brooklyn, the most influential presence in the clubhouse. He's loud and cuts anyone and everyone to shreds with his one-liners. Definitely an inner-circle Met. Needlessly sensitive to criticism, though, and likes to tell reporters who write too harshly about him, "I'll have to send one

•

of my boys to visit you." The beat writers assume—and pray—that he's kidding.

ANTHONY YOUNG
A former strong safety for the University of Houston who could have played in the NFL, he brings a mean streak to the mound. Endured a miserable first full year, some of it bad luck, but showed promise as a short reliever after being shifted to the bullpen at midseason. Wary of the press but a friendly, lively man.

PAUL GIBSON
Intelligent, witty, bespectacled, looks more like an accountant than a major leaguer. Has only so-so talent, staying in the big leagues with a combination of finesse, brains, and the good fortune to have been born left-handed. A New Yorker from Center Moriches, Long Island, he gravitated toward John Franco and thereby gained immediate acceptance into the inner circle.

JEFF INNIS
A quiet, pensive relief pitcher who's stayed in the big leagues with an unorthodox, sidearm delivery. Most right-handed hitters find Innis's curveball difficult to solve, although left-handers have killed him over the years. Armed with a degree in psychology from the University of Illinois, Innis can disarm players and writers alike with his impersonations of anyone in the clubhouse.

TIM BURKE
A Bible-studying reliever acquired from the Expos in exchange for Ron Darling in 1991. An admirable man, he and his wife have adopted three underprivileged children, two from Korea, one from Guatemala. But he's a pitcher on the way out, having lost his sinker. Traded in midsummer for Yankees lefty Lee

•

Guetterman, another born-again Christian, who was cut loose after the season.

WALLY WHITEHURST
A good ol' boy from Louisiana who was happy sitting at his locker with a dip of tobacco in his lip and his hand-held golf computer game on his lap. Served the Mets well out of the bullpen, but failed to deliver when given chances to nail down a spot in the rotation. Traded in October for Tony Fernandez.

•

EDITOR'S NOTE

As this book went to press, John Harper left his position at the *New York Post* to cover sports for the New York *Daily News*.

THE Worst Team MONEY COULD BUY

FEBRUARY

FEBRUARY 21. PORT ST. LUCIE.

THE PHONE CALLS started a little before 9 A.M., which for baseball writers was like being awakened in the middle of the night. And in spring training it meant trouble. An early-morning call from New York—from a panicked editor to his Florida correspondent—was a sure sign that a hot story had broken somewhere. How toasty was this one? "You won't believe what I'm about to tell you," the bosses breathed into their phones.

A story had appeared on the Associated Press wire, detailing a stunning excerpt from Darryl Strawberry's new book: Strawberry intimated that Dwight Gooden had begun using drugs during the 1986 season. As the guys on the beat liked to say, there was real smoke here. *Smoke:* code word for controversy. A smoked-up, stoked-up, full-of-fire story is one that usually makes its home on the back page, where the *New York Post* or the *Daily News* can write a headline that'll grab you by the throat, pull you in, and not let go until you've finished the twenty-fifth paragraph. That's the lifeblood of a tabloid, and in this case, Strawberry had provided plenty of smoke.

In his book, co-written by Art Rust, Jr., the former Met hinted that Gooden's fall to cocaine had occurred well before he tested positive in March '87 and spent a month in New York's Smithers Alcoholism Treatment Center. Strawberry wasn't specific about whether Doc ever actually took the mound when he was high, or whether he'd used drugs during the playoffs and

•

World Series. But the mere suggestion of it was enough to send the baseball beat into a frenzy.

The boys in the trenches smiled at their own naïveté during the previous winter. Now, more than ever, it was obvious that the Mets would never get off Peyton Place. They should've known better than to believe GM Al Harazin, who'd vowed to make the Mets quiet and boring. Harazin had spent millions creating baseball's highest payroll of $44.5 million to erase the memory of a disastrous fifth-place finish, return the Mets to immediate contention, and bring the organization some peace and tranquillity. Here it was, not even a week into spring training, and the ghost of the Mets past was already whispering in Harazin's ear. Of all people: Strawberry, whom the front office had pushed out the back door in 1990. Straw was getting his revenge all right, dragging the Mets into an ugly controversy. And whether his allegations were true or not—most everyone in the Mets community thought it was just Darryl being Darryl, reckless, wrong, lovable—the story sat like a rock on the back page of the tabloids for three days.

The crisis-hardened Mets writers were instantly in midseason form on February 21, hurrying to the spring-training headquarters in Port St. Lucie, fanning out to all corners of the locker room. First Gooden, who backed away from any public comment. Next was Harazin, shaken and pale, saying he had no interest in or inclination to know what was in the book—nonsense, of course. And finally, the beat guys poured into rental cars and sped up Interstate 95 to Vero Beach, where they could talk to Strawberry themselves.

Never mind that everyone was already in spin control, including Darryl, who was backpedaling fast, dancing with the semantics. "I didn't mean Doc was actually using drugs. I just said I wouldn't have been surprised. You guys are stirring up the shit again, as usual." That was Straw, all right: never too precise with the language, never really thinking about what he said—or in this case, wrote. Actually, the entire crisis dried up quickly, compared with past Met fire storms. Still, the first

•

gunshot of 1992 had been fired, and in a small way it represented yet another failure by the front office. A quiet 1992? Not quite.

The Mets' golden era began in 1984, and for seven years the baseball at Shea was terrific, full of energy, almost eliminating the Yankees from New York's consciousness. But by 1992 the Mets had become the dynasty that never was, having squandered an embarrassment of riches along the way. Hailed as the most talent-stocked organization in baseball in the mid-1980s, the Mets had but one World Series appearance to show for seven years of great expectations.

As world champs in 1986, they gained a reputation for on-field arrogance, a team that thrived on being universally hated. But the arrogance was actually in the front office, which insisted on trying to tame its wild bunch and wound up paying the price with failure and much public humiliation. Frank Cashen, Joe McIlvaine, and Al Harazin, the stuffy management troika making the decisions, refused to acknowledge the powerful chemistry of its renegade ball club, baseball's answer to Al Davis's old Oakland Raiders. Within weeks of the victory, World Series MVP Ray Knight was gone, walking away in a $200,000 contract dispute, as was Kevin Mitchell, traded for Kevin McReynolds plus three others. Cashen and the others didn't realize or care that Knight and Mitchell, both legitimate tough guys, had been the muscle behind the Mets' strut. But that was just the beginning.

Soon Wally Backman was gone, then Lenny Dykstra and Strawberry, Bob Ojeda and Ron Darling. Even Rick Cerone, who came along in '91 and became a savior as the number one catcher for a few months, was too political for the club's liking. Along the way, the Mets became something of a laughingstock, their supposed arrogance all that remained of the grit and toughness of '86. It wasn't all the brass's fault. If Keith Hernandez and Gary Carter hadn't gotten old in a hurry, if Dwight Gooden hadn't lost some of the magic in his right arm, maybe none of the other moves would have seemed so significant. But

•

7

when the Mets failed to live up to their billing, image became job one.

Owner Fred Wilpon, in particular, wanted to homogenize his ball club, and began stressing family values long before the Republicans tried to make it an issue in the '92 presidential campaign—with much the same success, as it turned out. It was Wilpon who ordered Al Harazin to go hire Jeff Torborg to replace Buddy Harrelson. For years Wilpon and fellow owner Nelson Doubleday had been delighted to sit back and watch their management team make all the baseball decisions. Neither man wanted the publicity—or the public ridicule—George Steinbrenner had always received as the high-profile owner of the Yankees, at least until he was suspended by then-commissioner Fay Vincent.

Wilpon had grown up in Brooklyn and played on the same high school team as Sandy Koufax; he thought of himself as a savvy baseball man, and began to assert more influence on the baseball decisions as the Mets' glory faded. He was a benevolent man who made an effort to learn the names of employees from top to bottom in the organization and was well liked because of it. Occasionally he'd ask a security guard or an usher how his family was doing and peel off a hundred-dollar bill, saying, "Buy something for the kids." But he wasn't going to sit by and watch his ball club go into the toilet. As early as midsummer 1989, when the Mets were playing below expectations, a couple of players overheard Wilpon at the batting cage warn then-manager Davey Johnson, "I hope this team isn't going to quit on us." Still, Wilpon had given Frank Cashen free rein to make the call on Davey Johnson, who was fired in May 1990. But after Harrelson—Cashen's choice to succeed Davey—failed miserably, leaving the Mets no choice but to fire him in September '91, just before Cashen turned over the job of GM to Harazin, Wilpon got involved.

He wanted a manager with a reputation for winning and handling the dreaded press. Just such a man—or so it seemed—practically fell in his lap when Chicago White Sox owner Jerry

•

Reinsdorf whispered to Wilpon at an owners' meeting that he'd be willing to let Torborg talk to the Mets, since New Jersey was home for his manager. It was hardly a noble gesture on Reinsdorf's part, considering that his trigger finger was getting itchy anyway. An impulsive decision-maker in the Steinbrenner mold, Reinsdorf was less than thrilled with Torborg's strategy from the dugout and he was telling close associates that the situation was beginning to resemble that of the Chicago Bulls, whom he also owned. There, Doug Collins had turned the lowly Bulls into winners, but soon Reinsdorf decided Collins wasn't the man to take the club to "the next level," and fired him in favor of Phil Jackson, who quickly coached the Bulls to two NBA titles. Similarly, Torborg had turned a downtrodden White Sox team into winners, but when they started stagnating in 1991, Reinsdorf was asking people he trusted, "Can he get us to the next level?"

There were no such questions about Torborg's character, however. He was family and discipline and everything the Mets' management wanted in their ball club. So Harazin, without interviewing even one other candidate, went out and made Torborg one of the highest-paid managers in baseball, giving him a four-year, $1.9 million contract. Then, just as quickly, Harazin remade the team in Torborg's mold, bringing in what the GM called "character guys," good soldiers like Eddie Murray and Bobby Bonilla and Willie Randolph, who weren't about to start trouble in the newspapers. But it wasn't long before controversy was haunting them again. It had been this way for the Mets ever since that ground ball trickled through Bill Buckner's legs in the infamous Game Six of the '86 World Series. The baseball gods seemed determined to make the Mets pay dearly for that miracle inning and eventual world championship, because the subsequent years were a blur of injuries and turmoil and screaming headlines. A stunning playoff loss in '88 to an inferior Dodgers team even turned their one other season of accomplishment into a terrible embarrassment.

•

* * *

This is where we begin, as beat writers who have spent far too many Friday nights in St. Louis or Cincinnati or Houston rewriting game-story leads on deadline because Straw lasered a home run off the clock in Busch Stadium or Doc watched in horror as Mike Scioscia took him deep. Klapisch and Harper. Or Harper and Klapisch, depending on whether you give priority to age or seniority on the beat. Quality of work? Let's not open that discussion here, where the spill of blood would make an awful mess. Suffice to say the competitive drive runs high on both sides. How could it not? Klapisch and Harper. The *News* and the *Post*. The rivalry is cutthroat: tabloid wars till death or a joint operating agreement, whichever comes first. The two papers have been trying to kill each other off since hard times and suburban dailies began alternately putting the *News* or the *Post* in financial peril some ten years ago. Both papers, losing money because of overstuffed union payrolls and dwindling ad revenues, have come close to shutting down completely in recent years. *Post* publisher Peter Kalikow, who bought the paper in 1988 from Rupert Murdoch, threatened to close it down in September 1990, and only an eleventh-hour buyout agreement, as well as mass layoffs and pay cuts accepted by the rank and file, kept the presses going. Only a month or so later, the *Daily News* unions went out on a strike that became so bitter that the parent company, the Chicago Tribune Company, sold the paper in April '91 to British magnate Robert Maxwell. Seven months later, Maxwell drowned in an apparent suicide, just as authorities were learning that his empire was collapsing in huge amounts of debt. In December '91 the *Daily News* was put up for sale, declaring bankruptcy, and didn't emerge safely until January 1993, when Mort Zuckerman, publisher of *U.S. News & World Report*, bought the paper for $36 million.

No sooner was the *Daily News* settled than the *Post* entered another crisis. It came literally within minutes of suspending operation on January 24, before financier Steven Hoffenberg stepped in to rescue Kalikow from bankruptcy. As this book went to press, the paper was in the process of being sold to Hoffenberg.

Through all of this, the uncertainty lent a new urgency to competition for stories and put a harder edge on the business of reporting sports, the section that sells the tabloids. And nowhere has the fire been stoked more furiously than at Shea Stadium, at least not since the mid-1980s, when the Mets became the sexiest team in New York, and therefore the most visible beat in the newspapers.

Why are we doing this book? It's not for the joy of working together, put it that way. We go together about as well as HoJo and Gregg Jefferies used to turn a double play in that infield from hell of a few years ago. It figures. Klapisch is a pitcher, pitched at Columbia University in the seventies, still pitches in a good semipro league in New Jersey. Harper was a shortstop and second baseman, played at the University of Bridgeport also in the seventies, finally retired to golf and sportswriting after staying in too many Motel 6's playing fast-pitch softball around the country.

Klapisch thinks he's hot stuff because he went to an Ivy League school and once struck out Ron Darling in a game against Yale. Harper thinks he's big time because he played on a national-championship fast-pitch team in Connecticut and got himself a ring as big and showy as any worn by World Series champs. Klapisch thinks like a pitcher—thinks the damn game belongs to him and swears that every ball in the hole was a routine play that a good shortstop would have had in his back pocket. Harper thinks like an infielder—curses the pitcher for taking too much time diddling with the resin bag and going to 3-and-friggin'-2 on every batter, and swears he's keeping the sore-armed wuss on the mound in the game every time he has to move a step to his right to field a ground ball.

Klapisch has the ego of the players he covers. He made a splash quickly on the beat in the mid-eighties by cozying up to

•

the likes of Gooden, Strawberry, and Darling, stroking their own egos with overwrought prose about their muscular fastballs or breathtaking home-run swings. He's a born tabloid writer, willing to indulge the bullshit excuses and temperamental nature of baseball stars for the sake of the job and the likelihood that it will earn him an exclusive story here and there. He infuriates other writers, particularly Harper, with his penchant for smokin' up a story, slickly turning a seemingly innocuous quote into something warranting a screaming headline. In short, Klapisch wants the back page as badly as his editors want something outrageous to put there every day, and he'll use the stiletto he carries on the job if the competition gets in his way.

Harper has an attitude, thinks he knows the game better than Whitey Herzog and Tim McCarver combined just because he used to slide like Pete Rose. He won't talk to players who don't get their uniforms dirty, not if he can help it anyway. He's not as comfortable around the ego monsters as he is around the Keith Millers, the Mackey Sassers, the Tim Teufels. He plays the tabloid game, works the corners of the clubhouse mostly in an effort to trump Klapisch on any given day, but has little tolerance for the money-inflated egos and statistic-driven selfishness that dominate baseball in the nineties. Harper fights for the back page too, but he'd rather strut his viewpoint across the column logo; the *Post* gives more column freedom to its beat writers, and it kills Klapisch that Harper is constantly jumping in with his holier-than-thou opinion on some Met-related issue, trying to prove to everyone that he's the toughest guy on the beat.

For five years we've been clawing at each other. Friends, sometimes, but neither would turn his back on the other. It's the nature of the job, the paranoia that comes with the territory, always wondering if the guy two seats down in the press box is working on a story that is going to blow the lid off the beat. On the road you travel together, eat together, play pickup basketball together, then put up the professional wall

•

while working the clubhouse. More and more, however, the Mets have become the common opponent, a great clubhouse turned cold and miserable toward the press. How did it happen? How did the team with the brightest future in the game fall apart so quickly? That's what we have come together to explore in detail.

So here we were, having migrated south again to escape the winter and live in our rented condos for two months. Port St. Lucie, a quiet, rural town that has grown into a jungle of Pizza Huts and Burger Kings and Blockbuster Videos since the Mets moved here from St. Petersburg in 1988, isn't Palm Beach, but it beats shoveling snow up north. In truth, Palm Beach, the glamour kingdom that sits an hour to the south down I-95, would have been a more appropriate winter home for the '92 Mets, the largest collection of millionaires ever assembled in team sports. And while only a minority of players actually looks forward to spring training and its six weeks of meaningless baseball, the start of a new baseball year always brings high hopes. Spirits were especially high on this team: The Mets had something to prove after their August collapse and fifth-place finish in '91, the first time in seven years they hadn't taken a pennant race deep into September. More significant, Harazin had put together a team of high-profile names, and players are more easily seduced by star quality than even fans are.

They believed they would be great, nothing less. But there were omens, terrible omens, for the season that lay ahead. Never mind the baseball: when ballplayers rekindle friendships in Florida there are more exhilarating adventures to pursue. Namely sex and golf, and as spring training began, both now came with a price. Or so it seemed. The Magic Johnson retirement had thrown a scare into hundreds of pro athletes who had come to accept sex as one of the rewards of their profession, but it had absolutely terrified the more nocturnally rambunctious of the Mets.

No one fit that category more than shortstop Kevin El-

•

ster. For years he'd pounded beers with the inner-circle Mets, a shrinking group that once had included Ron Darling, Bob Ojeda, Keith Hernandez, Wally Backman, Lenny Dykstra, David Cone, Darryl Strawberry, John Franco, and to some degree Doc Gooden, Frank Viola, Mackey Sasser, and Daryl Boston. In fact, Elster came to personify what the Mets of the eighties really were: good-looking, well dressed, wealthy, ultra-cool. When Elster first arrived at Shea in 1986, he was loathed by the veterans for his arrogance, but by 1989 he was fully accepted in the clubhouse. He could still be remarkably smug with reporters, but teammates gravitated toward him. Keith Hernandez was asked one day whom he considered his best friend among the Mets. In a room that still housed Darling, Ojeda, Dykstra, and Cone, Hernandez nodded at Elster and said simply, "Him."

It wasn't because of any real star status: Elster was a terrific fielder but below-average hitter and hardly one of the Mets' more vital components. Elster wasn't rich by baseball standards, never earning $1 million in a single season. And compared to Darling and Hernandez, Elster was a relative unknown on the society pages. Yet he had a magical touch with women. He thrived in a climate that was rife with sex. Every-where the Mets went—city to city, bar to bar, hotel lobby to hotel lobby—there were women to be scooped up and de-voured. Even the ballparks provided fertile hunting ground.

Sometimes all it would take was eye contact with a pretty woman in the stands and a smart ballplayer would have his lead. In Elster's case, one day in San Diego—he was sitting in the dugout in street clothes, having gone on the DL with a bad shoulder—it meant sending one of the clubhouse boys after a local beauty. She was pretty, all right, staring at Elster di-rectly, her smile an invitation. "Go see who she is," Elster told the kid. "Tell her I want to meet her."

It was a long shot, but well worth a try, especially since Elster was divorced and not breaking any laws—even club-house rules, for that matter. Friends' and teammates' wives

•

and girlfriends were off limits, of course, but beyond that the world was one big orgy waiting to happen. Incredibly, Elster hit the jackpot that day at Jack Murphy Stadium, in more ways than one. Not only did the woman agree to meet Elster, but she was the girlfriend of one of the Padres players, one Elster didn't know personally. By game time Elster had arranged for a rendezvous. By the third inning, they were together in the players' lounge adjacent to the visitors' clubhouse, and they weren't there to talk. At one point Darryl Strawberry, passing by on his way to the clubhouse between innings, poked his head in. Elster and the woman were near the height of passion.

"Hey, Ellie, how 'bout saving a piece of that for me?" Straw said, then walked on, chuckling. These were the Mets, where winning and sex were equal parts of the universe. And it wasn't limited to the Mets. In fact, the locker-room sex scene from *Bull Durham* is more common around the big leagues than the public knows. As Dave Cone once put it, referring to baseball players in general, "If you're talking about the number of guys who get a little head in the back of the bullpen during the course of the season, you're talking about a pretty large number."

The Mets had their own private lexicon when it came to sex. A "gamer" described any woman looking for sex. A "spinner" was a small woman with a good body. A "mullion" was an ugly woman, and a "stone cold mullion" a particularly homely one. And, of course, ballplayers don't make love. They "crush" women or "nail" them. Sometimes they just "beat it up."

The lingo wasn't meant to imply actual violence against women, though the choice of words is surely offensive and perhaps subconsciously revealing. Ballplayers come to think of sex as both a reward for their privileged status and a source of competition among themselves. Chasing women is practically an extension of the ball game, extra innings, as it were. Who's gonna score, who isn't? The conquest is what really counts. So when a player has "beat it up" it means he's had terrific sex—

•

which is open for discussion the next day. "Hey, you nail that little spinner last night?" is the usual opening line among ballplayers just arriving at the clubhouse.

Of course, that's the question posed to a player who'd been seen leaving a bar with a woman, usually a single Met. Other

A ROOKIE'S WORLD
—B.K.

THE YEAR WAS 1983, my first season writing baseball for the *New York Post*. I was in St. Petersburg covering spring training, equipped with nothing more than my Columbia education, a few years of varsity baseball, and, after graduation, two years of general-assignment work at the *Post*.

I'd never covered baseball before. My editor didn't seem concerned. "Just kick some ass," he said merrily. So in that first week, Mets PR man Jay Horwitz introduced me to Dave Kingman. I extended a sweaty hand. Kingman just stared and walked away. "Dave doesn't really like the press too much," Horwitz said, trying to explain. "I was hoping he'd give you a break because you're new."

Not quite. I quickly learned that first-year reporters can be devoured in a big-league clubhouse. The rookie is so easy to spot, too. He's the one who won't ask questions in a group interview (too worried his question will sound stupid), the one who misses deadlines (can't decide what to write), the one who misses too many stories (no sources in the clubhouse).

The rookie will also give himself away with his open awe in the clubhouse. I know I did: My mouth dropped when I saw the luxury that surrounded the Mets. Lockers three times the size of what I'd been accustomed to in college. Multiple sets of uniforms, all freshly laundered, hanging in each locker. I saw George Foster peel off his jersey after a morning workout and toss the shirt on the ground, and instantly, seemingly from nowhere, a clubhouse boy scurried across the room to pick it up. The jersey was hurried to a back room, where an enormous washing machine was laundering all the Mets' uniforms. Right next to the washing caldron was a mammoth dryer, nearly the size of an airplane engine. Within twenty minutes, Foster's jersey had been washed, dried, folded, and returned to his locker. Foster didn't seem to notice, or even care.

The other beat reporters seemed amused by my shock, not really doing much to help in my orientation. Not that I expected it, but when I missed a few stories in the opening week of camp, I was asked a not-so-delicate question by my editor back in New York. "Pardon me for bringing it up," he said, "but when the fuck do you intend to start working?" Before I could stutter out an

players are more discreet, opting for "room service." That's shorthand for spending the night upstairs in the hotel room, arranging for a past pickup to simply come to the door.

This glorious eighties ride was finally shattered by Magic Johnson's shocking AIDS disclosure in November 1991. Elster

---

answer, my boss had unceremoniously slam-dunked the phone.

I'd started to realize how alone I was on the beat—I knew no one, knew nothing—when I was sitting in the clubhouse one morning. The Mets were on the field working out, and the other beat writers were in the press room, no doubt devising new ways to stick it to the *Post.* I was reading a local newspaper, flipping through the college basketball scores, when Tom Seaver walked over and ripped the paper out of my hands.

Without uttering a word, he took the paper across the clubhouse, sat at his locker, and began reading. I was appalled at his audacity. I wasn't that many years removed from college, and I was still in touch with memories of frat-party brawls, when even an innocent bump in a crowded room would result in a thrown punch. Obviously, I couldn't clock Tom Seaver, but I had to do something. Only, what?

I'd grown up idolizing Seaver, not knowing in my youth how arrogant he could be. Even the Mets were to experience his chill in 1992: In July, the club held a Tom Seaver Day at Shea, which was rained out. When the Mets tried again in September, they forgot to check the WPIX-TV schedule, not realizing Seaver had a broadcasting commitment with the Yankees. The Franchise, offended at the Mets' oversight, declined to attend his own party.

But there it was, 1983, and Seaver, in all his iciness, had brought me to a crossroads. I was about to learn the difference between rooting for a player and covering him. At that moment I had two choices. The first was to do nothing, let Seaver win. Maybe he would've told his teammates how he'd humiliated the punk from the *Post.* Maybe Seaver would even tell some of the other, older journalists about it, letting them enjoy a good laugh. Or maybe Seaver would've kept silent, letting the incident remain our ugly little secret. I wasn't sure, but I couldn't take a chance. I chose the second option.

I took a breath and walked across the clubhouse to Seaver, yanked the paper back, and sat down right next to him. I didn't say a word. I didn't even look at Seaver. I just continued reading the local hoop scores.

After a moment of terrible silence, I heard Seaver chuckle. "Well done," he said as he walked away, having successfully taught me a lesson. After ten years covering the Mets—five at the *Post,* five more at the *News*—it's still the best lesson I've ever learned: Never back down.

•

remembered being on an L.A. freeway when he heard a news-caster break in with the bulletin. Elster was so unnerved he practically drove his Porsche into a guard rail. "I really didn't have control of the car for a couple of miles," Elster would say later. Eventually he pulled into a shopping mall to walk around, compose his thoughts. There he found hundreds of shoppers huddled around appliance-store TV sets and radios, desperate for more news, hoping there'd been a mistake. It wasn't just the kids who'd been devastated. Grown men and women were crying openly.

"It was as if the president had been shot. The place came to a standstill," Elster said. Soon after, a deeper and more insidious fear came over him. After so many years with the Mets' traveling sex show—How many women had there been? A few dozen? A hundred? Hundreds?—he began to wonder about his own health. There were a number of nagging symp-toms that normally wouldn't have merited a second thought. But in the post-Magic era, who knew for sure anymore?

Elster was suffering from the flu, a nasty one that had hit him in October and wouldn't go away. His stomach was jittery, twitchy, the nights riddled with bad sleep. When, by late No-vember, there had been no improvement, Elster finally asked his doctor for an AIDS test. The five days that it took to screen the blood were, in Elster's words, "just pure, fucking hell." He called friends for support, talked to his parents deep into the night, even called Klapisch in New York one day, not even starting the conversation with "hello."

"Tell me I don't have AIDS. Tell me I'm all right," Elster pleaded into the phone. Klapisch reasoned with the shortstop: He wasn't gay, had never used drugs intravenously, had never received a blood transfusion. Nervously, Elster said thanks, hung up, and waited out the remaining terrifying days until the results came back: still HIV-negative. The symptoms were the result of an ulcer, aggravated by too much anti-inflammation medication, taken over the course of an entire summer for a weak throwing shoulder. An ulcer at the age of twenty-six. Ironically, in the nineties, that was good news.

•

Even though Elster had survived the scare, he was never the same. Because of his ulcer, he was no longer drinking come the spring of '92, and he'd found a steady girlfriend, deciding it was time to stay home at night. "Never, ever going through that again," he said. Indeed, like other single Mets, he poured himself more thoroughly into another addiction: golf.

Then there were the married players, who now had more to worry about than their wives finding out that there weren't lights on the golf course—"night golf" being an alibi that one prominent Met once used to explain a moonlight rendezvous. Somehow it was a fitting if hilarious tale, because if there is a more consuming pursuit than sex among ballplayers—other than accepting free drinks, that is—it must surely be golf.

Ballplayers are obsessed with golf, which makes them no different from millions of Americans, except they don't have to get to their local course at four o'clock on a Saturday morning to ensure themselves a tee time. They live in a fantasy world; the best, most exclusive courses are only a phone call away: Oakmont in Pittsburgh, Riviera in L.A., Medinah in Chicago—if it's not ranked in *Golf Digest*'s Top 100, ballplayers don't want to play it. Of course, they don't make the phone call—they tell Mets PR director Jay Horwitz to set it up. *Jay, get us a tee time at Pebble Beach for the off-day in San Francisco, will you? Yeah, a foursome—Bonilla, Coleman, Saberhagen, and Sasser. And tell 'em if we gotta pay we're not playing.* Yes, the status of a major leaguer carries great clout when it comes to green fees. Getting on is nothing; getting on for free is what it's all about. Why not? The average club pro is like the rest of the adoring public, delighted to do a favor for big-league ballplayers, especially if it means shaking their hands and getting tickets for that night's game.

And so they play and play. In the eighties the golf bags would come streaming in on the conveyor belt at the airport when the Mets arrived in town—so many that it was comical. Charlie Samuels, the equipment manager, whose job it was to load and ship the luggage from city to city, airport to stadium, would walk around mumbling, "Is this the fuckin' PGA Tour

•

or a baseball team?" It wasn't unheard of: Most teams forbid their players to play golf on game days, but some teams allow players to ship their bags and play on off-days. The Mets just took it to an extreme, seemingly another way of flaunting their superiority complex. It could be embarrassing if they'd just lost two or three straight, but losing streaks were rare for most of the Davey Johnson era. And the thing was, Davey was the most serious golfer of them all, good enough that he played a little on a PGA satellite tour after he retired from baseball. For that matter, Cashen, the diminutive GM, was as fanatical about golf as his players were. He made at least one West Coast trip every year—even in '92, after he'd stepped down as GM—mainly so that he could play Riviera, which was one of his favorites.

In fact, golf seemed to be about the only common ground Cashen and his manager shared for a while, so different were they: The GM was as conservative and proper as the bow ties he wore, while Davey was loud and loose, at heart a cowboy who, to paraphrase former Oakland Raiders quarterback Kenny Stabler, believed in reading the scouting reports by the light of the jukebox. When Davey lost his touch with his ball club, however, Cashen decided that golf had become an abused privilege, and he demanded more discipline. Davey fought him right to the end. When the Mets got off to a bad start in '89, Davey made a show of banning golf—and card games in the clubhouse—on the road. It appeased Cashen and gave the press something to write about, the end of Club Met and all that. Then, two days later, Johnson, ever the players' manager, held a private meeting with his team to tell them he was just trying to keep the press and management off their backs; golf and cards were fine, he said, but just be a little more discreet: *Do what you want, but don't let Cashen or those fuckin' reporters know.* Eventually Johnson's refusal to bend to Cashen's demands, his refusal to play sheriff when the Mets began coasting too much, cost him his job. But as long as he was manager, the golf course was as open to his players as the hotel bar.

•

Yes, in those days the Mets barnstormed in foursomes. Darling, Ojeda, HoJo, Elster, McReynolds, Dykstra, Backman, Teufel, Carter, Sasser, McDowell, Knight—virtually everybody played. They played on off-days, game days, anytime, any weather, and always for money. For most it was twenty, maybe forty dollars a side, but if Dykstra was involved, the payoffs were usually in the hundreds. In '88 the joke in the clubhouse was that Lenny was losing so much money to McReynolds on the golf course, he would have to sign his postseason check right over to the left fielder. For all of them the money just heightened the competition. Indeed, in some ways, gambling, like sex, seemed to be just another way of keeping score, of living for the rush of catching a Nolan Ryan fastball just right and hitting it out of sight. The quest never ends: As such, eighteen holes were rarely enough. The boys would play as many as forty-five holes on off-days, a mere twenty-seven on game days.

Finally, the end of Davey meant the end of golf during the season—Cashen deemed it a finable offense except on off-days. Of course, that didn't stop Darling and Ojeda and Viola and Teufel from strolling ever so casually through a hotel lobby at 7 A.M., with golf shoes, gloves, and balls in plastic laundry bags, on their way somewhere to play with rented clubs. Players would follow a similar strategy in '92, since Torborg had the same policy.

Although the preseason was a different story, with golf as much of a tradition as happy hour, Torborg *had* been brought in to break tradition, at least recent tradition as it applied to the Mets, and he didn't want to hear about golf. Right from the start, his five-hour workouts were keeping the Mets at the ballpark deep into the afternoon, making it tough for the players to get more than eighteen holes in before sunset. Worse yet, the local St. Lucie West Country Club was guilty of sacrilege: no more free golf. There it was, a notice on the bulletin board in the locker room. The Mets were still welcome to play, but due to a change in management, they would now be asked to

•

pay thirty-five dollars for each round. This didn't seem like a terrible hardship for baseball's highest-paid team. No fewer than nineteen players were guaranteed of making $500,000 or more in 1992, and ten had multiyear contracts guaranteeing them at least $2 million per year. Yet this injustice was the talk of the locker room early in camp. "Wait till they ask us to play in their charity tournament," one player said. "We'll all be busy that day."

Often ballplayers don't mean to sound so utterly self-absorbed; it just comes naturally after a while. Big leaguers are trained early to reach for their wallets only in emergencies. And why not? On top of the 1992 average major league salary of $1.014 million, players were handed fifty-eight dollars a day in meal money on the road. Every year they are paid by various sporting-goods companies to wear gloves, spikes, wristbands, batting gloves, even T-shirts under their uniforms. They are paid cash, most of it under the table, to show up somewhere and sign autographs. They are paid, in the form of gift certificates or merchandise, to go on radio or TV after a good game. They are encouraged to show up at certain nightclubs in exchange for free drinks. When they are forced to pay for something, there is almost always a deal involved. In most cities on the road, there is a store that caters to ballplayers, offering huge discounts. That's when you see players spend money.

In Atlanta there's a shoe outlet, Friedman's, where players order pairs by the dozen. One day in '92 the owner joyfully related that Dodgers outfielder Eric Davis had spent twenty thousand dollars the last time he'd stopped in—bought hundreds of pairs for family, friends, and himself. Sound absurd? Players think nothing of spending ungodly sums on clothes, jewelry, cars, stereos, anything that makes them look good and feel good. Travel days, when a team is flying out on a charter flight right after a game and players on most teams are required to wear a suit and tie, are virtual fashion shows: all these nouveau-riche ballplayers dressing up in eight-hundred- to thousand-dollar suits—mostly to outdo one another. As they

•

file out of the locker room, attaché cases in hand, they could be a group of IBM executives . . . except for one thing. Virtually none of them wear socks. Custom-made suits, gleaming dress shoes, and bare legs. It's a league-wide statement of some sort, as if to draw the line on dress-code conformity. On the black guys it's not so noticeable, dark skin under dark pant legs. Even tanned ankles don't look too bad. But there's nothing quite so, um, chic as Mackey Sasser or Gregg Jefferies, their pasty-white ankles practically glowing between their pants and shoes, going sockless.

Not all of them dress to kill. Randy Myers, a small-town guy through and through, took pride in dressing down, wearing the same corduroy sport coat all season. Rick Cerone was big-city, but he refused to get caught up in dressing to impress, preferring casual sport coats. Most, however, can't resist spending their money to maintain a certain image. What twenty-seven-year-old can? It might as well be Monopoly money at times, they make so much at such a young age. Once, with the Mets embarking on a nine-game road trip beginning in Montreal, Ron Darling overslept. With a plane to catch, the pitcher decided he didn't want to fuss with packing and left his house with little more than toothpaste and a razor. "Figured it'd be easier just to shop when I got here," Darling told a couple of reporters the next night, after spending a few thousand Canadian dollars in the shops on St. Catherine Street that afternoon.

They've got the dough, all right. And where many of the more highly paid players once went to great lengths to hide their salaries from teammates in the interest of clubhouse harmony, now it's a topic for both serious discussion and clubhouse humor. On the first and the fifteenth of the month, traveling secretary Bob O'Hara makes the rounds in the Mets clubhouse, handing out paychecks, often with writers going about their business of interviewing or visiting. Occasionally a player will invite a writer to have a look. A few years ago, when

•

he was living somewhere in the $2 million-a-year neighborhood, Gooden handed his paycheck to Klapisch one day.

"Need some?" he said, laughing, as Klapisch gawked. The check, *after taxes*, weighed in at sixty-four thousand dollars.

One day in L.A. during the '91 season, Rick Cerone grabbed John Franco's paycheck and began waving it in the air. "Fuckin' guy's a crook," Cerone began, his voice carrying throughout the small visitors' clubhouse as writers turned to watch. "Look at all those zeroes. How many innings you pitch so far this year, Johnny? How many? Thirty? You pitched thirty innings yet? You're stealing money, Johnny. You're stealing." Perhaps only Cerone had the veteran status to take on Franco, the street-tough lefty and unchallenged clubhouse needling king, and players and writers were howling. Franco laughed himself before lashing back at Cerone, labeling him an over-the-hill charity case who hadn't earned his paycheck "since leisure suits went out of style."

In the age of huge contracts, the details of which wind up in the newspapers anyway, money is only a sensitive subject during contract negotiations or when players are being asked to spend it unnecessarily—on the golf course, for example. Thus the outrage over the St. Lucie West Country Club's new policy. But soon enough word filtered through the clubhouse that the St. Lucie West club pro had moved on during the club's change in management, and was working now at the Meadowwood Golf Club, some twenty miles north of Port St. Lucie. The course wasn't considered as challenging as St. Lucie West, which was less than a mile from the Mets' complex, but someone quickly learned that players would still be comped there. And soon enough, Vince Coleman and Bobby Bonilla, making $9 million between them in 1992, were among some of the players preferring to make the thirty-minute drive to Meadowwood rather than pay the thirty-five dollars at the course virtually across the street.

* * *

•

Of course, you'll find a reporter or two on a spring-training golf course as well. Most baseball writers regard the spring as their rightfully earned payback for the previous October, during which they'd worked four straight weeks covering the end of the regular season, the playoffs, and the World Series. By the time Game Seven had arrived, the average beat guy had covered his 140th game of the season.

So come February . . . well, most sports editors are unable or unwilling to intrude on this two-week grace period before exhibition games begin, although Greg Gallo—the tyrant/editor who made the *Post*'s sports section so powerful in the eighties—once said, "It pisses me off to even think of you guys down there."

Gallo, who now edits a horse-racing newspaper in New York, must have enjoyed a private laugh somewhere on this February day because the Mets beat writers' comfortable world had just evaporated. Here they were, surrounding Gooden, looking for a quote, getting on board for yet another season's merry-go-round. And there to choreograph was Jay Horwitz—sort of the White House spokesman, except Horwitz was never really privy to any of the club's inner workings. In truth, Horwitz had a thankless job: Mets management blamed him whenever the club was hammered in the papers, and reporters constantly hissed at Horwitz for trying to run interference for his players.

Little did Horwitz know he would become the point man for the most glamorous, most scrutinized, most controversial team in baseball when he was hired in 1980 to be PR director of what was then merely the most pitiful team in baseball. By then he'd earned a reputation for being innovative in attracting publicity, which the Mets desperately needed. He'd worked for three years as sports information director at NYU, his alma mater, and then for eight in the same position at Fairleigh Dickinson University in New Jersey. He'd managed to get little FDU on TV and in the papers regularly by calling the media's attention to the likes of a forty-seven-year-old fresh-

•

man football player, a forty-three-year-old priest who played hockey for the school, a second baseman who set an NCAA record by getting hit by a pitch 128 times in a season, and a first baseman who worked part-time in a munitions factory. Anything out of the ordinary and Horwitz was on the phone, selling an idea for a story. The first baseman was a perfect example: "One of the papers ran a picture of him holding a bomb at work, and we got picketed by an antiwar group at our next game," Horwitz recalls proudly.

That's Horwitz. He's defined by his devotion to the job and his warped sense of humor. He delights in dropping fictional items into the daily press notes on occasion—always on April Fools' Day—and watching for the fallout. More than once an unsuspecting reporter has written the bogus note into his copy: In the mid-eighties the *St. Petersburg Times* ran a note during spring training explaining that because Rusty Staub had few family members or friends in the area, he was inviting fans to bring him gifts on his birthday the following day. Staub knew nothing about it and was embarrassed when several fans showed up with presents for him. "Rusty didn't have a great sense of humor," Horwitz recalls. "At the Welcome Home Dinner that spring he hired a guy to smash a pie in my face, and he said if I did it again he'd have cow shit dumped on me. I didn't put Rusty in any more of my gag notes."

But he found other ways. In spring training a couple of years ago, Horwitz wrote that Jerry Mathers was a guest at that day's game, in Port St. Lucie to promote his new book, *Musings with the Beaver*. The beat guys saw the note and decided to carry out the joke, so Horwitz put sunglasses on Klapisch and had the P.A. announcer introduce him as "The Beaver" from the press box between innings, while the crowd stood and cheered. Later in '92 Horwitz would enjoy his finest moment: CBS-TV announcer Sean McDonough fell for a note claiming that infielder Chico Walker was the nephew of musician Jr. Walker, and that he'd be going on tour with Jr. Walker and the All-Stars after the season, playing second guitar.

•

McDonough read it as fact over the air while Tim McCarver, who knew of Horwitz's antics, fumbled for something to say, not sure whether to believe it or not. In a dreadful season, the gag made Horwitz's year.

Of course, the brass didn't always appreciate the humor, but for Horwitz it was his chance to have a little fun with a job that over the years had become more difficult than he had ever imagined. The Mets led the league in rehabs, starting with Gooden's in 1987, and Horwitz was always the man leading the player through the forest of TV cameras and microphones in and out of Smithers. And there were plenty of other problems. For a while it seemed some Met always needed shielding from the TV lights: From Keith Hernandez testifying at the famous cocaine trial in '85 to four Mets being arrested at Cooter's Bar in Houston in '86, to Gooden testing positive for cocaine in '87, to Strawberry getting arrested for pulling a gun on his wife in 1990, then entering Smithers himself, Horwitz was practically becoming a fixture on the tube, as recognizable to the public as the players. "My aunt in Arizona called my mom once in a panic," Horwitz recalls. "She'd seen me on TV coming out of the courtroom in Houston in '86 and thought I'd been arrested."

As the crises mounted, Horwitz's patience became more and more strained. He was too protective of his players at times, ready to throw a cross-body block at any TV cameraman who wouldn't give ground or box out any writer who didn't know when to say when. As such he'd been called many names by many people in his twelve years as the PR point man—goon, intimidator, babysitter, media-basher; he was even dubbed the "publicist from hell" in one magazine story. But in this case, Gooden was simply a friend, maybe the best friend Horwitz had had among the hundreds of players he'd served in the decade. In fact, Gooden was the only player who ever repaid Horwitz for his countless favors with a gift, presenting him a couple of years ago with a gold I.D. bracelet, his name spelled in diamonds. So now when Horwitz saw Gooden

•

being swallowed by reporters—"Doc, we need just a word or two about Straw's book"—Jay's first order of business was news suppression.

"Guys, guys . . . look, Doc isn't going to have anything to say, okay?" Horwitz said, stammering mostly, searching for a polite way to tell the beat guys to get lost. Actually, reporters weren't unsympathetic to Jay, as honest and hardworking a PR man as you'll find in baseball. Disagreements and even heated arguments with Horwitz were inevitable, given the explosive nature of the Mets' beat, but most reporters had a soft spot for the publicist from hell, particularly when it became obvious that Frank Cashen would never, ever give him the title VP of public relations.

It was the reward virutally all PR directors in baseball received for doing the dirty work of playing bodyguard for the organization, but Horwitz simply didn't fit into the Mets' blue-blood prototype. He was unorthodox in his ways, scatter-brained, too close to the players. The Mets preferred polish and a touch of elitism in their executives, even though their most visible owner, Wilpon, was, at his roots, just a Jewish kid from Brooklyn. Yet Wilpon affected the same WASPy or even lace-curtain Catholic arrogance that oozed from co-owner Double-day, Cashen, Harazin, and many of the junior executives on the way up. The younger execs would sit at management's long table in the press dining room, enjoying dinner before a game with their ties thrown over their shoulders in corporate salute; Horwitz, ever busy with some last-minute detail, would wind up squeezing in a meal during the national anthem, eating from a paper plate in the press box, rarely failing to leave a stain of spaghetti sauce on his own tie. Poor Horwitz, the franchise's ugly duckling; he was Bronx-born, blue-collar, a foot soldier to the end.

Actually, Horwitz knew the reporters had to ask Doc the questions about Darryl's book, and the press knew Horwitz had to act as a buffer. It was all part of a well-rehearsed scene, played out year after year while the Mets lived in the Scandal

•

Hotel. Sooner or later, every Mets player seemed to look to Horwitz for protection, but Gooden had been the most shielded of all, arriving as a teenage phenom back in 1984 with an untouchable fastball and a penchant for finding trouble. It was just small-change trouble at first, fibbing about an ankle injury, causing a scene at a rental-car office, but then big trouble followed when Gooden tested positive for cocaine in the spring of 1987. Five years later, Gooden had grown immeasurably, had come to be adored by the organization in the same way that Strawberry came to be scorned. He no longer needed Horwitz's protection, only now the ugly drug-abuse memory was being thrown in his face and the PR man felt obligated.

"Guys . . . please, could you do me a favor? Please." Horwitz was almost begging. Doc took it calmly, as usual, though. He stood by his locker, taking swings at imaginary fastballs, smiling a gentle smile, shaking his head, and letting Strawberry's charge go without any form of retaliation. Later Gooden would say privately, "You know, I could bury Darryl if I really wanted to." What did he mean? Gooden wouldn't amplify. For years there'd been whispers about other drug problems in the Met clubhouse. In '87 one rumor, which said another Met would shortly join Gooden in Smithers, became so widespread that Marv Albert brought it up during a national pregame show on NBC. Speculation naturally centered around Strawberry, because he was close to Gooden and because he'd made it no secret that he enjoyed the nightlife. Nothing ever came of it, however, and eventually the rumors ran out of steam. If Doc knew something, he decided not to use it against his old buddy. Gooden seemed to take Darryl's trespasses without any real anger, just as he'd let it pass when Straw failed to show up at his wedding back in '87, accepting the explanation that Strawberry had an endorsement commitment in Los Angeles that day with Eric Davis.

While Gooden was hurt that Strawberry would raise the specter of his cocaine use, but was willing to let it slide, teammates were angry. "I love Darryl," said Kevin Elster, "but he

•

fucked up. What he did was wrong." At another locker, Dave Cone smiled wryly and said, "I guess Straw forgot the things he used to do before he found God." Indeed, Strawberry had recently made a much-heralded conversion to born-again Christianity, although the news was met skeptically by his former teammates. "He'll be back on the streets soon enough," said one of Darryl's closer friends on the Mets. If Darryl was so close to the heavens, his old friends wanted to know, how could he possibly seek to injure his compatriot?

The only way to know was to ask Straw himself. That's the beauty of covering spring training. Unlike the regular season, when the teams are scattered around the continent, the Mets were no farther than an hour from the Braves, Expos, and Dodgers, and only slightly farther from the Yankees, Astros, and Twins. Finding Straw was easy enough: jump into the rental, cruise up I-95 to Vero Beach.

The ride was exactly thirty-three miles, a straight shot of smooth, triple-laned highway. The speed limit is sixty-five through most of Florida, but only the meek obey. "Press emergency," the reporters howled as two carloads pushed the speedometer to seventy-five and better. Even at that speed, Florida's Porsches and Mercedeses went streaming by as, somewhere, a Florida state trooper waited, his Mustang 5.0 ready to take on Europe's most muscular challengers.

"I can take any car on this highway," a trooper once told a New York reporter he'd pulled over for speeding. "If I feel like catchin' them, I do." The newsman pointed at his own speedster, a Toyota Supra Turbo, and said, "What about this baby?"

The trooper half-laughed, half-spit, and said, "Don't make me laugh, son."

Ah, spring. Another Met spring. A week into it and the throttle was already opened. Where was the road heading? Anything was possible for this team, as the men who ran it knew all too well by now. "I never expected to learn so much

·

about the law in this job," Horwitz had said once, summing up his tenure as PR man–bail bondsman. Only no one, not Horwitz, not Harazin, not even the team psychiatrist, Dr. Allan Lans, was prepared for the next exit ramp, and the month of hell to which it led.

FIVE TRAITS BALLPLAYERS LOOK FOR IN WOMEN
1. Large breasts.
2. A willingness to have sex on the first night.
3. A willingness to leave the room soon after sex.
4. A willingness to leave the player alone until the next time he's in that city.
5. Large breasts.

•

MARCH

MARCH 11. PORT ST. LUCIE.

T HE DAY BEGAN like so many March days in Port St.
Lucie: The beat reporters were lounging in the press room,
putting off writing yet another spring-training story they knew
would have no life. After so many years of Darryl and Keith,
and Davey and Cashen, and more Darryl and more Keith, the
1992 Mets offered nothing to the boys responsible for the day-
to-day dispatches. Nothing meant . . . nothing. Eddie Murray
had already made it clear the press wasn't welcome at his
locker. Bobby Bonilla, even in the opening days of his Met
tenure, proved to be an empty quote: He spoke a lot but said
little. That's an art the majority of players and decision-
makers in sports attempt to perfect, ever afraid of saying something that could come out the wrong way and haunt them
forever. "Again," Bonilla would say, "I'm just here to be one
of the guys. People want to focus on the money but I don't
think about it. Again, I'm just very fortunate that I was in the
right place at the right time to become a free agent. I don't
want to make waves, I just want to play baseball and help us
win. Again, wherever they want me to play, whatever they
want me to do . . ." Zzzzzzzzzz.

To reporters there's nothing worse than a dull player, and
the Mets' ultraconservative management was finding more and
more of them. Of course, dull didn't always mean dull: Sometimes it just meant extremely cautious. Daryl Boston, a
backup outfielder, was as popular with both teammates and

•

reporters as any Met. In a social setting he always seemed to be on the move, gliding from one corner to another in the bar, working the women in between downing beers with the boys, always looking like he was having the time of his life. In fact, nobody showed up with more different women on his arm than the Mayor. He didn't discriminate either: Black and single, Boston squired women of all races around town, and usually in style. No one dressed more elegantly or traveled in more limos than Boston, or DeBo, as he was also known. The lifestyle seemed to fit too, for he had the long, lean body and the athletic grace of a star, even if his game didn't earn him that kind of status.

Boston hadn't lived up to the potential scouts saw in him when he was drafted out of high school as the seventh pick in the country in 1981. Writers who saw him play high school quarterback in his hometown of Cincinnati say he made the wrong career choice, insisting he could have been an NFL signal-caller. He'd shown up as a Met in May 1990, picked up on waivers after the White Sox, managed by Torborg at the time, released him. A few weeks later the Mets made their first trip to Cincinnati; after the first game, an extra-long, gleaming white limo pulled up in the tunnel outside the clubhouse. Reporters were intrigued: Whose was it? "DeBo's," Strawberry said. "He's showing me and Doc the town tonight."

Boston was suspicious of the media, having been labeled an underachiever in Chicago. As a Met, on the other hand, he enjoyed great press as he stepped into the center-field vacuum created by the trades of Lenny Dykstra and Mookie Wilson, and played solidly. Soon enough he was the most animated Met when it came to casual conversation, talking with reporters about basketball or kidding with them about his late-night exploits. But as soon as the notebook opened, Boston clammed up. He responded to even innocuous spring-training features with shrugs and one-line answers, refusing to offer the slightest opinion, emotion, perspective, anything.

It was comical: "DeBo," a reporter friendly with him

•

would say, "this is ridiculous. Give me something to work with here. I'm trying to make you look good, for chrissakes."

"Can't," Boston would say. "Just happy to be here, man, you know that."

What was he afraid of? Nothing except his career. Like many players, Boston lived with an unspoken fear that this grand life could be stolen from him at any moment if he opened his mouth and the words somehow came out wrong, either in the way he spoke them or in the way reporters wrote them. Starting in high school, star players are told over and over by coaches and advisers to be wary of the press—the enemy. The notion is reinforced as they move up the organizational ladder, so much so that it becomes ingrained. Eventually some dare to think and speak freely, while some refuse to take the chance of being misquoted or misinterpreted. In Boston's case, it didn't make him a bad guy, and eventually the beat guys gave up on him, content to joke with him about his zest for women instead of asking him to analyze his batting slump or the state of the team.

Problem was, more and more players like Boston were the rule in the Mets clubhouse. Willie Randolph hadn't survived thirteen years as a Yankee in the Bronx Zoo for nothing; he was another nice guy who'd long since mastered the art of the safe quote. Vince Coleman was Vince Coleman, hostile and suspicious. There were other good guys—Dwight Gooden, John Franco, Dave Magadan, Mackey Sasser, Pete Schourek, and Todd Hundley were among the more media-friendly—but there was little of the charisma for which the eighties Mets had become famous.

Only a few years earlier, a trip to the Mets camp was guaranteed to leave your notebook smoking. The daily routine started at approximately 8:30 A.M., when you first walked in the clubhouse door. For the next ninety minutes or so, the Mets were yours: a human buffet table from which to select the day's story. Even in their most turbulent years, covering the club in spring training required a series of daily player features, and it

•

helped to have an idea or two in mind when you reached the ballpark. But even if you didn't, cruising the clubhouse would solve your problem. They were the glory boys then, a team full of charismatic characters who loved seeing their names in the papers. You only had to keep your eyes and ears open. In terms of one-day shock value, nothing compared to the day in '87 when scrawny Lenny Dykstra burst through the doors, his muscles exploding from his skin, his face having disappeared between two fleshy cheeks, his neck a block, his legs and arms swollen beyond recognition. Wally Backman looked up and said, "Lenny, what the fuck happened to you?"

"Dude, been taking some of those good vitamins, you know?" Dykstra said, his eyes turning into little slits as he grinned. Steroids? Dykstra just laughed. But how else could the little center fielder have put on thirty pounds of muscle? Anyone who knew Dykstra knew he didn't have the discipline or the work ethic to spend an hour in the weight room, let alone a winter. Besides, that was Dykstra: a crazy kid who'd do anything to make himself better, more famous, and above all, filthy rich. Nobody played harder, nobody dived into more outfield walls in the name of winning, but beyond that, Lenny was obsessed with money. He gambled wildly, needed the action on anything and everything—golf, cards, you name it. The gambling got him in trouble in 1990, when baseball investigated him for having written a check for a gambling debt to an ex-convict, but it didn't curtail his thirst for the spoils of wealth. From the moment he proved he could play as a Met, he wanted the big money that big numbers could bring, and by '87 he was blaming Davey Johnson for keeping it from him by platooning him with Mookie Wilson in center field. Dykstra became bitter, to the point where it affected his play. Johnson finally lost patience with Dykstra, and the Mets made the mistake of trading him rather than handing him the everyday center-field job, which, when he finally got it in Philadelphia, earned him the lucrative contract he craved.

Of all the Mets from the golden era, Dykstra was the most

entertaining for reporters because he was so reckless and so consumed with rumors and innuendo.

"Dude, we gotta talk," he'd whisper in your ear as he walked by. At his locker, he did most of the interviewing. "Whaddaya hear, man, am I gettin' traded or what?" Most of the time you'd end up repeating the latest rumor in the press room—no matter how outrageous—just to keep Dykstra happy, but usually his attention span evaporated after two sentences anyway. That was Lenny's way, fast and unpretentious. When he finally got his money and his fame, he seemed to change, though. He'd always thought he was invulnerable, but with money he grew bolder, and his near-fatal car crash in '91 seemed to be a culmination of his excessive lifestyle.

But in the eighties Dykstra was still a kid, so honest he never bothered to hide his impatience with the interview process. "Lenny, got some time this morning?" a reporter would ask. Dykstra, puffing hard on an early-morning cigarette before the workout, would say, "Dude, you know I've got nothing to say."

"Lenny, people want to read about you."

"Dude, you've asked me all the questions before. I've given you all the answers. You know what I'm gonna say. So go ahead and write the interview. Whatever you say I said, I said. I trust ya, dude." And with a friendly pat on the shoulder, Dykstra would leave you with an empty notebook.

That was never the case with Gary Carter, though. The standard rule in spring training—any time of the year, actually—was that if you were absolutely, desperately out of ideas, you went to Carter. That's because (a) he was always accessible, (b) he would talk forever, and (c) he would give you *something* usable out of the pages and pages of quotes that now choked your notebook. There was always plenty of self-promotion, for which teammates came to dislike him over the years. Indeed, they—Hernandez, especially—never got comfortable with that aw-shucks, nonstop smile, but Carter was one of the kindest and most accommodating Mets, ever there to rescue a

•

reporter on a slow day, even in bad times. And there was a certain comfort level in dealing with Carter: Whether or not he was full of shit, he was consistent and therefore in some sense genuine.

Davey Johnson had been a manager so sure of himself that

DARRYL AND KEITH

—B.K.

I FIRST HEARD THE rumblings at the tail end of the '88 playoffs. A player close to me whispered, "Hernandez is killing you in this clubhouse." The warning needed no translation: Behind my back, my old buddy Mex was raging about the column I'd written with Dave Cone for the *Daily News*.

You remember the Column. In it, Cone called Jay Howell a "high school pitcher"— resulting in a pummeling from the Dodgers in Game Two of the NLCS. It was a bad choice of words by Cone, and a bad decision by me to let it appear in print. Cone and I both admitted to our mistakes, but after he'd won Game Six, we felt our debt to the Met community had been repaid. But not to Hernandez, who was telling players not to speak to me, not to trust me.

Until then, I felt my relationship with the first baseman was healthy enough. At least I understood the ground rules of Mex's politics: He used me; I used him. Mike Lupica once called Hernandez the "Prince of Darkness," which drove Hernandez insane. Mex was obsessed more with Lupica than any other reporter, constantly bad-mouthing him to other Mets. Finally, one day in 1989, tired of listening to Mex's anti-

Lupica rhetoric, Lee Mazzilli told Hernandez, "The real reason Lupica makes you so mad is because what he says is true."

Still, Hernandez could help a beat reporter in a competitive clubhouse, and as long as you understood the distinction between his off-the-record and on-the-record dual personalities, you were fine with him. But by the tail end of the '88 season, right into the '89 spring training, Hernandez turned meaner, more distrustful than ever, perhaps because he was older, wearier of New York, a touch slower with the bat. It wasn't just the media who sensed Hernandez's metamorphosis.

Darryl Strawberry noticed Keith's darkening personality, too. Strawberry had his flaws, just like Hernandez, but there was always something less calculating about the way he dealt with people. In spring training of '88, Lupica had written an article for *Esquire* that quoted Strawberry at length questioning the professionalism of his teammates, including Gary Carter, Lenny Dykstra, and Backman.

As soon as the story ran, my assignment for the *News* was to gather player reaction. It wasn't a comfortable task, and Straw-

•

he gave his team complete freedom of speech. They ripped him in the papers and he ripped back. No problem, no grudge held. He enjoyed the newspaper game, in part because he knew how much the big headlines irritated Frank Cashen. In fact, Davey was always bitching about Cashen in the papers, wondering

---

berry was furious with me, believing I'd added fuel to the controversy. There was an awful, tense moment when Dykstra read a copy of the *Esquire* story at his locker, and, with Darryl only a few feet away, then looked up, his voice full of hurt, saying, "Straw, you buried me, man."

I used that exchange in the paper, covering the secondary angle of the story like any reporter would. Strawberry didn't understand—we didn't speak for days. Soon after, my father suffered a bad stroke and I was forced to leave the Mets camp. My petty quarrel with Darryl evaporated; I was more interested in seeing my father walk and talk again. Nine days later, I returned to Port St. Lucie. My father's crisis had passed, although he hadn't yet regained his speech or the feeling in the right side of his body.

I didn't want to be in the clubhouse. In my thoughts, I was still in the hospital with my dad. Moments after I reluctantly rejoined the Mets, more in a daze than anything else, I felt a hand on my shoulder. It was Strawberry.

"I heard about your dad. Tell him I'm praying for him," Darryl said. He offered his hand and we shook. The *Esquire* article was never mentioned again, and from that day, Strawberry and I never fought again. In fact,

during the crisis caused by the Cone column in the playoffs, Strawberry never sided with Hernandez. Gently, Darryl said, "Things got a little fucked up with Coney, huh?" It was his way of saying: Mistakes happen.

By spring training of 1989, Strawberry had severed whatever ties he'd enjoyed with Keith. In the early years, Darryl had let Hernandez serve as his mentor, but by '89 Strawberry rebelled, sensing weakness in the aging teacher. "Look at him, he's so fucking fat," Strawberry said one day that spring. It was true—Hernandez had gained weight over the winter. And he hadn't become any kinder to me. In fact, more and more players told me a confrontation was brewing with Hernandez over the Cone column. Even Cone was beginning to wear down.

"I hear every day that I can't trust you," Cone said. "It gets to you after a while." Hernandez was making it politically unpopular for anyone to be seen talking to me. He still had enormous influence in that clubhouse. So I surrendered to my first and—I made this vow a long time ago—my last moment of unprofessionalism. It was a mistake, and I learned from it. What I did was use a nugget of information against Hernandez that I knew would even the score.

●

41

aloud how the GM could deny him a contract extension—or the respect he deserved. So if the manager wasn't afraid to take on the GM in print, players figured anything was fair game.

Nobody took more license than Darryl Strawberry. He was so volatile, so unpredictable—even in spring training—

DARRYL AND KEITH

(continued)

In the fall of '88, I learned that Hernandez was subtly working against Strawberry in the MVP balloting. Darryl was a leading candidate, but so was teammate Kevin McReynolds. Hernandez was quietly telling reporters who had MVP votes that year—two from each city are given votes on a rotating basis every season—that McReynolds, not Strawberry, deserved the award.

Turns out Kirk Gibson won it, Strawberry finished third, and who knows how many votes Darryl lost because of Hernandez? By mid-March 1989, I wanted Hernandez to know that if he intended to make my life so bleak, it could work both ways. So one morning, when Strawberry was in one of his anti-Keith rages, I said, "You know, the man is no friend of yours."

"Fuck, I know that," Strawberry said.

"No, I mean he hurt you some last year in the MVP thing."

Strawberry's eyes narrowed. I continued.

"He told a few reporters K-Mac deserved to win."

"That right?" Strawberry said, playing it cool. But I knew the point had registered. Strawberry walked away, and the matter was dropped. I walked away, too, wonder-

ing what I'd accomplished. It was a moment of pure spite, and I didn't enjoy it as much as I thought I would. In fact, I regretted it instantly. What Hernandez said about Strawberry to other reporters off the record—no matter how destructive—was none of my business.

That night, I was told Hernandez and Strawberry were involved in a near fistfight at a Port St. Lucie bar. Hernandez didn't know where Straw's anger was coming from, and the hard feelings spilled over into the next morning, when the Mets were lining up for their annual team photo. When a photographer tried to position Hernandez and Strawberry together, Darryl snapped, "I don't want to sit next to no backstabber," meaning Hernandez. Hernandez shot back, "I'm tired of your baby crap," at which point the two started throwing punches.

It was a public-relations nightmare, with TV devouring every moment of it: teammates stepping in between the two, Strawberry screaming obscenities at Hernandez, going after him a second and third time. Strawberry stormed off the field, packed, and left camp. The workouts resumed, but the stunned press corps collected in the Met clubhouse. Everyone sort of laughed about it, but there was still a nervous tension in the air. Even the most senior writers in the group admitted they'd never wit-

that most sports editors would've been wise to assign one reporter to cover Strawberry, and just Strawberry. It was always something. In '88 Strawberry stirred the drink Reggie-style by ripping his teammates individually in a smoke-filled *Esquire* magazine article; in '89 he walked out of camp when the Mets

---

nessed such out-in-the-open hostility between teammates.

A few minutes later, when Davey Johnson was leaving his office on his way back to the field, he saw me and said, "Klap, you got a minute?" We were standing about ten feet from Hernandez's locker, and at that moment Keith was changing his spikes.

"I don't know how all this started," Davey said, "but Keith thinks you had something to do with that fight with Darryl." So. He knew. Someone had told someone who told someone. At that point, Hernandez shouted, "And don't you fucking deny it, Bob!"

In an instant we were in each other's faces, separated only by Johnson.

"You're totally unprofessional," Hernandez yelled.

"You know all about that, don't you?" I shouted back. Keith was mad, I was mad, and I wondered if, for the first time in my career, I was about to be punched by a player. If Hernandez wanted to go that far, I was ready, but it quickly became clear to me that this incident wouldn't escalate beyond words.

Hernandez let Davey remain between us, even though we were so close our noses almost touched. What really told me this outburst was more for cosmetic effect—probably for the other reporters in the room—was when Hernandez shouted, "Don't even come near my locker again—you or your fucking boss."

He meant Lupica. Hernandez thought Mike ran the *Daily News,* which actually wasn't far from the truth. But when Hernandez uttered the word "boss," he turned his face away from mine. To have left it there would've meant literally spitting in my face. And that, Hernandez knew, was a line even he could not cross, not even with a reporter he disliked.

We exchanged a few more epithets—Tom Verducci of *Newsday* called it a draw—before Davey finally pushed Keith out the door. Or more accurately, Hernandez allowed himself to be taken out of the room. We didn't speak for weeks, until Davey called me, Keith, and Lupica into his office and said, "This shit has to stop now." Mike and Keith, drawn to each other, I think, in a bizarre love-hate thing—two stars, you know—seemed to welcome the chance for détente. They did most of the talking, although they never did learn to trust each other, even to this day. Meanwhile, Davey and I looked at each other, smiling a smile that said: Baseball was never meant to be this crazy, was it?

•

•

refused to extend his contract, then came back and caused an uproar by taking a punch at Keith Hernandez while posing for the team picture; in '90 Strawberry was fresh out of a rehab center, the result of a violent confrontation with his wife that winter. Alcohol rehab, the Mets and Strawberry said, and some of Straw's teammates rolled their eyes, as if they knew there had to be more to it. In camp Strawberry was the subject of daily speculation, since he was entering his free-agent year. You could ask every day, "Darryl, you coming back?" And Strawberry would have a different answer every time you asked.

That was Darryl, who never did understand how completely he wore out the Mets' patience with his on-again, off-again declarations of his desire to go home to L.A./stay in New York. Ever in search of the father figure he lacked growing up, Strawberry was all too impressionable, listening to anyone who had his ear. People close to him say all he wanted was to feel loved, but Cashen got tired of feeding Strawberry's ego, and finally the GM let his impatience get in the way of his business sense and allowed his superstar to leave town. It was Strawberry who gave the Mets marquee value, who made the ballpark buzz with anticipation, who made the fans care passionately. They either loved him or loathed him, but they all wanted to know what he was like, what he was going to do next.

Like most star athletes, Strawberry was self-centered and egocentric, socially unskilled and not well educated. But Ron Darling, the Ivy Leaguer, once called Darryl "the very best friend I have on this team." Ever since he'd broken into the big leagues, Darling had been surrounded by people who wanted something from him: time or money or access to beautiful women. Handsome, intelligent, polite, Darling was the Robert Redford of the big leagues, and outsiders tried to force themselves into Darling's personal life, figuring baseball was just a stepping stone for a future career in politics or Hollywood. He came to disdain such hangers-on—"fucking greenflies," Dar-

•

ling called them—using ballplayers' slang for the human insects that buzz around money.

But in Strawberry, Darling saw none of the fake social graces, none of the pretentiousness. When Darling asked Darryl a question, he knew he was getting the truth. And like the rest of the Mets, Darling was fascinated by Strawberry's athletic skill. Nothing brought the ballpark to a standstill like a Strawberry at-bat. It's like Lee Mazzilli once said: "Every time Darryl comes to bat, I make sure I'm in the dugout because sooner or later he's going to hit the longest home run in the history of the game, and I don't want to miss it." Even in the clubhouse, Strawberry was set apart from the rest of the Mets. He was a six-foot-six thoroughbred, taller and stronger than any of his teammates, and he enjoyed showing off his muscles. He'd walk past a reporter shirtless, flex a bicep, and say, "Don't you wish you had guns like these?" In the clubhouse, however, where bodies are open to inspection and locker-room humor, teammates joked about Strawberry's more private natural gifts. Once, as Straw headed for the shower, Dave Cone laughed and said, "I'd like to have that 'Johnson' just for one day. I'd like to see how much my life would change."

*   *   *

The deeper the Mets take us into the nineties, the warmer those golden-era memories become. In the spring of '92, Strawberry's book was the only controversy in camp, at least through the first ten days of March. Management had seemingly won its war with the press, putting together a team that was going to sell newspapers with its play on the field. There was barely a shred of day-to-day intrigue in this camp—not even a single struggle between platooning players—so the seven beat writers were showing up at eight-thirty, looking left, looking right, and sadly asking one another, "What the fuck is there to say about this team?"

And these were *veterans* who were stumped. Marty Noble

•

from *Newsday* had made a living in the eighties cozying up to Keith Hernandez, gloating in the mini-exclusives Mex would give him in exchange for gushing praise. Noble, more than anyone, embodied the spirit of cutthroat competition that defined the New York newspaper beat. He enjoyed keeping his distance from the other writers, certain he was more talented, wittier, and smarter than his colleagues. Tall and blond, he'd developed a huge gut over the years. We couldn't understand how a former athlete—he'd once been a pretty good high school basketball player from Waldwick, New Jersey—could allow himself to become so obscenely out of shape, but Noble reveled in his image. No one cut a more distinctive figure among reporters, and that's what he sought.

He once told a story about having called Ted Simmons, now the Pirates' GM, in pursuit of a story. "He didn't recognize my name when I told him I'd interviewed him a couple of times," Noble said, "so I said, 'You know, the blond fat guy from New York.' He said, 'Oh yeah, Marty, how ya doing?' "

Noble took some needling from players about his gut. "Yo, Marty," Ron Darling once called out, standing next to an exercise bike in a visitors' clubhouse. "You ever meet Larry Lifecycle? He could help you see your toes again." Noble laughed. He enjoyed the attention.

His obsession with the job grated on his fellow beat writers, however. He annoyed them to no end with his habit of circling back after the manager's daily press conference to have a personal audience with Jeff Torborg. He knew it wasn't kosher; Torborg didn't have time to do one-on-ones with everyone, and as such there was a professional agreement among the writers that everyone got him at once. But Noble loved to create tension on the beat by bending the rules. He drove Jay Horwitz crazy the way he operated, and other writers as well. He infuriated Joe Sexton of the *Times* to the point where Sexton wouldn't talk to him, and they spent a year and a half on the beat together, at times sitting side by side in the press box without so much as saying hello.

•

Dan Castellano from the *Newark Star-Ledger* was quite the opposite. On the beat since the late seventies, he was liked by all the players because he didn't rely on a tabloid's venom. He had no enemies on the beat either—everyone confided in Big Dan; he was that trustworthy. Of all the Mets who warmed up to Danny, no one trusted him more than Lee Mazzilli. He became closer to Castellano than to his own teammates, and, as one Italian to another, referred to Danny, in brotherhood, as "Wop."

Joe Sexton was the *Times*'s answer to New York's tabloid wars, put on the beat in 1991 to give the city's elitist newspaper a reporter who was willing to trade punches with the *News* and the *Post.* Sexton was intense, intelligent, the thirty-year-old son of a prominent New York lawyer, and anti-establishment in every way. A radical by newspaper standards, he found himself instantly at odds with Torborg and the organization.

Steve Adamek of the *Bergen Record* was full of opinions and nicknamed the Shell Man—a reference to the old TV commercials featuring the Shell Answer Man—because he seemed to have the answer to every question ever posed in a press box. Finally, Ed Christine of the Westchester Gannett newspaper chain, owned by *USA Today,* was a former marine who had served two tours in Vietnam. Hence, nothing in the sports world fazed him, least of all a hostile Eddie Murray or Vince Coleman. Christine, a martial-arts specialist, would often boast to the boys on the beat of his prowess on the battlefield, and, after a few late-night beers, would make vague threats against any player who might be "stupid enough to fuck with me."

Despite accumulated knowledge, experience, and street smarts, the New York writers were tapped dry by early March. For once Sid Fernandez's weight wasn't an issue. He'd lost forty-five pounds in an off-season diet clinic. Doc Gooden's shoulder, recovering from arthroscopic surgery, was the biggest story, but progress was slow and steady and two weeks into camp it was the oldest kind of news. Howard Johnson was an

•

intriguing figure, having shifted from right field to center in his first full year as an outfielder. The Mets had to know it was a huge gamble, considering HoJo's fragile psyche. That, and the fact that Johnson had played a total of one month in the out-field. Did he have the instincts to play center? More signifi-cant, would failing at the new position ruin his confidence at the plate? But there was little to report until HoJo had played a couple of weeks of exhibition games, and besides, HoJo was in his second year of born-again Christianity, a conversion that had made him about as quotable as Daryl Boston. In a sense, Dave Cone was the new Darryl, a star entering his free-agent year, only he wasn't going to make it an issue in the newspa-pers.

The quiet was unnerving, and reporters quickly discov-ered that Torborg wasn't going to provide much help. As cour-teous and articulate as he was, he went out of his way to make sure nothing he said turned into a headline. In fact, the man-ager was careful never to utter an opinion on much of anything, for fear that it might offend someone. Ever the politician, he left himself room for policy reversal or a change of mind if the winds started blowing in the wrong direction.

Torborg was a perfect fit for Mets management, a man as well educated, as conservative, and as concerned with image as his bosses. His résumé read like that of an athletic director: a B.S. degree in education from Rutgers University and a mas-ter's degree in athletic administration from Montclair State College. He did his master's thesis on the effects of platooning in baseball, which is only fitting, since, as Mets fans would quickly learn, he is a slave to the percentages. More precisely, he's a product of his education, a man who goes strictly by the book in virtually every way, allowing computer printout num-bers and rigidly defined roles for his players to dictate game strategy, while enforcing traditional baseball protocol as his code of discipline for his players.

After a brief stint as manager of the Cleveland Indians in the late seventies, he'd become a coach with the Yankees.

·

Then, in the early eighties, he was offered the head baseball job at Princeton University, and, indeed, college is where he would be more suited, in the way that Rick Pitino is more suited to coach college basketball than pro, and Lou Holtz to college football. Problem is, unlike football and basketball, there's no money to be made in college baseball, and when George Steinbrenner, who liked having a college-educated man on his coaching staff, offered Torborg a lucrative multiyear deal to remain a Yankee coach, Torborg passed on Princeton. Religious and a nondrinker himself, Torborg wanted to teach and discipline his players in a controlled environment, and basically treated major league millionaires with a college mentality. That was fine for the White Sox, a young team hungry for guidance. The Mets, however, were full of wealthy veterans who would not take kindly to Torborg's constant daily meetings or his rule forbidding players to drink on team flights.

Torborg had survived ten years in the big leagues as a light-hitting catcher, seven with the Dodgers, three with the Angels. As a manager he sounded as insincere and superfluous as Tommy Lasorda, except Lasorda knew he was doing schtick when he talked about bleeding Dodger blue, his players knew it, and he knew they knew it. Torborg tried to make New York believe he was earnest and candid, but within a few weeks the city realized this was a manager obsessed with image. No other manager had ever taken to the airwaves like Torborg, on the twenty-four-hour sports-talk radio station WFAN twice a day, putting his spin on the day's events. Mets fans weren't interested in a well-polished manager or his well-polished, empty answers. All they wanted was a manager who could make the eighties return to Shea. The Mets had promised New York a better, brighter leader in Torborg, someone to erase the memory of Buddy Harrelson. But what they would soon learn is the Mets didn't look or play much differently under Torborg than they had under Harrelson.

Of course, Torborg didn't get so knotted up and overwhelmed by the interview process as little Buddy, who would

•

jot down what he considered clever one-liners to spring on the press after games. But even though Torborg was more sophisticated, it quickly dawned on the beat writers that his answers weren't any more insightful. At this point in the spring, most questions from the press revolved around the lineup or how the Mets matched up against the rest of the National League. Torborg met these queries with the most ambiguous of answers, maybe a smile and an anecdote or a simple "I know what you're saying" to make writers feel comfortable. Torborg avoided substance. He insisted he needed more time to evaluate the Mets, the league, and—no doubt—the press. In other words, he was exactly what the brass wanted, part of a franchise seemingly bound by a pledge to make New York forget how much fun a baseball team could be. Sitting there every day writing next to nothing in your notebook, you couldn't help but think about Davey Johnson sitting in that same chair, saying, "I expect us to go out and dominate our division." Eyebrows would raise all around the room and Davey would simply look at you with a "Yeah, that's right" smile, knowing his every word would end up as a headline somewhere back in New York.

Then Frank Cashen, who would digest the New York papers the next day, would send his manager an angry memo. Photocopied stories would appear on Davey's desk, his quotes highlighted in yellow, with notations from the GM that screamed, "Did you actually say this? How could you say this?" Davey loved that. It meant he'd made the little white-haired GM a little crazier than the day before.

Those days were over now that the Jeff Torborg administration had assumed office. No one disliked the new manager— it was impossible, actually—but in a way he just made everyone miss Davey and the old Mets even more. And that didn't bother the front office in the least. "Sorry we can't help you out this year, guys," Al Harazin would say smugly. The brass, per Cashen's orders, had always kept its distance from the local papers, but the gap had been widened by the strain of reporting on an underachieving ball club and a front office

•

whose golden touch in dealing for the likes of Hernandez and Carter and Cone had turned leaden.

Harazin was more interested than Cashen in maintaining a working relationship with the press, but he was coldly corporate too, a lawyer first and last. The new boss created some hard feelings on press row by effectively banning reporters' children and their families from the spring-training press room. PRESS ONLY, the sign atop the door said, although the beat guys took that as a warning to keep the public out. (It wasn't uncommon for a lost fan to wander in, looking for the ticket office.) But one day Joe Sexton's wife and two young daughters accompanied him to a spring-training game and waited in the press room until they could pick up their game tickets. The room wasn't much, cinder-block walls with not a window in the place. It was a dungeon compared to the lavish press room at the Dodgers' spring training home in Vero Beach, a sprawling room overlooking practice fields, complete with a big-screen TV and a full bar where writers, coaches, and others enjoyed a predinner cocktail and talked baseball. Still, it was the only room where the Mets could serve lunch to scouts, writers, and their own executives before a game. The Sexton family sat at one of the tables that day, waiting for their tickets, and it rubbed Harazin the wrong way. He told Jay Horwitz to "do something" about the situation, and what choice did poor Horwitz have except to stammer and tell Sexton there would now be a new policy for the press room. The Mets never seemed so petty.

* * *

Then came the news. Who knows how the Mets might have turned out differently if not for the news that hit camp on March 11? There are some members of the organization who believe the '92 Mets were doomed the day the St. Lucie Police Department released the chilling statement that three Mets players were being investigated in the wake of a rape accusation.

Rape. The word swept through the Mets' camp, shatter-

·

ing the lazy calm the front office had strived to create. No one actually walked into the St. Lucie County Sports Complex and read the announcement to the Mets or the press corps. Instead, local news reporters were tipped off first, and it wasn't long before all the reporters were on the phone to their New York offices—baseball writers turned crime reporters—saying, "You won't believe this . . ."

Needless to say, the New York offices were overwhelmed by the news. No one enjoyed the idea of covering a rape investigation—even the headline-starved editors knew it would be a terribly tense assignment—but finally the Mets had made news again. If it had to be a sex crime . . . well, it wasn't the newspapers who'd brought the charges. If anything, it was the Mets who'd created their own hell.

Word of the players' identities spread quickly that day, but no one could be absolutely certain. The St. Lucie police wouldn't reveal them and Al Harazin stood outside the executive offices, looking ashen, saying only that the club had no comment. The new GM's voice actually shook as he spoke to reporters, and for the first time in a long while, his eyes lost that cold look. Harazin seemed to be pleading with the press for a little compassion.

It did make for a difficult crossroads. We were being asked to cover an alleged crime involving players with whom we were also asked to mingle and establish relationships every day. No faction of this nation's press corps comes in closer day-to-day contact with its subjects than sportswriters, certainly not in a more threatening environment than an often-hostile locker room. In itself the job of baseball reporting has conflict of interests—developing sources about whom you also are writing critically at times—but this was a much more delicate situation.

The Mets responded by calling a team meeting and stressing that no one should speak to anyone—teammates, club officials, reporters—about the accusations. Players took the warning to heart, fearing the possibility of being subpoenaed if the case went to trial. Reporters and their newspapers, meanwhile, wrestled with the question of revealing the names. All they knew for certain was that the rape allegedly had taken place in Port St. Lucie a year earlier, March 30, 1991. Without police sources to confirm the names, none of the New York papers would print them that first day. The next day, however, police made public the address where the alleged rape had occurred, and reporters were stunned to learn it was a house Gooden had rented the previous spring. His family had been with him in Port St. Lucie then, so it didn't sound right. But it was later learned that Gooden's wife and kids had returned to their home in St. Petersburg in late March, before the alleged crime took place. In any case, when *The Miami Herald*, quoting police sources, revealed a day later that Vince Coleman and Daryl Boston were the other players involved, the New York papers followed suit.

By then every paper in New York had dispatched a news or crime reporter to Port St. Lucie to take the burden of covering the rape story from the baseball writers. Shirley Perlman from *Newsday* and Bob Gearty from the *News* were Florida-bound within two days. Details began to emerge: The woman was from New York, claimed to have met the players at a local bar, offered Gooden a ride home, went into his house to use the bathroom, and allegedly was pounced on by the players in question. The story was given sensational treatment by all three New York tabloids, but no one made quite the same splash as news reporter Andrea Peyser of the *Post*. Sent down to report on the rape, she camped out in the beach bars and wrote stories detailing the pickup game between players and groupies. She interviewed some of the women hoping to meet Mets players and identified players like David Cone and Daryl Boston as having sat at the bar with girls on their laps. SWING TRAINING screamed the front-page headline in the *Post*, and though there was nothing terribly shocking about ballplayers picking up women in bars, it infuriated the players and the organization, adding to the emotional atmosphere surrounding the rape allegation.

Through it all, it was Doc who made the issue so trouble-

·

some to the baseball writers, who'd covered him for years. Boston was single, so his main fear was being charged with a crime. Coleman, like Gooden, was married, but otherwise there was no comparison as far as damage to reputation. Gooden was revered in New York, but now, well . . . it seemed that one day he was the youngest pitcher ever to win a Cy Young Award, a genuinely good guy for whom reporters had gained enormous respect, and the next he was an alleged rapist, someone who supposedly lured a young woman into his home, then attacked her with the help of Boston and Coleman. It didn't seem to fit, and it gnawed at reporters, perhaps players as well, creating a tangible tension in the locker room.

Meanwhile, news as well as sports reporters from papers all over the country were flooding the tiny locker room, some looking for information for rape stories, some assigned to write about the mood of a team already on trial in many ways. Players became more and more agitated, bumping into reporters and TV cameras at every turn. "Someone's gonna get their ass kicked in here one of these days," John Franco would say out loud, to no one and everyone. Finally, the Mets limited locker-room access, handing out pink passes to "baseball writers only," Jay Horwitz said.

It was a powerful story charged with unspoken emotion, simply by virtue of the racial angle. Three black players and a white woman: Whatever the underlying reasons or prejudices at work, there was little doubt that the story received more attention, and perhaps was treated more sensationally, because of its interracial nature. In New York racial tensions had heightened in recent years because of violent incidents, specifically several cases of seemingly unprovoked attacks between the races—white kids beating a black teenager to a pulp apparently as some sort of racial message, and vice versa. Sociologists were being quoted on TV news shows saying race relations were more strained than ever, in New York and elsewhere, and only a month or so later the strain exploded into horror when the Rodney King verdict set off riots in Los Angeles and around the country.

Then there was the matter of the Mets' own racial makeup. The color of the clubhouse had changed dramatically in recent years: During the eighties the Mets had been the whitest team in baseball—Gooden, Strawberry, and Mookie Wilson were the only blacks on the ball club during its golden era. The franchise was attacked for it occasionally in the media, and a bitter George Foster, whose skills had diminished considerably, cried racism when he was benched in 1986—even though he'd been replaced by Kevin Mitchell, a black player. Foster was soon after released. Still, there was never any evidence that Cashen or anyone else in the organization dictated such a color scheme, and the Mets' success kept the grumbling to a minimum. While Mookie, strictly a family man, kept to himself, Strawberry and Gooden mingled easily with the white guys; Strawberry, especially, became close to Darling and then Cone and Elster and was very much a part of the inner circle.

In that way the Mets had been different. On most ball clubs the social cliques are inevitably divided along racial lines. Even on close-knit teams, the whites, blacks, and Hispanics tend to go their separate ways on the road, whether it's dinner on an off-day or beers after the game. By '92 the recent arrivals of Vince Coleman, Anthony Young, Eddie Murray, and Bobby Bonilla on the Mets had changed the complexion of the clubhouse in more ways than one. Gooden and Boston gravitated toward the new guys and the Mets had their first truly black clique in the clubhouse since Wilpon and Doubleday bought the team. Now, here were three black guys in the middle of an awful scandal: It was fuel to feed the worst kind of racial stereotype, and it made the matter all the more delicate for the all-white management of the Mets, and for that matter, the seven white beat guys.

You couldn't approach Gooden without thinking of the possible charges that hung over him. Though he was remarkably composed, seemingly unfazed in the face of such humiliation, the small talk was strained, terribly false. "Got nothing to hide from," Gooden told a reporter in a private moment. "This is a joke." Of course, everyone wanted to know his response to

•

the allegations, but the best he could do, even off the record, was whisper side-of-mouth comments such as these. In the meantime, the story mushroomed even further when it was revealed that the alleged victim had dated Dave Cone earlier the same spring. Stories quoted various sources saying the woman had met Gooden at the bar on the night in question to make Cone jealous after their brief fling had ended.

The days were filled with rumor and innuendo, as everyone kept waiting for the cops to show up with handcuffs and formally present charges. The paranoia level doubled among the beat reporters. The sight of a police car anywhere in Port St. Lucie made you wonder where it was heading. Once, three of us were going out for a bite to eat at dusk when we spotted a cop coming from the general direction of Daryl Boston's condo. Should we? We'd better. And off we went, just on the hunch that something was happening. Anthony Young, Boston's roommate, answered the door when we knocked, and looked as if he'd seen a ghost. "I know you guys aren't here to see me," he said, backing away quickly.

Boston came to the door wearing his thousand-yard stare, a menacing look that could scare off even the most hardened reporter. But his tone was surprisingly gentle that day. "If the police have been here to see me, I ain't heard about it," he said. He and the reporters all stared at their feet, not sure what to say next. It was another false alarm.

Into its second week, the investigation widened to include Ron Darling, who was said to have been linked, along with Cone, to the woman, now known to be a thirty-one-year-old Manhattan architect. The case file, opened when the investigation was concluded, would show that Cone had indeed been involved with the woman, and had engaged in a night of group sex with her, her friend, and Darling, the third married Met to be entangled in the scandal. But neither Cone nor Darling played any part in and told police they had no knowledge of the alleged rape. At the end of the '92 season, in fact, Cone said he had yet to speak so much as a word to Gooden, Boston, or

•

Coleman about the affair. "There was so much fear of being called as a witness that nobody talked to anybody about anything," Cone says. "Whatever happened that night, only those guys know, and my feeling is that no one else will ever be sure what the real truth is."

Although he never faced the possibility of arrest, in some ways Cone endured the greatest humiliation. Only five months earlier in Philadelphia, on the final weekend of the '91 season, he also had been accused of rape. Police quickly dismissed the allegation, lending credence to the claim Cone later made that he'd been set up by a spurned groupie.

But that was only the beginning. Soon after Cone was linked to the alleged rape victim in Port St. Lucie, he was named in a lawsuit by three New York women, charging that he'd exposed himself to them in the Mets' bullpen in 1989 and masturbated in front of them. Actually, the women had filed the suit months earlier, only it was merely sexual harassment then; widely known as groupies, the women had accused Cone of threatening them during a game at Shea Stadium, and Cone admitted going into the stands, saying the women had been taunting some of the Mets' wives. After the rape scandal hit the papers, linking Cone indirectly, the women amended the suit to include the masturbation claim. The women gave their story to Andrea Peyser of the *Post*, and the story ran on the front page, sending another tremor through the Mets' shaken organization. When Cone saw it, he was beyond embarrassment. He was now, like most Mets, simply numb.

MARCH 27. PORT ST. LUCIE.

AFTER ALL THAT had been said and written, it was a cartoon that pushed the Mets over the edge. But then, it wasn't just any cartoon. There it was, on Page Six of the *Post*, perhaps the most widely read page in the city, famous for its gossip and general outrageousness: A pitching coach was on the mound, yelling to Cone in the dugout: "Are you almost finished

.

warming up yet?" Cone could be seen only from the waist up, but the cartoon left no doubt about where his hands were. He had an expression of, well, arousal, and teammates on either side were staring down at his crotch in stunned disbelief. The Page Six cartoon humbles some public figure practically every day, but no one could remember it previously tackling the rather delicate subject of celebrity masturbation. Cone was neither surprised nor enraged. "I almost expected something like that," he would say later. But John Franco was practically in a state of seizure. The Mets had a night game scheduled, and Franco was waiting when Cone arrived at the ballpark that afternoon.

"That's it, Coney," he barked. "The motherfuckers have gone too far now. We're gonna do it."

Cone didn't have to ask Franco what he meant. The little lefty had been quietly rallying the troops for days, like a union leader gathering his forces for a strike. It was the Brooklyn in Franco—he needed to retaliate in some form. He'd decided a boycott of the press was the only way the players could hit back. A few days earlier he'd pitched the idea to Bobby Bonilla, figuring Bonilla's support would carry great weight in the clubhouse, and Bonilla was all for it. Cone himself had talked them out of it once already, figuring it would be like lighting a match to a flammable situation and worrying that it would make him look small. It wasn't Cone's style; he'd long since proven himself to be one of the all-time stand-up players of any generation, willing to take responsibility for mistakes rather than hide or conjure up alibis. When he saw Franco's fury this time, however, Cone knew it was hopeless. "I couldn't even begin to reason with Johnny that day," he would say later. "His mind was made up."

Small as Franco was, at five-eight and 175 pounds, there were few players willing to take him on when he was in full rage. You didn't see it often. On the surface he was all laughs, maybe the funniest clubhouse needler in baseball. He was bright and witty and crackled with street-smart wise-guy one-liners, shooting at anything that moved.

His gift was that he could insult most anyone and everyone without drawing blood. More than once he'd defused potential clubhouse problems. In 1990 Bob Ojeda was angry at Buddy Harrelson for removing him early from a game, and, with Ojeda being bounced in and out of the rotation that year along with Ron Darling because the Mets had six starters, it was a delicate issue. Yet Franco, a close friend of Ojeda's, had the entire clubhouse howling the next day by doing an impersonation of a baby crying, high-pitched voice and all: "Waaah, waaah, I didn't want to come out of the game. Waaah, waaah . . ." It went on for minutes. Anybody else and it would have started a brawl. Franco was so uproariously funny that Ojeda had to laugh, and that afternoon he and Harrelson met to iron out their differences.

That was the beauty of Franco: He created laughter that was vital to a baseball team. As such the mood of the clubhouse almost always took its cue from him, but there was a hard, bitter edge to him too. Growing up in Brooklyn made him plenty tough and inherently suspicious, but losing both of his parents—his mother to cancer, his father to a heart attack—over an eighteen-month period in the late eighties hardened his shell just a little more. He was wildly protective of family and friends, ever ready to come to the rescue. When the fuse to his hair-trigger temper was lit, people ran for cover. He could remind you a little of Tommy, Joe Pesci's character in *GoodFellas*—*Man, this guy is crazy.*

In a crowded bar in San Francisco a few years ago, Franco was enjoying a few beers with teammates when some guy with a ponytail accidentally bumped Ojeda. Ojeda paid little attention, but when the guy bumped him again, Ojeda said something and the guy gave him a go-fuck-yourself look. Instantly, Franco was in his face, breathing fire.

"You bump him one more time," he said, "and I'm gonna wrap that fuckin' ponytail around your neck and hang you with it."

The offender, considerably bigger than Franco, was startled by the relief pitcher's fury. He apologized and moved off in another direction. Franco's teammates howled and ordered another round of beers.

As much as his teammates loved him, they were wary of Franco too. Once Ron Darling was standing with a couple of writers in a bar, and somehow the subject turned to the tough guys on the Mets. Darling pointed across the room to where five or six of his teammates had gathered. "I'd take my chances against any of them but that little fuck," he said, referring to Franco. "He's dangerous."

No wonder Franco rarely had problems with reporters.

TRAPPED ON PAGE ONE

—J.H.

O VER THE PHONE, the night editor spoke the words most sportswriters dread: "They want it up front." Up front means the real world of cops and gangsters, and politicians who talk and say nothing. Up front means your story transcends sports, and the bosses want it right up there next to the murders and Mayor Dinkins.

I knew it was coming. What could be juicier for a tabloid than a story of a woman accusing three Mets players of rape? Still, I cringed at the thought. The news and sports sides of a newspaper are separate worlds in most every way. It's not like the old days, when sports pages were filled with flowery prose about the feats of the Yankee Clipper and the Boys of Summer. For years sportswriting has been at least as confrontational as covering cops or politicians, and often more so, given the egos of pampered, millionaire ballplayers who resent the increased scrutiny of a prying media. Writing throughout the eighties about drug scandals, labor warfare, and contract language,

not to mention the likes of Darryl Strawberry, hardened the most romantic of sportswriters. Yet the folks on the other side of the newsroom still like to giggle about how much fun life must be in the "Toy Department."

The clash in philosophy is inevitable. In general, sportswriters enjoy more freedom to analyze, offer perspective, even entertain, in their copy, mainly because it's no longer enough to report the facts about ball games their readers have watched via TV coverage, which is becoming more sophisticated all the time. News side doesn't have to worry that Tim McCarver has already explained in detail how the bank robber pulled the job, and besides, speculating on murder suspects is slightly more libelous than publicly suggesting the star shortstop may soon be traded.

In any case, it's rare when a sportswriter can recognize his own story after it's been moved up front and edited. Thus began my three weeks of hell, as the allegations of a

His status in the clubhouse worked to his advantage—pick a fight with Franco in print and you never knew how wide-ranging the consequences would be. He wasn't afraid to embarrass you. He'd ripped into Harper earlier in the spring in front of teammates over a couple of lines in *The Sporting News Yearbook*—a free-lance assignment—that portrayed him as less than dominating in his two seasons as a Met. But he didn't hold grudges—ten minutes after screaming at Harper, he was joking with him again about something else.

We were both his confidants and his foils. He manipulated

---

gang rape became the hottest story in New York, given front-page, sensational treatment by the newspaper with the most famous front-page headlines in the business. All of the beat writers were caught in the middle, given the task of trying to maintain relationships with players who were the focus of scandal. But the *Post* has a way of capturing such stories with front-page headlines that range from more outrageous to more daring to more creative to just plain funnier than those of the other tabloids. HEADLESS BODY IN TOPLESS BAR was a classic that sold many a T-shirt as well as newspapers. BEST SEX I EVER HAD, a commentary on Donald Trump by Marla Maples, was the talk of New York for a while. In many ways the front page of the *Post* personifies the spirit of a city renowned for its chutzpah. The headlines are supposed to touch a nerve, which is great as long as it's not your nerve.

Indirectly, mine was very much exposed during the frenzy of the rape story. Especially when Andrea Peyser hit town. Peyser, a news reporter at the *Post*, was sent to Port St. Lucie to take over the brunt of the rape coverage, allowing me to go back to the Mets. All the New York papers sent news reporters, but only Peyser gained a measure of instant fame by hanging out in the beach bars, interviewing groupies, observing their interaction with players, and writing about the whole scene. She caused an uproar among the players by naming names and detailing their actions. It made for good reading in New York and, in truth, the groupie phenomenon was a legitimate story since it gave readers a better understanding of the setting as well as the psychology involved in the alleged rape. Of course, Peyser didn't have to worry about asking the same players how their fastballs were coming along. I did, and life got pretty difficult in the clubhouse, especially when one story lumped Bret Saberhagen, married with children, in with single Mets David Cone and Daryl Boston, describing him jumping into a car with a young woman upon leaving the Jensen Ale House.

"Why should I ever talk to you again?" Saberhagen said angrily when he saw me the next day. "It's your fuckin' paper. That was [Kevin] Elster's girlfriend who gave me

•

us like perhaps no other player in the clubhouse when he wanted good press, most recently a few weeks earlier when he was coaxing an overpriced $8 million contract extension from Al Harazin. The smart ones all do it, usually in subtle ways, when courting favor. They have a way of making themselves more available, more candid, sometimes a little more friendly. They'll whisper off-the-record information about the status of their negotiations, as if they've suddenly taken you into their

---

TRAPPED ON PAGE ONE
(continued)

a ride home. The story doesn't say that anywhere, though, does it? What if my wife sees that story? I'm out for a hamburger and a few beers and it looks like I'm pickin' up some bimbo.''

What could I say? I apologized to Saberhagen, and later asked Peyser about it. She stammered through an explanation but clearly had no way of knowing if the girl in question was Elster's girlfriend providing a lift or a groupie making a connection, because she hadn't asked anyone. At best it was reckless journalism; at worst it was libelous.

But in her mind, Peyser was crusading for truth. She was also selling papers, and her editors wanted more. She wrote a column denouncing the baseball writers for covering up for players' sexual habits, refusing to report the truth. She didn't seem to understand that a reporter assigned to cover a baseball team would not last a week on the beat if he—or she—was keeping score in print of which players were out picking up women after the ball games. If a player's nightlife is somehow affecting his performance, then it's an issue, but otherwise, why is it anybody's business? If a presidential candidate is sleeping around, the public has a right to know. A ballplayer may be a public figure as well, but the country's trust is hardly at stake.

In any case, tension was building, and it boiled over when Peyser astonished everyone by marching into the locker room one morning, knowing it would cause a commotion and give her another story. Sure enough, Saberhagen and Cone confronted her, demanding an explanation and an apology for the apparent injustice done to Saberhagen. While Peyser coolly gave answers, Jay Horwitz was in full panic, announcing that the clubhouse was closed and herding as many reporters out the door as he could, then returning to break up the Peyser mess. Peyser did write a column about her locker-room experience, and she remained in Florida for another two weeks, but I didn't see her again. She didn't call, didn't come to the press room, apparently

•

confidence. Wise to it or not, writers inevitably get sucked in, seduced partly by the need to deliver the story, and sometimes by the charm of guys like Franco.

Nobody had a livelier relationship with the press corps than little Johnny. He loved needling, insulting, even commanding the beat guys. Every morning coach Barry Foote closed the clubhouse for a team meeting at nine-fifty, ten minutes before the players were due on the field, and Franco took

---

having decided that I was as much the enemy as the players were.

Still, the war continued. The Mets scandal was the hottest story in town, and papers hungered for new angles. Sports editor Bob Decker fended off demands from news editors who wanted me to give them names of married players I knew for sure cheated on their wives—presumably so Peyser could tail them. Indeed, battle lines were drawn in the newsroom. In the afternoon editorial meetings, news-side people became careful not to tip off sports about certain stories on tap.

In particular, the sports department was kept in the dark about a front-page story that detailed the lawsuit brought by three groupies against Cone for allegedly exposing himself to them and masturbating in the bullpen. Thus, I had no warning of what I was walking into the next morning. Cone, to his credit, didn't hold me responsible, but other players lashed out at me in his defense. Indeed, that story was the low point of the scandal coverage. The three women phoned Peyser the Crusader and told her

they were amending a previous suit against Cone to include sexual harassment. Peyser wrote it hard, quoted their lawyer, but didn't bother to check the background of the women, all well known around the New York sports scene as groupies who came on to players in hotel lobbies and outside of team buses, exposing and fondling themselves. Cone was no saint, but Peyser was out of bounds. Giving these women such a forum for publicity, portraying them as victims without a hint of a character check, wasn't journalism at all.

Three days later, Darryl Strawberry responded to the accusation against Cone by calling the women "pigs" and describing some of their public sexual gestures. The story had many of the same ingredients as the one accusing Cone, but this one, which I wrote, was taken "up front" and then buried on page thirteen. "And they wonder why people become bitter about the press," Cone said softly the next day. In this case, I couldn't disagree.

•

63

great pleasure in counting down the second hand on the clock. Then, in his best Brooklyn accent, his voice boomed throughout the small room: *"All right, yuz motherfuckers, geddout. All of yuz. Out."* As the writers paraded toward the door, Franco would usher them out by the nicknames he'd given them this spring: Klapisch was Moe Green; Harper was Jimmy "The Weasel" Fratianno; Dan Castellano was Clemenza; Joe Sexton was Jughead; Ed Christine was G.I. Joe; Marty Noble was Baby Huey; and Steve Adamek was Tweety Bird. The references to *The Godfather* weren't unusual. For the most part, Franco didn't mind the inevitable mafia jokes he fielded as a heavyweight Italian from Brooklyn, but he liked to put a little fear in writers now and then.

Franco could turn on the writers, and quickly. In the case of the boycott, the baseball writers weren't the enemy, but Franco's loyalties were rigid. The cartoon was especially annoying to him because he didn't care for the *Post* at all. The *Daily News* and *Newsday* could be as rough or rougher on New York teams, but the *Post* seemed to strike more nerves with its back-page headlines. Franco, in fact, was convinced that the *Post* had it in for him. By the nature of his job, a closer is vulnerable to harsh headlines when he blows a save and perhaps the game, but Franco insisted that the *Post* was tougher on him than any other paper in town. One headline in particular, written in late June 1992, would reinforce his belief. DOWN THE JOHN the back page screamed after Franco, who was until then having a superb season, had blown a game. It was more humorous than cruel, as back-page headlines go, but it was the type that might start a fight for the beat writer. Nothing gets writers in more trouble than headlines written by editors who don't have to worry about showing up in the clubhouse the next day. Their job is to sell the paper, plain and simple, with a back page that grabs the attention of readers at the newsstand. Anything clever and catchy is nice, but clever and catchy and delivered like a left hook to the chin is better.

At the *Post* the man responsible for most of the back-page

•

beauties was night editor Pat Hannigan. A no-bullshit editor, Hannigan was a legendary high school athlete himself in Westchester County, New York, some twenty-five years ago, and had little sympathy for the overpaid prima donnas he saw in pro sports these days. Give him the opportunity and he loaded the gun. THROW-JO STRIKES AGAIN, one headline read back in '89, when Howard Johnson, having a much-publicized problem throwing to first base, made a fatal error. CRYBOBBY was bannered across the top of the back page the day after Bobby Bonilla made his infamous call to the press box to protest an error. Then there was the headline in 1988 after Dave Righetti, struggling at the time as the Yankees' closer, lost a game: RAGS GAGS AGAIN. Gulp. Current Yankees radio broadcaster Michael Kay was covering the team for the *Post* at the time, and he figured his only hope was to beg forgiveness. Upon entering the clubhouse that day he went straight to Righetti and apologized for the headline. Righetti understood that Kay hadn't written the headline and didn't hold a grudge. That made him a rarity; writers almost never write the headlines for their stories, but most players don't want to hear that. It's your name on the story, you take the heat. Franco, fortunately, was another who understood the writer wasn't to blame for DOWN THE JOHN, so he merely shook the paper at Harper in the clubhouse the next day and muttered, "Why does your fuckin' paper hate me so much?"

In that sense, for all of his temper, Franco could be eminently fair. Which makes it that much more puzzling that he was an instigator of the boycott. In any case, Franco called a meeting to propose immediate action on the boycott, and the players voted unanimously in favor of it as a way of protesting media coverage they considered an invasion of privacy. In truth, not all of the players were in favor of the idea. At least a few thought Gooden and Boston and Coleman and Cone had brought on their own problems, and why shouldn't they have to face up to them? But no player was about to stand up and say so in such an emotionally charged meeting. The boycott

•

was a childish response and some knew it, but there was no stopping it now.

Funny thing was, the beat writers were delighted by this development. The Mets were boring us to death. The news of the rape allegations had broken two weeks before, but it seemed like two years. Not only had Harazin and Torborg succeeded in removing virtually all charisma from a locker room that only a few years earlier overflowed with it, but the Mets were playing with no more style than they talked.

For weeks our eyes kept telling us that New York was in for a huge disappointment. Not to mention Harazin. More than anyone else, this team was his baby, his first statement as a rookie GM. It was particularly important to him because he'd come up on the business side of the organization, a lawyer who was far more a numbers cruncher than a talent evaluator. He'd never played, coached, or scouted baseball past the Babe Ruth League stage, and he was highly sensitive to the question of whether he knew the game well enough to warrant his new position. He'd earned celebrity status and back-page praise, however, by acting boldly over the winter to reshape a passionless, heartless team that had quit on Buddy Harrelson in 1991. He wasn't going to bring back the spirit of '86, but he was determined to disinfect a germ-infested clubhouse. So he hired Torborg; overspent wildly on free agents Murray and Bonilla; traded whipping boy Gregg Jefferies and duck hunter Kevin McReynolds for Bret Saberhagen; and signed one more solid citizen, Willie Randolph.

On paper the players looked wonderful. Under the hot Florida sun, they looked like a fifth-place team. They were slow and heavy-legged, in the field as well as on the bases, and the ball never seemed to jump off their bats. Bonilla looked overweight and moved like a tank in right field. Murray barely moved at all at first base. Randolph's bat was slow. Howard Johnson was doing the polka in center field. Kevin Elster couldn't throw to first base. Todd Hundley was hitting .120. Vince Coleman had already pulled up once on the bases, protecting a tender hamstring.

•

We saw it, we talked about it, and to some extent we wrote about it. But you can never be sure of what you're seeing in the spring; when the adrenaline throttle is opened come April, it's often a whole new ball game. Baseball writers learn not to judge a team harshly in March, not in print anyway, for fear of looking foolish when the bell rings.

For days writers who covered opposing teams, gathering information to make their season predictions, had been asking us what we thought of the new Mets, and for days we'd been replying in unison: "They stink." Yet most of us wound up picking the Mets to win the NL East anyway. The Pirates had been weakened badly, we thought, by the defection of Bonilla and the salary-related trade of twenty-game winner John Smiley, and no other team looked ready to emerge. Gooden, meanwhile, seemed to be progressing nicely from shoulder surgery; Saberhagen was unhittable; Sid Fernandez was off the beer-and-pizza regimen; and Cone was Cone. Pitching, it was easy to rationalize, would cover a multitude of Met sins.

So, win or lose, the Mets had convinced us they weren't going to be much fun to cover. But the boycott was new and different, cloak-and-dagger stuff. It became the story. And though the novelty quickly wore off, at least there wasn't the daily pressure to work the clubhouse and deliver a juicy story with hot quotes from some disenchanted player—although each of us lived in fear that someone else on the beat would convince a player to speak out and break the boycott. But soon it was clear they were taking the idea seriously, and we were more than willing to keep our distance. Certainly other reporters seemed more disturbed about the boycott than we were. As a whole, journalists tend to get self-righteous in these kind of matters. *How dare they not talk to us.* That type of thing.

In fact, when the Mets beat writers nominated Cone in November 1992 for the Good Guy Award, annually presented by the New York chapter of the Baseball Writers Association of America in appreciation of a player's candor with and courtesy toward the press, several Yankees writers and baseball columnists howled in protest, saying we'd be sending a message that what the Mets had done in spring training was okay. We thought we'd be sending a message that we weren't small and petty enough to be influenced by some silly boycott. But Cone was voted down in favor of Yankees reliever John Habyan, a player so obscure as to demean the importance we place on the award. Nothing personal about Habyan, but asking a no-name middle reliever to be nice to the press is like asking him if he wants a raise. Next year the Mets writers plan to nominate Charlie Samuels, the club's equipment manager, for the award.

* * *

While the beat writers celebrated the boycott, Mets management fretted. Al Harazin had tried to talk Cone—who was the player rep—out of the action before it became official. He feared a backlash from New York fans tired of all the nonsense. At this point the Mets' image was not unlike that of Bill Clinton in his presidential campaign, both soiled by scandal and sensationalized by the press. Clinton talked his way past all of that. The Mets talked themselves into believing that silence was the answer. Seven days had passed without a player uttering a single quotable sentence to a reporter. But the emotion of the moment had passed. After a day or two many of the players had returned to exchanging small talk with reporters in the locker room. Hello, how ya doing, how's your golf game, and of course, how's your team doing in the pool?

The NCAA basketball tournament gives players an opportunity to play with their Monopoly money, in the form of their own little office pool. Teams are picked at random, fifty dollars each. The brackets are drawn on cardboard and tacked to the wall. Fifty bucks is a lot to pay for the privilege of getting Southwest Missouri State, but that's the price of being in a big-league pool. Besides, there are plenty of other pools from which to choose. It's not the money that matters; players crave the action. Pools form in every corner of the clubhouse. For various amounts of money, players pick the games all the way through the tournament, earning points for every game

•

they predict correctly. Some players wind up in so many different pools, with so many different teams, they're not sure which
way to root through the first couple of rounds. But they've got
action. When you see players throwing fifty- and hundred-
dollar bills around like that, it's not hard to understand how
someone like Pete Rose or Lenny Dykstra could go over the
edge gambling. When you're young and strong and hitting
.300, it must seem as if the money will always be there if you
need it.

Even while exchanging pleasantries, however, the players
seemed to be hardening their stance. Many enjoyed being left
alone for once, free not to worry about being surrounded at
their locker by a swarm of writers. And Bonilla was advocating
making their message more powerful. "If you really want to
hurt them," Bonilla stood up and said during their first meeting, "you've got to take [the boycott] into the season. Then
they'll know we mean business." When they broke camp and
left Florida on April 2, that was the plan. But Harazin and
other major league baseball officials were in a panic. The Mets
were playing an exhibition game against the Orioles in Baltimore on April 3 to christen Oriole Park at Camden Yards, the
new gem of a ballpark situated on the Baltimore harborfront.
It was basically a photo opportunity for the troubled sport of
baseball, a day when this gorgeous, old-style stadium would
give baseball writers a chance to romanticize about the game
and its history rather than focus on money and spoiled ballplayers. But not if this boycott was continuing. So with the
encouragement of commissioner Fay Vincent and Harazin,
leaders of the Players Association had also flown in and met
with Cone, asking the players to consider ending the boycott.
Cone called a meeting, where Willie Randolph and Dave Magadan appealed to their teammates to end the boycott, telling
them the message had been sent. Bonilla again made the point
about taking it into the season, but the majority decided
enough was enough. The media was alerted and Cone read a
statement before the assembled masses, saying the boycott,

•

regrettable but necessary, was over and the Mets would be a stronger, more unified team for their action. It sounded nice, but you had to wonder how many players believed as much. As Cone himself would say, looking back after the end of the season, "Well, I wanted to believe it."

•

APRIL

APRIL 6. ST. LOUIS. METS 4, CARDINALS 2 (ten innings).

T HE DÉJÀ VU washed over the press box in the ninth inning: reporters rolling their eyes at one another, ready to dismiss the "Hardball Is Back" slogan as just so much hype. Here, on opening night, the Mets had been smothered for seven innings by Cards right-hander José DeLeon, and, aside from Bobby Bonilla's solo home run in the fourth inning, the Mets had offered no reason to believe they were any better than the club that had slogged through spring training.

Oh, they'd had the alibi machine working, all right. Let us get to the business of baseball, the Mets said, and all the scandals will melt away. The New York fans, eager to believe their icons, nodded politely and waited. And waited. So here they were, in the tenth inning, having rallied to tie the game with a run in the ninth, staring at Lee Smith and his ninety-four-mile-per-hour heat, when Vince Coleman reached on a bunt single. Willie Randolph sacrificed him to second, and when Bonilla strode to the plate, you couldn't help but think—especially in this setting—that moments like these used to belong to Darryl Strawberry.

All you had to do was look to the depths of the stadium and the big clock way, way up above a runway in the right-center bleachers. Ah, 1985: Who could ever forget the home run Darryl Strawberry hit off lefty Ken Dayley that silenced a boisterous crowd and kept the Mets alive as they chased the Cardinals that last week of the season? It was Year Two of the

•

73

Mets' Return to Glory and Strawberry's breathtaking blast seemed to be a promise of untold feats ahead for both a team brimming with spectacular young talent and a hitter already perhaps the most dangerous in the game at age twenty-three. By then the Mets had learned that Strawberry had a flair for the dramatic, and though he would never live up to the expectations his talent created, Straw would never lose that penchant for delivering in a big moment. And no matter what the Mets said, they paid $29 million for Bobby Bonilla in large part to make Strawberry's memory disappear—or, more precisely, to resurrect Darryl's ghost. No one had hit the ninth-inning homer in 1991, the first summer Straw spent in L.A., and the front office learned fast how much Strawberry's mere presence in the lineup—as a guy pitchers feared no matter if he was slumping or streaking—meant to the Mets. Not that the suits-and-ties would ever admit to making a mistake: Strawberry's name had become an unmentionable around the brain trust at Shea. The players were a different story. They hadn't all liked him or his constant yapping, but they knew how vital he was to the ball club. As David Cone said privately after the Mets made only a token effort to keep Strawberry from leaving, "They better have a plan, a real plan, or this decision is going to cost people their jobs."

Only they didn't have a plan, or, by then, a farm system. The Mets had been largely rebuilt from within by Joe McIlvaine, whose run as scouting director from '81 to '85 landed such talent as Dwight Gooden, Lenny Dykstra, Roger McDowell, Dave Magadan, Randy Myers, Kevin Elster, and Gregg Jefferies through the amateur draft. McIlvaine drafted Jefferies in June '85 and then moved up to vice president of baseball operations in October; since then the only number one draft choice for the Mets to even reach the big leagues was third baseman Chris Donnels, and he flopped so badly the Mets left him unprotected in the expansion draft in November '92 and he was taken by the Florida Marlins. Of course, the Mets weren't drafting as high once they began winning, but that hardly

•

accounts for the talent drought created by a series of poor drafts. Roland Johnson, the man who had replaced McIlvaine as scouting director, finally paid for his mistakes in September '92, when the club "restructured" their scouting department, making vice president of baseball operations Gerry Hunsicker the new supervisor of scouting and development, while creating a three-pronged scouting system with Johnson as one of the regional directors.

By the end of the '90 season, the Mets were already feeling the pinch. With not an impact hitter in sight to replace Strawberry, Frank Cashen made the incredibly misguided decision to sign Vince Coleman, a turf-created stolen-base specialist, then promptly stepped down as GM when the club responded with a fifth-place finish. Al Harazin was sure he'd solved the problem by waving $29 million at Bonilla—Darryl with a smile, as one employee of the organization whispered. Trouble was, Bonilla wanted no part of Darryl's legacy, not during off-season press conferences, not in spring training, not even now, in the tenth inning against Smith. "I just want to be one of the guys," he'd say, and reporters would raise an eyebrow, wondering how a man earning $29 million could expect anonymity.

For years in Pittsburgh, Bonilla was content to let Barry Bonds be the Pirates' version of Strawberry—loud, combative, even obnoxious, but, like Darryl, a man who bragged of being a money hitter and often delivered. By contrast, Bonilla came off as a happy-go-lucky kid just delighted to be in the big leagues. It was a perfect image to project in the nineties to a public that was sick of all the seemingly unhappy millionaires baseball's brave new world of finance had wrought. But Bonilla never understood the void he was walking into at Shea, a fact that eluded him even after he took Smith deep to right in the tenth inning, providing a Strawberrian moment in his very first ball game as a Met. His swing didn't have the speed or grace of Strawberry's; Bonilla wasn't that kind of pure power hitter. He simply muscled the ball with the brute strength of an offensive tackle, which he resembled in appearance. At 250

•

pounds—at least that's what the beat guys were guessing his thickened waist line added up to—he was hardly streamlined, but oh so powerful, and when he caught a fastball like that of Lee Smith's just right, well, not even Strawberry could make a ball disappear faster.

The Mets mobbed him, the high-fives devouring Bonilla all the way into the dugout and—after John Franco put the Cards away in the bottom of the tenth—into the clubhouse too. The Mets seemed more than happy. They were sure that after all the madness in Florida, this was an omen of better days ahead, a sign that Bonilla was the man to lead them back to the promised land. In the clubhouse that night, Cone went so far as to say, "We haven't had a leader like Bobby since Keith Hernandez." That was a stunning endorsement for a man who'd played a total of ten innings as a Met. But that's how desperate this team was for somebody to believe in again. After losing Straw, after seeing Davey Johnson and Buddy Harrelson both fired in less than eighteen months, the renegades and all the rest needed someone to say, "Climb on my back, boys."

Instead here was Bonilla, standing at his locker, handing the mantle right back to the Mets. "I'm not here to be Darryl Strawberry," he said. "I'm not here to hit forty home runs." It was as if Bonilla already feared the ramifications of hitting two dingers in his first game. Questions came from every corner, every angle: How did it feel to win a game in such heroic fashion? "All I did was get good wood on the ball," Bonilla said, unable or unwilling to play along with the media.

The New York press was looking to celebrate the moment, write overheated prose about the path of the home run, the emotions that surrounded it, the evaporation of all the spring-training ugliness, and here was Bonilla splashing cold water all over our notebooks. Nothing wrong with a little modesty, but right then and there it made you wonder if Bonilla could handle his role as designated savior. Strawberry delighted in such moments: "You're born with bat speed," he'd say with a sly smile, "but you've gotta be fearless too when the game's on the line."

•

Bonilla wouldn't dare be so bold. In the most human sense, it was admirable, but for a man in his spot it was an unacceptable retreat, one that foreshadowed trouble in the coming months. If you're going to play the free-agent game and auction yourself into becoming the highest-paid player in baseball, you'd better be willing to take the responsibility that comes with the money, not run from it.

There was no such restraint on the front office end. Al Harazin was walking around the visitors' clubhouse at Busch Stadium, drinking freely from a large cup of beer, his ego on display. New York had spent an entire winter praising Harazin for his signing of Bonilla and here was the dividend, paid out on the very first day. Sweeter yet for the rookie GM, he had been ridiculed by elements of the baseball community as a modern-day George Steinbrenner, raising the ceiling on baseball's salary structure to an outrageous level. The charge had wounded Harazin, who defended his signing of Bonilla by saying he was merely the victor among "four or five clubs who would have made him the highest-paid player in baseball." But it was Harazin who'd bid the highest, prompting one American League executive to bitterly ask a reporter in private, "Who wouldn't look like a genius if your owners tell you there's forty-five million dollars available for the payroll?"

So now Harazin was full of Take That swagger in the clubhouse—answering questions from the press with a beery flush on his face. Reporters were only too happy to fire away, just relieved there was finally a GM on the grounds willing to speak at all. Harazin's presence, after all, was a huge departure from Cashen, who, at sixty-four, had finally run out of patience with modern-day baseball. As GM in Baltimore, Cashen had presided over the legendary Orioles teams in the sixties, back in an era when there were no million-dollar salaries, no free agency, no arbitration lawyers or slick agents with which to deal. Cashen never made the transition to the eighties, never accepted that money had become just as much a part of baseball as the pennant races, and that if his old Orioles favorites

•

were still around today—Boog Powell, Brooks Robinson, Frank Robinson, Dave McNally—they'd have agents, too, looking for guaranteed millions.

Instead, Cashen turned colder and angrier as the years passed, harboring a particular dislike for reporters. That was odd, since Cashen had once been a sportswriter for the now-defunct *Baltimore News-American*, covering horse racing. But as with baseball, Cashen refused to accept change in the newspaper industry. It irritated him that papers covered his Mets so aggressively, so harshly. What happened to the good old days in Baltimore, when the press practically revered Cashen? Actually, he had been praised as a savior upon taking over as GM in 1980, but began to take some heat when the Mets showed no improvement or promise after a couple of seasons. Then Cashen was hailed for acquiring George Foster and bringing back the Franchise, Tom Seaver. But that only set the club up for a memorable and image-damaging faux pas: Cashen left Seaver exposed in a player-compensation draft after the 1983 season, thinking no one would take the high-salaried, aging star, then watched in shock when the Chicago White Sox selected him. As it turned out, Seaver's departure left a spot open on the staff in the spring of '84 for a young phenom named Gooden, but at the time Cashen was worked over and pummeled by the old guard on the baseball beat, hardened vets who'd covered seven straight years of awful baseball, including five last-place finishes by the Mets. Maury Allen of the *Post* and Dick Young of the *Daily News* were quick to throw punches in print, as was the new hot shot in town, Mike Lupica. Even the *Daily News*'s Jack Lang, who rarely went looking for a fight, railed against Cashen and the Mets over the Seaver affair. And though the Mets were soon bolting into contention, Cashen regaining his status as a genius, the GM's bitterness toward the press had cemented, and he would grow only more aloof. Often Cashen would warn Joe McIlvaine, who enjoyed the give-and-take with reporters when he came to power, to tone down his remarks to the press in the best inter-

•

ests of the ball club. Cashen wanted the press to know as little as possible, always regarding the writers as the enemy. In a quiet moment in spring training of 1983, Cashen pulled Klapisch aside. He told the rookie reporter, "Use this job to get yourself something better, maybe television or something. This isn't what you want to do the rest of your life, is it?"

For the last few years of his tenure at Shea, Cashen did his best to avoid the press, obviously uncomfortable when he was finally cornered for an interview. He could be an engaging man with the same reporters if they wanted to talk about his beloved golf game or something equally harmless in casual conversation, but he'd turn the warmth off instantly if the questions got tough.

Harazin, on the other hand, loved publicity, loved to see his name in the paper, loved to be heard on WFAN. Harazin's legal background helped him respond to tough questions with seamless answers. But as he ascended to the throne of GM, a simple question haunted him: Did he belong there?

The Mets didn't exactly respect him as a baseball expert. In fact, when Harazin was still a fledgling lieutenant in the Cashen regime, he acquired a nasty nickname. The Mets policy for almost a decade has been to send one member of the front office on all road trips. The players liked Joe McIlvaine, nicknamed Father Joe because of his background in the priesthood—he attended a seminary in Philadelphia and almost ended up wearing the collar. McIlvaine was a gentle man, trusting, and above all, knowledgeable about baseball. Cashen, for all his bitterness, was always an honest man, and no one questioned his credentials when it came to evaluating talent.

But Harazin? For some reason, the Mets suffered their most brutal road trips when Harazin served as chaperone. Soon enough, he was nicknamed the Black Cat for all the bad luck he brought, although none of the players could quite muster the nerve to tell Harazin to his face. Instead, the locker room would fill with sounds of cats' meows when Harazin would walk through the door. The bespectacled former lawyer was oblivi-

•

ous to the ridicule, of course, although some Mets eventually became so brazen about it, they'd meow even when Harazin was within a few feet of them.

By the mid-eighties, the long-range blueprint called for Harazin and McIlvaine to succeed Cashen, with McIlvaine making the baseball decisions and Harazin working the dollars. It would've been a fine fit. With Cashen's blessing, the two VPs were already working in concert, each respecting the other's particular skill. Trouble was, by 1990, with Cashen still clinging to power, McIlvaine got tired of waiting, and he accepted the GM position in San Diego. In a sense, Cashen had the perfect job: He let McIlvaine and Harazin do most of the hands-on work, while he would spend time . . . well, the day before he was fired, Davey Johnson told a reporter off the record, "Just once, I'd like to have a job description for Frank Cashen. I mean, what does he do?"

Cashen was unaware of the remark, but Johnson was doomed by then, anyway. Twenty-four hours later, he would be dismissed, ending a two-year war that was nasty and often personal. With Davey out of the way, Cashen could aim his rifle at the next target, Darryl Strawberry, whom he also considered a threat, too full of ego, too dangerous to leave in the clubhouse for the rest of the nineties. Cashen knew Strawberry's public longings to play in L.A. were really nothing more than boyish fantasies, but Cashen was too old for such nonsense, and decided he'd prove the Mets could do nicely without Darryl. In the end, his four-year offer of $15.5 million to Strawberry wasn't peanuts, but Cashen knew it wasn't in the ballpark with the Dodgers. "Biggest fuckin' mistake Frank ever made," Strawberry would say that off-season. Who knows? If Cashen had hurried up and let McIlvaine climb into the cockpit, the Mets might've had a different look in '92. Perhaps Strawberry never would've left.

Cashen, meanwhile, had staked his reputation on letting Strawberry walk. "We'll be a better team without Darryl within two years," he said the day Straw signed with the Dodg-

•

ers. When the Mets bottomed out instead, Cashen decided to get out of the way, and Harazin became the GM immediately after the '91 season. It was no easy task, taking over after a shocking fifth-place finish. But no one felt sorry for Al, not when it became obvious he'd been given carte blanche by owners Wilpon and Doubleday. When he used the ocean of dollars to sign Bobby Bonilla and Eddie Murray, Harazin was looked upon with great skepticism around baseball. One AL executive said, "We'll see what Harazin's got when it comes time to make a trade, not in signing free agents."

Actually, Harazin impressed the baseball world with his first major trade, following his own off-season plan nicely in using offensive surplus created by his free-agent signings to acquire Bret Saberhagen, considered one of the top five pitchers in baseball. To get Saberhagen and utility infielder Bill Pecota, Harazin gave up Kevin McReynolds, Gregg Jefferies, and Keith Miller. It was a gamble, given Jefferies's offensive potential, but after all the years of misjudgments by the front office, Harazin had read the climate around the Mets accurately, sensing the need for sweeping change, and the free-agent cash he had spent had given him the ammunition to seduce a sixth-place team like Kansas City, which desperately needed manpower. It wasn't anything clairvoyant, but Harazin did deserve plaudits for getting it done. He had the intellect for the job, all right, but he was as consumed as Cashen had been with filling the locker room with good soldiers, paying little mind to the fact that a thick skin and a certain swagger are the personality traits that seem to flourish in New York, certainly among players being paid a pirate's treasure.

A GM can't put together a team anymore without considering what role money will play in shaping the personality of the ball club. Often there's a misconception about fat-cat-itis: In some cases big money steals a little of the desperado in ballplayers, but others are affected in quite the opposite way. Spoiled and pampered or not, there's guilt at work for most any player making millions to play baseball, and it creates such

•

insecurity that they rail at the slightest public criticism, fearful of damaging their good name. Like Bonilla, they want the money but not the burden of responsibility. Image, image, image—ballplayers in the nineties live in fear of having their image tainted because they have to justify the money. Bonilla was a classic example, a man who drowned in his own righteousness in '92, simply afraid to tell the truth.

More than ever, teams need some sass in a clubhouse—players who aren't consumed with their public personas. Is it coincidence that the only teams that have won in New York since free agency came along have been the hard-ass Yankees of Munson and Nettles and Reggie and Billy, and the fuck-you Mets of Backman and Dykstra and Hernandez and Carter? In some ways that's all chemistry is, having enough players with the balls to say, *Fuck you, I don't care what they think or you think, I don't care what's in the papers, I don't care if this guy throws at my head, I'm gonna kick their ass and yours too if you're not right there with me.* That's what the Mets missed about Knight and Mitchell and Backman and the others who were dismissed too quickly. It's an attitude no amount of earnestness can buy, a toughness you can feel around certain teams and certain players that isn't defined in numbers or character references. It has nothing to do with being a prick or a gentleman once the game is over. Ray Knight was one of the great gentlemen of sports, but he'd put you in the hospital if you were standing between him and winning a baseball game, and too fuckin' bad if somebody didn't like it. That kind of toughness on a ball club is the most precious quality in sports, especially in a city where the newspapers won't let you hide. The Mets had it, and management didn't appreciate it—that was the sad part. Now Harazin had no idea how to recapture it.

Did he have any baseball instincts? The players in the Mets' locker room, many of whom saw Harazin only as the man who had squeezed them in off-season negotiating sessions, had little faith. More than one player in recent years has delighted in telling a story about Harazin that became legendary

•

around the locker room. Harazin was touring the back fields at the Mets' training complex during spring training one day, observing the club's various minor leaguers go through the day's drills. He was particularly impressed by an outfielder's arm, to the point where he wondered aloud if the organization should consider converting him to a catcher.

"We might," said one of the Mets' minor league coaches, standing nearby, "if he wasn't left-handed."

No, Harazin couldn't shed his image as a lawyer first, a financial hatchet man second, and a baseball exec third, just because he was the new boss. Players aren't impressed by law degrees; they want to know if a guy has ever played the game. The Mets accepted McIlvaine because he'd toiled as a minor league pitcher and then worked his way up the baseball ladder through scouting. Harazin had done his time in the game himself, having bought into baseball as owner and GM of the Orioles' Double-A affiliate in 1972 and spent the next twenty years in the game, corporate side or not. But it just wasn't the same. He was never an athlete; indeed, he freely admitted he'd never worn a pair of jeans as an adult. That was why the sight of him more than once at the batting cage in March, wearing a rubber sweat top under a golf shirt like a coach or player made for a great sight gag. Harazin was trying hard to be one of the boys, but it remained a very tough sell.

Oh, Harazin pulled hard on that beer after Bonilla's opening-day blast. Little did anyone know it would be the Mets' finest moment of the season. At the time, it was merely a moment to savor for Harazin, for Torborg, for Bonilla. For the writers, it was merely a means to an end. The beat guys had skipped the Camden Yards game and the exhibition series with the Yankees in New York, so we hadn't seen the players since the media boycott had ended, and all of us had sensed a lingering tension in the locker room before the game.

One player had sidled up to two reporters and whispered a warning: "Don't sit on the stools."

"The stools?"

•

"Yeah, it's a pet peeve of some of these guys. Came up during the boycott."

"Come on."

"Yep. Bugs the shit out of some guys."

It had always been common practice for a reporter to pull up an available stool from the next locker to interview a player. If the neighboring player returned to get dressed or whatever, his stool was quickly returned to him. Nobody ever seemed to mind, but suddenly it was an issue. And so was loitering: Jay Horwitz was scurrying around handing out press releases, warning writers that standing around in the locker room was now considered loitering and highly discouraged.

Loitering? The beat guys had a good laugh over the charge. Fans always seem to think reporters are the luckiest people on earth because they get to wander around the locker room, but in truth it's uncomfortable under the best of circumstances. You're on opposition turf—there's no avoiding the antagonistic nature of the job—and the majority of players don't want you there—it's as simple as that. Yet standing around is unavoidable. Players don't exactly sit at their lockers waiting for you to come interview them before batting practice. They're off eating a burger in the players' lounge, taking a whirlpool, sleeping off a hangover on the trainer's table, or watching *Gilligan's Island* on TV in a back room somewhere. You hang around waiting to grab a guy when he's at his locker dressing or shooting the breeze with another player. Loitering? Right.

But this too had been a hot topic for the players during their boycott grievance meetings. Horwitz took pains to assure the beat guys that the complaints weren't aimed at them, but rather the unfamiliar faces of out-of-town writers or columnists whom the players trusted even less than the regulars. In their most paranoid moments, players were sure reporters were eavesdropping on their conversations, looking for a gratuitous remark that would somehow become a headline.

So we had gone upstairs to watch the game, convinced of

•

a certain hostility in the air. The euphoria of the postgame celebration was irrelevant, and our questions lingered. A.J.'s would provide some answers. A.J.'s was the closest thing St. Louis had to offer to a New York–style nightclub, with ear-splitting music and dozens of midwestern women trying to look Euro-chic. Whatever its trappings, A.J.'s was appealing mostly because it was located on the ground floor of the Adam's Mark Hotel, where the Mets stay—a comforting thought to any player on his seventh or eighth beer of the night. The location ensured a mixture of players and writers in the bar after games. The routine was always the same: Both groups kept their distance until the beers took effect, then the barriers disappeared.

On this night it wasn't long before John Franco, celebrating his first save of the season, sent over a round of beers to a table of five writers. A peace offering? Franco laughed off the question when he came by the table. "Fuck yuz all," he said happily, which in Franco's happy mood was Brooklyn for "Let's put it behind us." It would always be this way with Franco. When it came to putting reporters in their place for a team cause, it wasn't personal, it was business. Soon enough some of the other players wandered past, and indeed it seemed to be business as usual. The friendlier guys waved a bottle of beer our way, maybe stopped by to tell a joke or two, the others pretended we didn't exist. There was doubtless more animosity than ever in the Mets' locker room toward the press, but we were finding out it was more the result of the personality bypass the club had undergone via management's scalpel than a direct result of the tense spring or the boycott. Basically, the state of player-press relations seemed to be returning to normal, especially with word filtering out of Florida that the rape case against the players was close to being dropped.

Then there was Dave Cone, never normal but always entertaining, always willing to swap a couple of stories at the bar with the writers. When he came past our table, we pulled him over, offered congratulations on a strong opening-day pitching performance, and began to work him for details of the tumultu-

·

ous spring. But it was clear that Cone was still unsettled by the trail of scandal that had followed him around Florida, and he said he didn't know if he'd ever feel free to discuss the trials and tribulations of his past few months.

Still, Cone was Cone, as unpredictable as he was uninhibited by conventional baseball boundaries. And soon enough the conversation at the table turned to basketball. Five or six of us planned to play the next morning at the downtown YMCA, and as soon as Cone heard this, he leaned in and said, "Count me in."

MCCARVER AT THE MIKE

—J.H.

WHEN DEION SANDERS made a spectacle of himself in October '92, soaking Tim McCarver with tubs of ice water in retaliation for comments made on TV, sportswriters everywhere sympathized with McCarver, yet said a silent thank-you. For once it wasn't a writer at the mercy of some overindulged millionaire ballplayer. For once the public could get a sense of just how childish players can act when their egos get bruised. And for once, since much of the incident was caught on camera, the world got a glimpse of just how naked a reporter can be made to feel in a locker room.

It was hard to believe none of his teammates made a move to restrain Sanders in his repeated dousings, considering that McCarver is as heavyweight a broadcaster as there is in baseball these days. But a gang mentality often prevails in a locker room, and then again, McCarver is anything but the typical glad-handing, ex-jock broad-

caster. To some players, he's more annoy ing than sportswriters.

His sin, of course, is that he doesn't pu his punches on the air. McCarver's honest and insights have made him the premie baseball analyst in the country; in othe words, he's no hatchet man, but as an e> player, he's in uncharted waters, daring t criticize his own fraternity brothers.

To McCarver, however, any other wa would be phony. "Praise without criticism ludicrous," he says. "For praise of a guy t be meaningful and credible, you have to cr icize too, rather than just be an ex-athlet sucking up to these guys."

Most players don't see it the same wa As a result, McCarver has managed annoy many a Mets player during his te years working their games. They're alwa complaining to writers, of all people, th "McCarver buried me on the air last night Usually that means McCarver pointed o

•

86

"What?"

"I'm in," Cone said. "Count me in. What time you playing?"

Cone had been making noise about playing basketball with the writers for years. He'd missed the Lockout Games, a week or so of full-court basketball under the sun when writers and players put aside their animosities during the '90 lockout in Florida, and ever since then he'd longed to show off his high school point-guard skills. But this was out of the question, a star pitcher playing during the season—especially this season,

that So-and-so had no business missing the cutoff man with a throw, allowing the tying run to move into scoring position; or blundered badly in trying to stretch a double into a triple with the Mets trailing by two runs in the eighth inning—something like that. McCarver will drive the point home emphatically in the interest of explaining the finer points of the game to viewers, and by the time a player hears about it, from a wife or father watching at home, it sounds in translation as if McCarver suggested ten years of hard labor as punishment for the crime.

Rarely do players actually confront McCarver or go public with their complaints, however. Deep down they respect him for his knowledge as well as his twenty-one-year career as a catcher in the majors. In a general protest of McCarver's candor, Eddie Murray doesn't talk to him, but to that McCarver chuckles and says, "Eddie doesn't speak to a lot of people. Big deal."

The one Met who was willing to take McCarver on publicly at Shea was Davey

Johnson. They had been Phillies teammates and friends in the late seventies, both viewed as potential managers. McCarver had chances to manage, approached by the Expos in 1984 and the Twins in '86, but found more money and less aggravation in the broadcast booth.

There, his perspective was so enlightening, his analysis so insightful compared to that of other broadcasters, that McCarver became one of the reasons the Mets were such a happening in New York in the eighties. But he drove Davey crazy by repeatedly pointing out on the air that the Mets played their outfielders too deep, especially the opposite-field outfielder. It often seemed as if McCarver would no sooner say Darryl Strawberry was much too deep in right field than someone like José Lind would dump a soft liner at Darryl's feet for a run-scoring base hit. Johnson didn't dispute McCarver's point, but argued that he'd rather an outfielder like Strawberry play a few steps deep than play shallow when he wasn't comfortable going back on the ball.

•

since Cone had put millions of dollars on the line, turning down a $16.8 million offer from the Mets in January to play free-agency roulette.

"Come on, Coney," someone said, "you can't do that."

"Why not?"

"Why not? You've got twenty million dollars riding on this season, you've been getting killed in the papers all spring, and you're gonna take a chance on breaking an ankle playing hoops?"

"Fuck it," Cone said, laughing. "I'll be careful."

Nobody thought Cone was serious, but he insisted on getting a wake-up call in the morning, and hopped out of bed when

---

MCCARVER AT THE MIKE
(continued)

They debated the issue occasionally, once loudly in the trainer's room while players and coaches gathered to listen. If Strawberry was so uncomfortable, McCarver said, why didn't Davey have him take enough extra fly balls until he *was* comfortable going back on them? Davey said it couldn't be done, and the argument raged on.

Finally, when Frank Cashen spared the manager's job after much organizational debate at the end of the '89 season, but fired coaches Bill Robinson and Sam Perlozzo, Davey was stung for his friends and lashed out. Rather than rip Cashen for singling out scapegoats, he told the newspapers that McCarver's constant harping on outfield positioning got Robinson fired.

"It was the most ludicrous thing I ever heard," McCarver says.

After Davey was fired in May '90, he again had harsh words for McCarver, say-ing he hadn't been a good enough player to criticize as much as he did. The two haven't spoken since.

"I bear no animosity toward Davey," says McCarver. "If a guy wants to hold a grudge, so be it. I always felt I was fair to Davey."

Fairness is all a player should ask from the media. McCarver says it's all he ever asked as a player, but, like so many people around the game, he thinks money has changed baseball for the worse, creating what amounts to a paranoia among players who need to justify their huge salaries.

"You can't just take the money and leave the responsibility in the wings somewhere," he says. "That's what's happening, and fans sense it. In a lot of cases, fan perception is wrong, but in this case, it's right. Players are so insecure that when something goes wrong, the first thing they ask is 'Why are you always picking on me?'"

•

---

it came, on his way to the downtown Y, where the lunchtime pickup games take on the importance of Bulls vs. Knicks in the eyes of the St. Louis regulars. Something about the Y's in St. Louis and Pittsburgh—the locals foul with intent to maim and then take every single call to judge and jury before resuming play. The games aren't for the faint of heart, and into that setting stepped Cone, hangover and all. The beat guys were just praying he'd have the sense to play it cool, shoot some jumpers, run the floor, and stay away from trouble. We should have known better.

Cone mixed it up from the start. More of a driver than a shooter, he managed to spend most of his time in the lane, where he relished contact, exchanged elbows, pushed on defense like the local boys, and generally fit right in with the animals out there on their lunch hour. Some of the regulars had come to recognize the Mets writers, mostly because Gooden had come over one day just to shoot around a little. But none of them recognized Cone, whose five-foot-eleven, 180-pound frame hardly identified him as a pro athlete. As it turned out, that was a blessing, because an hour or so into the day's play Cone suddenly squared off with some guy who looked like a former high school linebacker, and both were pushing, shoving, and cursing. Every writer in the gym, fearing the possibility of reporting that *Cone was carted off to the St. Louis police station yesterday after a brawl in a downtown YMCA,* raced to intercede. But Cone was in a rage, lunging at this ox, who seemed more amused than angered by the explosion of temper.

"I'll kick your ass you push me like that again you sonofabitch," Cone hollered.

"Fuck you, pal."

Now the ox and Cone were trying to get at each other, while the rest of us kept them apart.

"Fuckin' asshole," Cone yelled, glaring at the guy. "That the way you play around here? That's horseshit."

"Fuck you. Go on back to New York if you can't handle it."

Several of us were trying to talk some sense into Cone,

•

reminding him he didn't need another lawsuit, and finally he backed off. By now it was nearly one o'clock, and everyone agreed to call it a day. Remarkably, none of the Y regulars yet had a clue they'd just broken up a fight involving one of the Mets' star players. One, in fact, tried to make light of the situation.

"You guys ought to be in the mood to go talk to Vince Coleman now," he said.

Cone didn't laugh. But at least he was cooling off. The rest of us just sort of looked at one another, shaking our heads. We'd become accustomed to Cone doing just about anything to be different or to get a laugh. Once he'd tied a piece of rope to his dick and dragged a five-pound weight around the clubhouse while players and writers, howling, bent over in reflexive pain—it hurt just to watch. And more than once Cone had sent a clubhouse kid, box of baseballs in hand, down to the visitors' clubhouse with instructions to ask a certain player to sign them as a favor. Cone delighted in hearing later how the player opened the box only to be repulsed by the smell of, well, use your imagination.

There was no doubt Cone enjoyed living on the edge, being different, challenging authority. Over the last year he'd become a heavy smoker, mostly it seemed so that he could light up in the clubhouse at any sighting of Al Harazin, just to see if he could produce a look of disdain from the GM. And when Cone went over the edge, as he did that night in Atlanta when he argued with an umpire while two runners circled the bases, he could laugh at himself and say that was the price he paid for playing with emotion. But the basketball incident seemed to put Cone on new and dangerous ground. He clearly had some self-destructive mechanism at work behind that altar-boy face, and every once in a while it just seemed to grab the steering wheel and hit the gas.

Still, Cone had emerged intact from playing hoops, and the Mets were undefeated. Suddenly, anything was possible for Jeff Torborg's ball club, at least for a few more hours. But then

•

the first signs of decay set in. The pitching staff was hammered in the next two games, allowing twenty-four runs, Tim Burke giving up a home run on his very first pitch of the season. That was a corporate wound as well, since Burke had been acquired from the Expos for Ron Darling the previous summer. Oh, how the brass had come to despise Darling and his intellectual, cynical view of his sport and particularly his bosses. It was a commentary on the club's feeling toward Darling that when someone asked Joe McIlvaine later that year if he'd be interested in signing him to the Padres, the former Met honcho shook his head and said, "Not in a million years would I take him."

Burke, meanwhile, was the Mets' kind of guy, a religious and in some ways remarkable man. He and his wife have adopted three children, two from Korea and one from Guatemala, who needed open-heart surgery. The problem was that, at age thirty-three, he'd lost the sinker that had made him an effective reliever in the late eighties with the Expos, and Burke had been tattooed regularly over the last season and a half. The Mets, desperate for a setup man for John Franco, had worked all spring with Burke on a new delivery designed to get more sink on the ball. But here he was, getting hit so hard in his first appearance of the season that he abandoned the new delivery immediately. The next night was equally disturbing, with Paul Gibson, acquired in a trade the front office thought would fill their annual void for a decent left-handed middle reliever, nuked for six runs in three and a third innings. It was a portentous event. The bullpen would kill the Mets, especially early in the season. But for the moment, the Mets dismissed it as a fluke. And, besides, there was other news to preoccupy the club: The verdict was coming.

APRIL 9. ST. LOUIS. METS 7, CARDINALS 1.

WHAT HAD BEEN an extraordinary and ugly spring seemed finally to come to an end in the seventh inning.

•

The telephone in the press box rang while the Mets were winning easily, on their way to splitting this first series of the season. Jay Horwitz took the call, then whispered to reporters about a "declination to prosecute."

No one was surprised by either the timing or the outcome. Word had spread through the media, leaked by police sources in Florida, that the state prosecutor had decided there wasn't enough evidence to take the case to trial. Most New York TV stations had sent crews to St. Louis for reaction to the expected announcement. The scandal-frenzied journalists spent the game hanging around the press box, bored by the mundane matters of baseball. As soon as the game ended, their dawn had arrived: A crush of minicams and klieg lights were hustled to a makeshift press conference in an equipment room adjacent to the visitors' clubhouse where Gooden, Boston, and Coleman would be waiting with statements. The scene there was a mixture of relief and I-told-you-so hostility. Although Bonilla defiantly said, "It's about time," the three players involved were merely grateful they were free of any more legal fears.

Stiffly they gave the announcement their blessing, saying they were glad the ordeal was over. But while the prosecutor's decision meant there would be no indictment and no trial, the police reports were now a matter of public record, already being gathered for tomorrow's newspapers. No wonder Dave Cone, seemingly unfazed by the headlines in March, suddenly looked ashen. Cone knew what was in the police file—word-for-word transcripts of interviews with the cops like the one they'd conducted with him as well as with the accuser, telling of sexual encounters involving not only Cone but ex-teammate Ron Darling. That's why Cone reached for a cigarette, dragged on it furiously, and said to reporters, "This will only add fuel to the fire of this whole unfortunate incident. There's tremendous relief here right now, but certainly no joy."

Other reactions to the announcement were predictable: The accuser's friends and family cried foul, claimed the players were given privileged treatment because the Port St. Lucie

•

police didn't want to humiliate the Mets, whose presence in their town meant big money for the local economy. The ballplayers, on the other hand, pointed to Mike Tyson's recent conviction for rape and claimed they were victims of their own celebrity. Said Gooden's attorney, Joseph Ficarotta, "It's a shame these players have had their names dragged through the mud based on uncorroborated allegations that are over a year old. These men were never charged; there was not enough evidence to charge them."

No one talked much about Coleman or Boston that day. Boston was a part-time player safe from the scrutiny with which a superstar lives. And neither the Mets' fans, the press, nor the rest of the team had much attachment to Coleman, whose first year in New York had been ruined by injuries. (One irony of this day was that Coleman had once again pulled up lame with a hamstring injury, and while he was telling reporters he intended to return to the lineup for the Mets' home opener twenty-four hours later, he was headed instead for another month on the disabled list.) Coleman had also long since alienated reporters with his surliness, and he had a piercing laugh that seemed to echo throughout the clubhouse, sometimes even during the quiet brought on by a tough loss. More than one player, after the announcement, would intimate they wouldn't have minded seeing Coleman sweat out a trial. "Think he would have been laughing then?" one player said.

The world would never know. The players were free of worry and the ball club could officially go back to baseball now as they headed for the airport, on their way to New York for the home opener. Historically the plane ride home was the scene of the eighties Mets' greatest war crimes, but this year would be different. In his first meeting with his players in February, Jeff Torborg had spelled out his team rules, including his decree that there would be no alcohol on team flights. What? Players snapped to attention, as if the manager had stuck smelling salts under each and every nostril. No beer? Was he serious? Good Lord, he was. It was a direct challenge to the

•

legacy of the renegade Mets, and it would be grounds for protest later in the summer, but at the time the players listened in silence as Torborg explained: "I've seen what can happen between guys on planes when they have a few drinks. I saw what happened with Billy Martin on charter flights. Someone says something after a tough game and things get out of control. I'm not trying to tell you guys you can't drink, but I won't have it on team flights. It's for the good of the team."

Torborg told them the story he would repeat to the press later in the season, how there was alcoholism in both his and wife Suzie's families, how he'd given up liquor himself fifteen years earlier at his wife's request, "for the sake of our two sons." Torborg left the impression that he'd pounded his share of beers in his day, recalling for reporters a college memory of throwing a fellow student out a fourth-floor dormitory window during a beer-inspired argument, saying how lucky he was the victim's fall had been broken, sparing serious injury. "It could have cost me my career," he said.

Nothing personal, of course, but the players didn't care a lick about alcoholism in the manager's family. They wanted to be able to have a couple of cold ones on a midnight flight after a one-run game while they bullshitted in the back of the plane about sex, golf, and the nastiest slider in the history of baseball, which had struck one or two of them out that night. Cone would say later in the year that he thought it was a good thing Torborg hadn't come along a few years earlier, because fifteen players might have stood up right then and there when he announced his policy and said, "Sorry, Skip, no can do."

By now, however, the ban didn't have nearly the same impact. There was a contingent of Bible studiers in the clubhouse, and while they didn't constitute a majority, their presence was felt. This was true not only in the Mets' clubhouse, but throughout baseball, as more and more players could be found attending Sunday chapel. It seemed to be still another way players dealt with the pressure of living up to bigger and bigger contracts. Among the Mets, Howard Johnson became

•

the most devoted to the Scriptures, approaching teammates and even a writer or two about the need for salvation. HoJo would pass out little booklets called *Our Daily Bread*, which offered a brief synopsis of the ways prayer could enrich the lives of the lost. "I thought you might be interested in looking at this," Johnson told Klapisch one day in 1991, pressing the booklet into his hand. "Let me know if you want to talk." Johnson was joined by Gary Carter, Tim Teufel, Tommy Herr, Tim Burke, and Lee Guetterman over the years, a group that served as a counterbalance to the other Mets' wilder lifestyles. These were Mets who could be counted on to disappear after road games—back to the hotel room, never to be found in a bar or nightclub. And certainly anyone who read the Bible would never venture to the back of the plane, where the hardest drinking always took place.

No drinking. The Mets were still numb from the no-booze edict when Torborg floored them again. In detailing his belief in a family philosophy, he announced that his wife would be accompanying him on virtually every road trip, and that on certain trips the club would extend invitations to all players' and coaches' wives to come along as well. "I know some of you guys might not like that," Torborg said, "but that's what I believe in. When you manage a team you can run it any way you want." At this point, at least a few players were ready to ask for oxygen. No booze was one thing; wives was something else. Even two or three wives on a road trip constituted a threat, because they became the eyes and ears for a network of spouses. A wife on a road trip meant no hotel lobby was truly secure, no woman picked up in a bar and brought back to the room could be transported in total secrecy. What if a wife walked into the same hotel elevator? Would she tell? Bob Ojeda used to tell a story of his days with the Red Sox in the mid-eighties, remembering a player who used to bring his wife on every road trip, and even worse, tell her everything the players did after-hours. The Red Sox were so outraged by this breach of trust that they finally devised a plan to retaliate: A party

•

95

was thrown on the road in one of the hotel rooms. The player in question was invited. Upon his entrance, the player was plied with liquor, practically force-fed alcohol for hours until he was nearly unconscious. His defenses finally broken down, the player was treated to a young, gorgeous groupie, courtesy of the veterans, who told the girl to do whatever she had to do to ensure the player cheated on his wife. That way, the player could become a part of the fraternity, once and for all, sworn to secrecy. At first the player resisted, and it wasn't until the other players held him down and literally placed the girl on top of him that sex finally got under way.

But such stories came from another era: pre-AIDS, pre–*Fatal Attraction*. Now Torborg's plan included making at least one trip a year an official wives' trip. That meant they could fly on the Mets charter, city to city, airport to airport, hotel to hotel, just like the players, free of charge.

It wasn't just the players who were shocked at the suggestion of a country-wide family outing, but the Mets management as well, which wanted the wives left at home for its own reasons. It wasn't just that wives meant days full of shopping and other distractions. To an old-school GM like Frank Cashen, wives didn't belong on the road for the same reason women reporters didn't belong in the clubhouse: Baseball was traditionally a man's world. The clubhouse, the playing field, the press box were all property of the old boys' network, and yet here was Torborg breaking all the rules. Cashen, still the CEO of the club, strongly resisted the request from the new manager, yet Torborg wouldn't let go and finally succeeded in making the St. Louis–Chicago trip in late June the wives' trip. The manager didn't win any friends with his innovation, at least not with most Mets. On the day the Mets left for St. Louis, a telling inscription was anonymously scribbled on the clubhouse blackboard: SIX DAYS OF HELL.

The wives had reason to feel they'd triumphed once and for all. Earlier in the season, a handful of Bible-study wives made a pact that if they saw anyone's husband cheating on the

•

road, they would tell. "It was like having an army of spies,"
one of the wilder Mets said after word spread through the
clubhouse. "It made you paranoid, wondering who was watching you, ready to go behind your back. Like having Nazis on
your team."

There already were nonplayers in the clubhouse who made
the Mets paranoid. Meet Dr. Allan Lans, who was retained by
the Mets in 1987 after Gooden emerged from the Smithers drug
rehab. Lans, a staff psychiatrist at Smithers, had been responsible for treating Doc, and the Mets wanted to be sure their ace,
back in the real world, didn't suffer a relapse. So Lans was
enticed away from Smithers to smooth Gooden's transition to
baseball, and the club was so pleased with the result, Lans was
hired that same year to preserve the collective sanity of all the
Mets. He was a funny, kind man with a dry sense of humor.
Interestingly, Lans's closest association was forged with Keith
Hernandez, the two working on crossword puzzles day after
day. Lans would occasionally approach an athlete who was
slumping, or one who was angry at management, offering com-
monsense advice about self-help. But unless a player came to
the doctor with specific emotional problems, he was uncomfortable prying. That meant Lans would spend weeks at a time
simply hanging around the Mets, killing time just like the
press. At times there were awkward conflicts, as a reporter on
deadline would have to wait out Lans's small-talk session with
a player. And other times, Lans found hostility from the players he was being paid to serve.

While sports psychology had gained acceptance on most
levels in this country, there was still a hard-core group of athletes
who resented that intellectual approach. There were some Mets,
Tim Teufel and Randy Myers among them, who felt that Lans,
however well intentioned, was an intruder. In fact, there were
some corners of the clubhouse that saw Lans as a pipeline to—a
spy for—the front office, and made sure to never, ever offer a
revealing thought to the doctor. Players now viewed Lans with
ever greater suspicion, simply because he had become part of a

•

Torborg-led regime that enforced a strict disciplinary code. It only made players long for the freedom of the old days even more. That freedom was typified by the 1986 flight from Houston to New York after the Mets had won the NLCS in a memorable sixteen-inning game against the Astros. The drinking went on for hours—foodless and heroic. The meals became ammunition for what became known as the greatest midair food fight in airline history. By the time the plane landed, the Mets had caused in excess of ten thousand dollars' worth of damage to that Continental 727, thanks to a party so wild, "even the wives were involved," one player said. Indeed, postseason was normally the only time wives were allowed to fly with the team. And on this flight, "Everyone was kissing everyone else's wife," a player recalled. "Hell, no one gave a shit at that point."

Within a day or two, the Mets received a letter from the airline alerting management of the damages. Before the start of the World Series, Frank Cashen assembled the team in the clubhouse and, waving the letter in the air, told them they were responsible for the costs. Davey Johnson calmly took the bill from Cashen and ripped it to pieces. "If it weren't for us winning that playoff," he said, "there wouldn't have been any party. We made this organization plenty of money. You pay it."

Was it any wonder the players loved Davey? The plane rides, like the hotel bars and the golf courses, were theirs to enjoy. The territory was clearly marked on-board too: coaches and broadcasters up front, Bible studiers in the middle, wild-siders in the back. Writers, who almost always flew with the team twenty or thirty years ago, rarely if ever do anymore. It's usually out of the question, since teams leave for the airport thirty to forty minutes after the last game of a series, while reporters are just heading back upstairs from the clubhouse to write. And it's one place where the ball club doesn't want to have to worry about reporters seeing or hearing something they shouldn't.

Not that the old Mets cared. The back of the plane was for drinking and they didn't care who knew it. Keith Hernandez always insisted that it was vital to the camaraderie of a ball club to have players get together and rehash the game over a few beers. "You can learn a lot just talking about the game in those settings," Hernandez would say. Of course, some would have trouble remembering the dissection of the game the next day, depending on the extent of the drinking. There were nights like that for Bob Ojeda, as he would admit years later after being traded to the Dodgers. "There were flights where I distinctly remembered my first couple of drinks," Ojeda recalled, "and the next thing I remembered was waking up in my hotel room, naked. Don't ask me how I got there. I just did."

The back of the plane was the place to find out about teammates—who was for real, who was full of shit. It may sound silly, but Ron Darling probably spoke for a sizable percentage of players when he said once, "I don't trust any player who doesn't drink beer." The air would be thick with smoke amid the poker games, empty beer cans, and minibottles of whiskey. Flight attendants were worked, cajoled, and flattered, and it wasn't uncommon to see one or two of them in the next town, off duty, visiting one of the players in the hotel. And there, in the middle of the party sometimes, would be Davey Johnson himself. "I treated my players like men," he liked to say. "As long as they won for me on the field, I didn't give a fuck what they did otherwise."

*   *   *

But on April 9, 1992, that era was a distant memory. The Mets took off for New York on a TWA charter, somber with the knowledge of the police transcripts that would hit the papers tomorrow. Players had their flasks of hard liquor to pour into a cup of soda, but it was awkward—men in their thirties, many of them, sneaking sips of booze like high school kids. There wasn't much conversation on the way home, some of the players would recall. Many retreated into the seclusion of their headsets. Some read, others stared out the window. The season groaned to a start.

•

APRIL 10. NEW YORK. EXPOS 4, METS 0.

FRIDAY ARRIVED WARM and sunny, an abnormally beautiful April afternoon in New York for the home opener. Unfortunately for the Mets, the timing of Thursday's announcement, freeing the players of any criminal prosecution, doomed the club to yet one more day of shame. Reporters were quick to seize the chance to satisfy New York's curiosity.

The accuser's story was printed in detail in Friday's papers, complete with her own crude stick drawings of the house, illustrating the various rooms and locations of the occupants during the alleged rape. She claimed the players had set a trap for her, Boston and Coleman emerging from a closet after she'd gone inside with Gooden to use the bathroom.

Included was her graphic description of forced sexual acts that she claimed left her in such a state of immediate shock and denial that, when the ordeal was over, she made the bed and even kissed Boston good-night before leaving the house. The description was numbing, and that was only her side. None of the three accused players had consented to interviews with police, but Cone's account of his brief relationship with the accuser made for titillating reading for commuters or Mets fans riding the No. 7 IRT to Shea for the ball game.

There was plenty about the rendezvous at Cone's rented house in Port St. Lucie with the accuser, one of her friends, and Ron Darling. Darling: the most glamorous of all the Mets in the eighties. Darling: the Yalie married to a beautiful model. Darling: now just another Met who would have a lot of explaining to do at home. Out of friendship, Cone had avoided mentioning Darling's sexual involvement with the women, but the accuser's friend had described various sex acts, from swapping partners among the foursome to one couple watching another. The newspaper accounts read like letters to *Penthouse*, and the tabloids were only too happy to pump up the volume all over again. The *Daily News, Post,* and *Newsday* all carried similar stories, accompanied by eye-catching headlines telling of METS'

•

WILD SEX PARTIES. It was hard not to think of Al Harazin, wanting to drink in the home-opener atmosphere he'd bought for the Mets, gagging instead on his morning coffee as he spread the newspapers at his breakfast table.

No, the dismissal of the case could hardly erase the stigma attached to the ball club. The Mets' brass was grateful it would be spared the disgrace of arrests, a trial, and possible convictions, but it hardly felt vindicated. Cashen and Harazin were much too rigid, much too conservative to chalk it up to life as surrogate fathers of pampered, irresponsible millionaire ballplayers. They wouldn't forgive and forget, no matter what they said publicly. Boston had to know '92 would be his final season as a Met. And Coleman would only make management regret the day they signed him even more as the season went along.

Only Gooden, Teflon Doc, was safe from reprisal. The nickname became an inside joke among the beat writers: John Gotti, the celebrated New York mobster, had been dubbed the Teflon Don in the papers until the law finally made a murder charge stick early in 1992. So now Gooden was Teflon Doc.

Of all the players involved in the scandal, he had the most to lose, yet he seemed unfazed by it all. Gooden would look a reporter directly in the eye and insist he'd done nothing wrong, intimating he'd been framed, privately dropping hints that he'd tell the real story once the case was dropped. But afterward, with the possibility of a civil suit still out there, Gooden said he wouldn't discuss the matter and never did tell his version. The Mets were left with a forever blurry picture, leaving Harazin to mouth the company line: "To me the critical thing is there was no criminal violation of the law. That's a big lift to this organization." As compared to jail terms, that is.

For the beat writers, it was hard to be satisfied with Gooden's answers on this subject, but it was harder to suggest to him he might not be leveling with us. Who really knew? The question of his involvement was left to each individual to judge, and as fate would have it, public response would be measured immediately, because Gooden was pitching the home opener, pitching for the first time since shoulder surgery the

•

previous September. His start would test his arm as well as the impact of the scandal. Would Mets fans boo the man who will be forever linked to the return-to-glory era of the eighties?

There was a smattering of boos, as it turned out, but that was all. Gooden was cheered as he took the mound, but not the way he had been in years past, since he first electrified New York in 1984 as a nineteen-year-old phenom with an unhittable fastball. Back then his timing was perfect, coming along to lead the Mets out of the cellar, and he was instantly adopted as the black Tom Seaver, the Franchise revisited. Gooden had arrived to rescue New York from a decade of dreadful baseball at Shea, and his reward was unconditional adulation. If anything, the drug rehab in 1987 only strengthened his hold on the fans—he needed their support, and they were only too happy to provide it. But this was different. Whatever the truth, the month of rape talk and speculation had left a bad smell. You could hear it in the cheering. It wasn't an opening-day, we-love-you-Doc response, but more like respectful applause that amounted to a plea of Say it ain't so, Doc.

Soon enough, however, the headlines faded and the incident seemed to scar Gooden no more than a couple of bad starts would. Even on this day, the crowd, hungry for baseball, warmed to him as the innings passed. He was giving them hope, throwing hard, getting outs against the Expos. When he was finally lifted in the seventh inning, Gooden received a standing ovation on his way to the dugout and tipped his cap in appreciation.

He wound up taking the loss because Ken Hill shut out the Mets, but he looked strong, better than anyone could have expected a month earlier. If this was his first start of the year, well, you knew fans were already thinking about the promise of June and July. Gooden himself was pleased. The adrenaline had pushed him to reach back more often for more juice on the fastball than he had in spring training, and still the shoulder cooperated. He too was starting to think he would be blowing hitters away by midseason at the latest. And now, finally, the scandal—if not the circus—was behind him.

•

The locker room was a sea of reporters, most of whom were at Gooden's locker after the game. As usual, Jay Horwitz was frantic as he tried to orchestrate. More than ever, his loyalty to Gooden was on the line, and damned if he was going to let this mob bully his friend. Horwitz stood near Doc's locker, ready to call a halt to the interviews as soon as he sensed the time was right. Then, suddenly, Horwitz spotted a TV cameraman climbing onto a table behind the crowd, trying to give himself a clearer shot of Gooden answering questions. Horwitz's face tightened. "Hey, pal, do me a favor, okay? Off that table right now." When the cameraman ignored Horwitz, he tried to reason with him. "This is our home. I wouldn't stand on a table in your living room. Now get down." When he again got no response, Horwitz grabbed the table and yanked on it.

The cameraman pitched forward and nearly fell into the pile of people below him, camera and all. "Hey, you scumbag," the guy hissed at Horwitz, but reluctantly he climbed down from the table, and Horwitz returned his attention to his player, another battle fought and won. Gooden, meanwhile, was handling himself capably, as always. No, he said, smiling into the battery of TV cameras surrounding him, he wouldn't comment any further on the rape accusations. "I'm here to talk about how I pitched," he said. The case, after all, was closed. On the first afternoon of baseball at Shea, despite the shame captured in the newspapers, that seemed to bode well for the Mets. That and six strong innings from Teflon Doc.

TOP FIVE GOOD-GUY METS, ALL-TIME
1. Dave Cone
2. Rafael Santana
3. Bob Ojeda
4. Keith Miller
5. Tim Teufel

•

MAY

MAY 3. ATLANTA. METS 7, BRAVES 0.

E DDIE MURRAY had parked himself in a recliner, eyes
fixed on the clubhouse TV. The L.A. Lakers were playing,
and Murray, who lives in Los Angeles, wasn't moving for anyone, certainly not the press. He knew the writers were waiting.
He'd slugged his four hundredth career home run in the win
against the Braves, and the milestone demanded an obligatory
quote or two from baseball's Angry Man.

Murray had arrived as a free agent during the off-season,
his defiance toward the media firmly in place. He'd feuded
bitterly with the press in Baltimore, where he established potential Hall of Fame credentials over twelve seasons, and then
held the media at arm's length during his three years with the
Dodgers. No one quite understood his fury, but he'd made it
clear that he considered writers the enemy. Still, as the year
began, the New York press was willing to make the effort to
provide Murray with the proper escort in his final strides toward Cooperstown.

The beat guys didn't want a war. Blaring headlines may
sell newspapers, but after three straight years of hammering
the Mets for being moping underachievers, we were deathly
tired of conflict and the inevitable confrontations with players.
Controversy energizes reporters to a point, raising the level of
emotions on both sides of the story, but too much of it dulls the
senses and wears down the spirit of intrepid reporting, especially in the intimidating setting of a professional sports locker

•

107

room. So when the new season dawned, all of the beat writers were looking forward to establishing a more harmonious relationship in the clubhouse.

This was particularly true now that Gregg Jefferies and Kevin McReynolds were gone. Only his teammates were more delighted than the writers to see Jefferies go, and suffice to say the press corps didn't chip in for a going-away gift for McReynolds either. For that matter, all New Yorkers had been happy to see the two of them go in the Bret Saberhagen trade. For entirely different reasons, they had come to personify the Mets' image as a team that whined more than it won.

Jefferies had been the focal point of a bickering, backstabbing clubhouse since he arrived as a twenty-one-year old "savior" in the '88 pennant drive. Ballyhooed by management and babied by Davey Johnson, Jefferies was in a tough spot from the start as the organization's golden boy. But his own personality bred the disdain that became so widespread among the Mets. Jefferies had been trained well technically: His father's prescribed eight-hour days of creative drills—swinging a bat underwater—and conditioning were practically legend by the time he reached the big leagues. But because of the cocoonlike environment created by his father, Jefferies was socially unskilled and so self-absorbed that he couldn't begin to grasp the resentment and plain dislike his arrogance and selfishness inspired. It wasn't a New York phenomenon—he'd been equally despised in the minors, where he played the prima-donna role to an extreme, routinely berating official scorers and cursing so loudly on the field that fans complained to the ball club.

Mike Cubbage, his manager in Triple A, became exasperated with Jefferies and more than once called him into his office for a private talk. Cubbage is a cerebral baseball man, educated at the University of Virginia, but he couldn't reason with Jefferies, who by then had already twice been named Minor League Player of the Year. Finally, Cubbage became so fed up that he appealed to Jefferies's sense of shame.

"Do you know how it looks and sounds when you come

•

back to the dugout cursing the way you do in front of all those fans?" Cubbage said. "How would you feel if your mother was sitting there in the front row?"

Jefferies shrugged and said, "She's heard it before."

The big leagues were no different. He wouldn't even pretend to listen to advice on hitting from anyone but his dad, and that was a problem when he was hitting .200 in July '89, his first full season as a Met. Hitting coach Bill Robinson finally arranged to have dinner with Jefferies's father on a West Coast trip in August to establish some sort of working agreement regarding the son, but nothing changed.

And Davey Johnson wouldn't intervene. In fact, Jefferies would be a major factor in Johnson's firing the following May. It was Davey who insisted, against management's wishes, that he could teach Jefferies to play an adequate second base, but more significant, it was Davey's coddling of Jefferies that damaged team morale beyond repair. It was a strange stance for the manager, because he was a man's man among his players, leaning on his veterans to police the clubhouse. But one thing about Davey: He'd sooner buy lunch for Frank Cashen than admit he was wrong about anything. In this case, he was convinced Jefferies would be a great hitter. "He can hit .300 standing on his head," he said once. And as a former All-Star second baseman with the Baltimore Orioles, Johnson was sure that he could work magic with Jefferies at the position. He made it his pet project in the spring of '89, and once Davey's ego got involved in something so fully, there was no turning back. So even when Jefferies was hitting .188 in late May '89 and making a mess of the double-play pivot, Davey was still hitting him second or third in the lineup, oblivious to the outrage it was producing in his locker room.

Still, Jefferies could have survived being a pet. To some extent, rookie Todd Hundley received similar treatment from Jeff Torborg in the '92 spring training, given the number one catching job ahead of Charlie O'Brien and Mackey Sasser despite nearly going 0-for-March. But Hundley, whose own fa-

•

ther, Randy, was a major league catcher who made a name for himself with the Chicago Cubs, was nothing like Jefferies. He was a tough, likable twenty-two-year-old who spoke up on the field as required but knew his place in the clubhouse, and the veterans, including O'Brien and Sasser, went out of their way to be friendly to him.

So it was neither an accident nor the result of a conspiracy that Jefferies had become the loneliest Met. It was sad, however, because he didn't know how to change. Hard as he tried, his attempts at needling teammates were always awkward, never in step with the rhythm of clubhouse humor. There was something oddly contrived about him: He told people that his favorite singer was Elvis Presley and his baseball idol was Ty Cobb, neither of whom was exactly a contemporary hero for his generation. Players figured it was just another way of creating attention for himself. "Yeah," a teammate once said, "and he wants to marry Marilyn Monroe."

So Jefferies was an outcast. The real problem was that he was also the future, as deemed by Frank Cashen and Joe McIlvaine, as well as Davey Johnson, all of whom were convinced the kid was another Tony Gwynn. They traded Wally Backman to make room for Jefferies, then they kept rearranging the infield while trying to decide if he would make his home at second or third base. By the end of the '89 season the players were disgusted with management over the Jefferies situation. It was fairly clear by then that the Mets wouldn't re-sign Keith Hernandez or Gary Carter, and Hernandez was especially bitter about it. Having decided he wanted to live in New York even after baseball, he wanted desperately to stay around for another few years with the Mets. But on the final weekend of the season, Hernandez, off the record, insisted it was just as well this way, convinced that management was blind to Jefferies's flaws. "They're going in the wrong direction," he said, "thinking Jefferies is the man."

Even as the club changed around him, Jefferies's status never improved. In the spring of '91 he was still the target of

•

the kind of practical jokes usually reserved for rookies. In fact, other rookies pulled pranks on Jefferies with the approval of the veterans. One day pitcher Terry Bross, a six-foot-nine-inch former St. John's basketball player, filled every pair of spikes in Jefferies's locker with shaving cream. Jefferies reacted badly, making a scene by accusing and threatening a couple of other rookies he thought were responsible, while the veterans watched from a distance in delight.

Even as Jefferies learned to stop sulking so openly at going 0-for-4 or being benched for a day, his obsession with his personal stats was all too obvious to teammates and their intolerance became practically universal. Not even Tim Teufel, one of the all-time nice guys in the big leagues, was immune. "Watch him when he gets a walk," Teufel once said in a quiet moment. "He's mad because that's one less chance to get a hit and add to his total. He's got the whole thing figured out, right down to the number of games and at-bats to break [Pete] Rose's hit record."

Some, like Howard Johnson and Kevin Elster, openly despised and mocked Jefferies. HoJo's resentment seemed to be a commentary in itself, since he considered himself the ultimate team man. HoJo had privately aired the kid out a couple of times during Jefferies's rookie year for acting selfishly, and the next spring he told reporters that if his behavior didn't improve, "he'll get his lunch handed to him in here." Jefferies, for his part, seemed to have a genuine fear of HoJo, once asking a reporter, "Why does Howard hate me so much?" When HoJo showed up in the spring of '91 a born-again Christian, the joke in the locker room was that he'd turned to the Lord to save him from a murder rap because he would have killed Jefferies sooner or later.

Others were more discreet about their feelings. The writers were amused by Ron Darling's hypocrisy when he came forward with a handwritten note in support of Jefferies in '91. Darling acted after he had been quoted in the newspapers stating a preference for Tommy Herr's defense. It was funny not

•

just because Darling, the Yale-educated ballplayer, unintentionally misspelled several words in his note but also because he was among the most avowed of the closet Jefferies haters.

Finally, when Jefferies faxed his infamous "open letter to the fans" to radio station WFAN in June '91, he sealed his fate. A few days earlier Jefferies had been moved again from third to second base, replacing the aging Tommy Herr, who wasn't hitting but continued to play good defense. Darling and Frank Viola spoke out, directing criticism at the club, not Jefferies, for again putting a priority on offense rather than defense. But Jefferies took the criticism personally and wrote a letter to be read over WFAN, basically pleading his innocence in this war with his teammates, saying he wanted fans to know he'd done everything in his power to become one of the guys, and still they continued to torment him. Obviously, Jefferies felt isolated and helpless, but the open letter was a typically childish, self-indulgent response that created only more clubhouse resentment, driving a wider wedge between him and his fellow Mets. Maybe if he'd gone on to hit .320, everyone would have forgotten. But when .300 proved elusive for a third straight season, Harazin, who wasn't linked as closely to Jefferies as Cashen and McIlvaine were, became convinced the kid would never thrive in New York, and by mid-August, when the Mets fell out of the pennant race, the soon-to-be GM knew he was going to trade the golden boy.

McReynolds was a different story. He simply played his way out of town. He personified the post-'86 passionless Mets. Acquired two months after the '86 World Series, he turned out to be the first big step backward for management. It was Joe McIlvaine's deal from the start. McIlvaine had wanted desperately to draft McReynolds out of the University of Arkansas in 1981, but Mets doctors declared the young center fielder too much of a risk coming off knee surgery. So with the fourth overall pick of the '81 draft, the Mets chose Terry Blocker, an outfielder who would play only briefly in the majors, and McReynolds went to the Padres, who had the eighth pick.

•

McIlvaine had plotted ever since for another chance to acquire McReynolds, and when he finally made the deal it seemed sensible enough, Kevin Mitchell and three prospects for an established power hitter and exceptional outfielder. Except McIlvaine was somewhat naïve in the matter of people and the chemistry among pro athletes. Mitchell, with his brute strength and rollicking disposition, was a vital piece of the Mets' personality. He and Ray Knight were the necessary muscle behind the Mets' on-field arrogance.

Indeed, if there was a pivotal night in '86, an episode that made the Mets feel bulletproof, it was the moment that Knight demonstrated his boxing skills, decking Eric Davis in Cincinnati with perhaps the best right cross ever thrown on a baseball field. Then, in the ensuing brawl, it took about half the Reds' roster to finally cage and control Mitchell's unleashed rage. The Reds were stunned by the Mets' show of force. Even Dave Parker, the baddest man in baseball at the time, had backed off when Knight invited him to step into the ring right then and there. The intimidation was genuine—no one ever looked at the Mets quite the same way again, themselves included. The Mets brass just didn't understand. Cashen, who could be astonishingly stubborn about money, refused to bend when Knight asked for a $1 million one-year deal following the '86 World Series. The Mets offered $800,000 and said so long when Knight wouldn't budge either. Knight let his ego drive him from a championship team, and wound up signing for only $500,000 with the Orioles, but Cashen's stubbornness cost the Mets far more in the long run.

As for Mitchell, the Mets feared that his street-gang background would lead Dwight Gooden and Darryl Strawberry into trouble, so they dealt him for a player who was as corporate as the Mets brass itself. McReynolds was a rotisserie player come to life, all numbers. Blessed with as much talent as most any player in baseball, he refused to push himself toward greatness. His passion was duck hunting in his native Arkansas, not baseball. He once admitted he didn't even particularly like base-

•

ball, that it was just a job to him—and it showed. He did play hard and teammates both respected and feared his quiet strength, but he didn't bleed for the game. He was known for his mad dashes out of the clubhouse to beat the postgame traffic. Most players agree there is something to be said for hanging around after a game, sharing the emotions of a great win or a tough loss with teammates. *Chemistry* may be an overused word in sports, but in an era of huge salaries with players behaving like corporations, the impact of true team unity and genuine closeness has never been greater. More than ever, teams seem to be looking now for a player with the spirit of a Kirk Gibson, someone who can galvanize a ball club; the Mets haven't had it since Keith Hernandez's legs gave out in 1989.

And while no one looked to McReynolds as a leader, his lack of interest could be disheartening. One night in September 1990 was particularly telling: The Mets were chasing the Pirates, and after having been swept in Pittsburgh a week earlier, they defeated the Bucs and their ace Doug Drabek before a full house at Shea to move within one and a half games of first place. Darryl Strawberry had hit a monster home run, the crowd had gone bananas; it was an emotional victory of the highest order. Yet minutes after the game, the door to the locker room opened and out strode McReynolds, showered and hurrying toward his car, seemingly oblivious to the moment. Even off the record teammates would rarely criticize McReynolds, having accepted him for what he was, but on this night Strawberry noted the left fielder's speedy departure and whispered, "What's with him anyway? If you can't enjoy this one with the guys, something's wrong."

That was McReynolds. He wouldn't take extra batting practice during a slump, wouldn't even talk hitting with the Mets coaches as his numbers began to decline sharply in '90 and '91. And he wouldn't do so much as a sit-up to get in shape. If there was a defining moment in McReynolds's Mets career, it took place in Pittsburgh in April '91. Returning from a minor

•

knee injury, he was instructed to warm up on the Lifecycle in the clubhouse, get the blood flowing in his legs before going out for batting practice.

Lifecycles had become the most common of conditioning machines, computerized exercise bikes that were found in virtually every health club and Y in America. So McReynolds got on the bike in the middle of the clubhouse. Then, while several writers standing nearby pretended not to notice, he motioned strength coach Keith Cedro to come over and show him how to operate it. It was only a year earlier that many of the same writers had angered McReynolds by writing that he looked and was playing like he was overweight. "You fuckers are poisoning people's minds against me," McReynolds had said with rare animation. But now it was obvious that McReynolds, a thirty-one-year-old professional athlete whose stolen-base total had dropped dramatically, had never been on a Lifecycle. Was it any wonder he was fast becoming just an average player?

And while management loved McReynolds because he kept his mouth shut, Harazin finally took note of the declining numbers in the winter of '92 and realized that his left fielder had become a media target. Mostly Harazin believed the public, and indirectly the press, would not embrace the Mets again without an image change, so he traded both McReynolds and Jefferies.

Eddie Murray was part of Harazin's answer. He brought All-Star status, and while he was no speech maker, by all accounts Murray had a passion for the game and a reputation as a willing leader. In other words, he was not another McReynolds. So the writers who would deal with him on a daily basis were hoping to find him a man of quiet substance—as Al Harazin had assured them they would—and glorify him for his accomplishments and his subtle genius as a hitter. All he had to do was let us canonize him. But, as we found out, Murray was a fiercely private and strangely insecure man. At thirty-six, he'd never been married. He came close once while still with the Orioles, but called off the wedding at the last minute after

•

many friends and family had flown in from Los Angeles. He was difficult to figure: In the clubhouse with teammates he was friendly, often going out of his way to make rookies and veterans alike feel comfortable. On the field he delighted in making conversation with opposing players, joking with anyone who wound up next to him on first base. He gave the appearance of a man who appreciated his good fortune in life and loved every minute he spent in baseball.

On TV he exuded a similar warmth for the cameras, bright and well spoken enough to come across as a thinking man's ballplayer. Yet he put on the coldest possible face for the writers, outraged by even the slightest criticism, seemingly a haunted superstar. His paranoia went back to his days in Baltimore, when he was criticized by Orioles ownership for lack of production during an extended slump one year. When a portion of the local media jumped on the anti-Murray bandwagon, he felt persecuted and held it against everyone who carried a notebook.

Sports Illustrated's baseball writer Tim Kurkjian, who covered the Orioles for the Baltimore *Sun* at the time, once wrote a story projecting Murray as a future Hall of Famer, and remembers Murray telling him the next day, "That's a lonely corner you're sitting in." Murray was sure that no one else recognized his accomplishments. But it wasn't long before Murray stopped speaking to Kurkjian over something he wrote. To this day, Murray won't speak a word to any writer from Baltimore. Kurkjian, who hadn't spoken to him in years, made an attempt during the Mets' season-opening series in St. Louis, and wound up in a heated argument with him in a hallway outside the visitors' clubhouse. Why was Murray so mad? Kurkjian had no idea. "With Eddie you can never be sure what it's about," he said.

It didn't necessarily have to be a writer. If a TV guy crossed the line, Murray put him on his list. Tim McCarver, for example. As one of the few ex-player broadcasters in baseball who dared to call an honest game, dealing out criticism as well

•

as praise when warranted, McCarver managed to anger his share of players during his ten years doing Mets games. But no one ever reacted to him like Murray. McCarver first introduced himself during the '89 season, Murray's first in the National League, before the Dodgers took batting practice one day.

"Eddie, Tim McCarver," the broadcaster said, extending a hand.

Murray just looked at McCarver and said, "I know who you are. You're the butcher."

McCarver tried to make light of it.

"Guess you're talking about my hands, huh?"

Murray shook his head and just pointed up toward the broadcast booth.

"Well, I guess I'm doing my job then," McCarver said as he turned and walked away.

McCarver was dumbfounded because as far as he could remember, he'd never said a word about Eddie Murray on the air. But when Murray became a Met, McCarver figured he'd give him the courtesy of another introduction, and once again extended a hand on the field one day during spring training.

Again Murray declined, barely acknowledging McCarver.

"Got tape on my hands," he said brusquely.

Again McCarver walked away, more amused than offended, but sure that he would never say another word to the new Mets first baseman.

Clearly, Murray wasn't going out of his way to change his stripes for anyone who didn't kiss his ass up and down. He'd set the tone for his tenure as a Met on his very first day in camp, keeping a horde of media waiting forty-five minutes for a press conference arranged by Jay Horwitz, then proceeding to warn writers there would be "focusing" days during the season when his locker would be off limits.

Writers kept their distance early, but Murray widened the gap when he wondered aloud one day why Joe Sexton of the *Times* was still in the clubhouse late one afternoon during

•

spring training. "The free food's upstairs," he said, fixing his glare on the reporter.

Three weeks into the season, Sexton wrote a story basically in praise of Murray for his productive start, but also mentioning his indifference and occasional hostility toward the media. A few days later Murray confronted Sexton in the locker room and they argued, though not loudly enough to make a scene.

"How can you write that I'm hostile?" Murray demanded. "I been hostile to you?"

"How about 'the free food's upstairs'?"

A DAY IN THE LIFE

—B.K.

So you want to be a baseball writer? Love the idea of traveling around the country, ballpark to ballpark, getting paid to watch home runs and strikeouts? It's not as glamorous as you might think. Like any job, there are days when you dream about being free, winning the lottery.

As a baseball beat writer . . .

You'll cover an average of 120 games a season, plus a best-of-seven playoff and another best-of-seven-game World Series. That means you'd better love baseball.

You'll write three stories a day, every day. The deadline for your first-edition dispatch is usually 7:00 P.M., which means you have to write a pregame feature on someone—a streaking player, or a slumping player, or one who's sitting and wants to be traded, or one who's been recently injured and depressed, or one who's ready to come off the DL . . . the possibilities travel into infinity. All this means you have to get to the ballpark around 4:00 to make sure you ha~ time to interview. Once batting practice b~ gins at 5:00, your access is almost nil.

Even if you write a terrific first-editi~ story, chances are you'll never see it. Yo~ piece runs in the paper's national editio~ which travels out of state.

Now your attention turns to your "r~ ning" story. This is a play-by-play account ~ the game, which has to be filed arou~ 11:00 P.M., or right as the game is ending.~ the case of the *Post* and the *Daily New*~ this edition reaches suburban Westchest~ Rockland, and New Jersey, sometim~ even parts of the five boroughs, if it's a lo~ game. So you'd better find new and int~ esting ways to describe a Dwight Good~ fastball, because night after night, th~ sands of New Yorkers rely on you. This~ particularly true on the nights the Mets ~ broadcast on cable. Parts of the city, incr~ ibly, still haven't been hooked up.

"That was a joke. How come Franco can throw you out of the locker room every day and everybody laughs, but I can't make a joke like that. You guys don't show me enough respect."

"Who you kiddin', Eddie? You weren't joking that day. You want respect, it works both ways."

In Atlanta the next night, Murray raised the issue again with Sexton, this time from across the locker room for the benefit of his teammates, but Sexton was on deadline and wouldn't be drawn into it.

Now, two days later, Murray sat in the recliner sur-

Think you're finished? Not quite. Your next-edition story is due by 12:30 A.M., which means you have approximately half an hour to work the clubhouse, return to the press box, and write another story. This one makes it to five boroughs, and even though 's the last thing you do every day, it's also he hardest. That's what makes this job so nique. You spend all day waiting for forty-ve minutes of anxiety, stress, creativity . . an explosion that usually leaves you viped out by 1:00 A.M.

So you go home, you sleep. If you have ids who want you to get up at 7:00 A.M., ough. If your boss wants to call at 10:00 nd ask why you didn't have So-and-so's flammatory quote that appeared in the ther paper, that's tough, too. It's part of he job. It doesn't matter that you and So-nd-so aren't speaking because your paper rote an inflammatory headline about him he week before. Editors don't understand e street politics of a clubhouse. Only you o, the baseball writer, who never, ever rites headlines. That job belongs to a mid-dle-level editor inside the office, one who never has to face the target of his 100-point abuse.

That's what makes honest men of most baseball writers. You go after a player in print, you have to be in the clubhouse the next day to see him. You learn quickly that major leaguers are really like the rest of us: some great guys, some jerks, the majority somewhere in the middle. And you do learn, too, because from February until October, you spend more time with the ballplayers than with your family and friends.

As a baseball writer, you spend fifty days away from home in spring training, another one hundred days on the road during the regular season, and then disappear for almost all of October for the postseason. By then, you'll have written over five hundred stories, some five hundred thousand words, flown twenty-five thousand miles, called your office fifteen hundred times.

That's not to say this is a bad job. Not at all. If you love baseball and love to write, it's the best way to spend your days on this

rounded by other players watching the basketball game—unapproachable. Sensing a problem, Jay Horwitz nervously sidled over to Murray and whispered a plea of cooperation into his ear, then shuffled away, his face panicked. Murray still wasn't moving. He sat, we loitered with nowhere else to go, since Dave Cone, who'd pitched a shutout, was icing his elbow. Five minutes passed, an eternity for a roomful of writers standing awkwardly in various locations, trying to act as if they weren't waiting for Murray.

A DAY IN THE LIFE

(continued)

earth. A baseball writer never has to worry about rush hour. He doesn't have to wear a jacket and tie to work. He has all his expenses paid for by his newspaper. He sees his name in print every day—and if you don't believe that matters, ask how many writers leave their bylines off their stories.

A baseball beat writer sees, hears, and knows practically everything that happens to his team. Often he knows more than the front office does. A beat guy becomes the father confessor to troubled players, to managers who rail against GMs, and to front-office executives who defame agents.

Players and executives say they don't read your stories, but as a beat guy, you know they're lying. Rule one in sports: Everyone reads everything. What appears in print has enormous influence, which is one of the reasons the Mets hired Jeff Torborg. He's better with the media than Buddy Harrelson was. As a baseball beat writer, you'll

have access to free tickets, but you'll learn quickly to ignore the idiots who ask for them all the time. You can get autographs, but you won't: It's unprofessional. A beat guy thinks most TV people would be lost without the information they get in the paper, but is secretly envious of the TV guy's salary.

A beat guy is a little jealous of the newspaper columnists, the guys who come around once a week or so, ask you for all the inside information, and then write it as if it were theirs. But that's all right. Mike Lupica gives the *News* legitimacy in the clubhouse, just as does Tom Verducci for *Newsday*. But the beat guy usually has to face the players the next day when the columnist has blasted a guy and then disappeared.

In fact, the beat guy has to swallow it all: editors' constant dissatisfaction, columnists who prey, players who are rude, and fans who think you're ruining their team. Still want this job?

•

"Fuck him," Ed Christine, one of the beat writers said, loud enough for some other players to hear. "I'm not waiting all day for this guy." None of us had much patience for Murray's act. It was late Sunday afternoon, we had a game story to write as well as a separate sidebar detailing Murray's feat, and there was a flight to Houston in about three hours.

Finally, as the Lakers fell hopelessly behind the Portland Trail Blazers, Murray rose and sauntered toward his locker, the crowd of reporters creeping after him. Pretending not to notice, Murray suddenly turned and marched to the food table in the center of the locker room, where he filled a plate. When he returned to his locker, again the crowd moved toward him, and again Murray, without the slightest acknowledgment of the reporters, suddenly departed, this time for the trainer's room. By then, Horwitz looked as if he'd swallowed bad clams.

"Y'all know that Eddie Murray don't talk," Daryl Boston called out to the reporters, half-mockingly. "Whatcha waitin' for? Eddie don't talk to you guys, you know that."

"Fuck him," Christine said again, this time a little louder. "I'm never talking to this motherfucker again."

Just then Murray emerged from the trainer's room. This time the crowd pinned him at his locker and he answered questions about the home run for a few minutes. Christine, true to his word, refused to join the interview, watching with a piercing stare from across the room. Meanwhile, the words were hardly worth the wait. Murray, as usual, offered little perspective or insight.

"It's a nice round number," he said of number four hundred. He's a bright man, but no matter how artfully we wanted to write about Murray's accomplishments, he wasn't going to talk to us. So while the Mets were playing decent baseball at this point, having just won two of three in Atlanta to go five games over .500, we were starting to wonder if Murray could single-handedly make covering the Mets an act of misery.

•

MAY 5. HOUSTON. ASTROS 5, NEW YORK 4.

I T W A S J U S T one bad inning, really. In a sea of so many
games, so many innings, so many forgettable moments, the
Astros' seventh inning against Wally Whitehurst was a mere
speck. But it's like that first hint of a sore throat, the very first
ache in the bones that says a cold is coming. Something about
that inning, and more specifically the postgame response to it,
whispered ominously about what kind of summer awaited Torborg and his Mets.

The Mets had gone into the inning trailing only 1–0. As
usual, Sid Fernandez was near-brilliant, but having been abandoned by the offense, he left the game staring at a tough loss.
These were the kinds of games when Fernandez slipped into his
one-syllable funks. Journalism-school students should be required to interview Fernandez on days like these.

"Did you have good stuff, Sid?"

"I don't know—ask Mel," he'd say, nodding vaguely in
the direction of pitching coach Mel Stottlemyre.

"Well, what was it that you threw to Biggio? Fastball?"

"I guess."

"Does it make you feel any better that you're throwing
well?"

"Yeah. . . . I don't know. Look, can I go now? Are we
finished?"

Before you could answer, Fernandez would trudge off to
the shower, wrapped in a towel that hid his jiggly flesh, and
you'd be left staring at your notebook searching for something—anything—that represented a self-analytical quote.
And, as always, even two minutes at Sid's locker had assaulted
your senses. He had this pregame ritual: On the days he
pitched, Fernandez refused to shower, shave, or even brush his
teeth until after the game. That meant Sid's locker was a combat zone for any eager reporter, but it didn't take long to realize
there was little reason to be there anyway. Fernandez wasn't a

•

bad guy. He was painfully shy and remarkably lacking in self-confidence for a pitcher who was murder on hitters. Deceptively overpowering because his unusual arm angle—he practically pushed the ball from a position tight against his body—made it tough to pick up his pitches, Fernandez was always among the league leaders in strikeouts and fewest hits allowed per game. The Mets had thought he'd develop into a perennial twenty-game winner until they saw him unravel year after year in crucial moments of close games. You could see it coming. He'd walk the number-eight hitter in a one-run game, get mad at himself, lose concentration and confidence, serve up a fastball that had no conviction behind it to a pinch hitter, and suddenly his victory had turned to defeat. Maybe it was due to his low self-esteem, the result of his constant battle of the bulge. He was prone to periods of severe depression when going bad. Two months earlier, he'd been so shaken by a poor performance in his very first outing of spring training, in Fort Lauderdale against the Yankees, that he sent word through Horwitz that he wasn't talking. Wasn't talking? In March? It was unheard of.

"Jay," said Ed Christine, who, of all the writers, was perhaps the friendliest with Fernandez, "tell that big pineapple to cut the bullshit. It's spring fuckin' training and we drove an hour and a half to watch him pitch and he's our only fuckin' story."

Fernandez eventually relented but he was practically inconsolable in the locker room. When someone wondered what he would have to do differently in his next outing, out of nowhere he snapped, "What the fuck you want me to do, quit?"

At such moments we felt we should be able to page the team shrink on a beeper phone. *Calling Dr. Lans. Code blue, code blue, Sid's about to jump. We'll stall him as long as we can.* As it turned out, however, Fernandez would be one of the very few Mets to distinguish himself in '92, pitching consistently well among the rubble of a rotten season. There was just no figuring El Sid. His heritage seemed to be part of his mystery:

•

a native Hawaiian, Fernandez never seemed completely comfortable in the States. A couple of years earlier, in a quiet moment, he'd said, "When I retire I'm gonna go home, climb to the highest rock on the island, and throw my spikes and glove as far away as I can." Over the years he began to loosen up with teammates and reporters but remained terribly inhibited in virtually all mass interview settings, and eventually you accepted him for what he was and learned not to count on him to help your story.

Still, it's a reporter's job to know his subjects, and you looked for clues at all times. A player's locker is his home away from home, and often it makes a statement of some sort, though more so at Shea than on the road. Though it doesn't seem to fit, Fernandez is a heavy-metal freak who litters his locker with concert memorabilia from the likes of Mötley Crüe and Def Leppard, as well as piles of compact discs and sometimes his own guitars. Former Met reliever Randy Myers had perhaps the most distinctive locker: It could have passed for a munitions supply store, filled with military and gun magazines, army boots, and assorted camouflage T-shirts and fatigues, as well as huge bottles of megavitamins—all testimony to Myers's obsession with power. Ron Darling, the Ivy Leaguer, kept philosophy books on his shelf, which Keith Hernandez used to say Darling never read but displayed for cosmetic effect. Hernandez, on the other hand, lined his locker with Civil War books, which Darling claimed Hernandez never read, either.

Dwight Gooden had so many factory-fresh gloves and spikes, courtesy of the companies with which he had endorsement deals, that a visit to his locker was like walking into a sporting-goods store. "Need one?" Gooden would casually ask a reporter, producing a glove so new you couldn't help but press the leather to your nose just for that terrific smell. Of course, almost every Met's locker was filled with letters from women. There were usually so many that players would simply toss them away. They'd learned to detect which were the ones written by teeny-boppers—the ones who professed simply to love

•

them and worship them, but not offer anything else—and which were from the more daring and sometimes more dangerous ones.

Oh, they were out there: women—and sometimes men—who'd send nude or near-nude photos of themselves. Usually they were accompanied by graphic notes asking for, or else offering, various forms of sex. Players would pass the pictures around the locker room but rarely pursue such propositions. Common sense prevailed, especially among the big-name Mets. Darryl Strawberry, who was the target of a steady deluge of Please-call-me letters over the years, professed to have never once responded to such a letter from a stranger. "What if it's a setup?" he asked.

Indeed, there was too much easy sex to be had in the bars, too many women to meet face-to-face in the ballparks, for the Mets to resort to pickups by mail. But even meetings in the flesh posed a threat. Legend had it that as a minor leaguer in the early eighties, a big-name Met—no longer with the club—unknowingly picked up a transvestite in a smoky southern bar. It wasn't until they began slow-dancing that the Met discovered his partner was a man. The player pushed the transvestite away in disgust, and had actually cocked his fist to throw a punch, but teammates—fearing the ensuing arrest and headlines—restrained him. On his way out the bar door, the Met told the man he'd eventually get his ass kicked, some way, somehow, but the transvestite simply cooed, "If you weren't so uptight, you'd have at least taken a blow job."

Even Fernandez, no matinee idol, got his share of propositions in the mail. But this May afternoon at Sid's locker in the visitors' clubhouse, there was nothing of interest, just Fernandez running through his usual unintelligible answers. The beat guys quickly fled Sid, leaving him to the Houston-based radio media. The New York press knew there was little time to waste in getting to the dugout, where Jeff Torborg was holding court. The fact that reporters had to find Torborg in the dugout and not in his office said something about the manager's

•

priorities. Before taking the job, Torborg had pursued all avenues toward increasing his yearly salary with some sort of broadcast deal. At first, he wanted a postgame TV show, but not even Harazin, in all his desire to cleanse the Mets' public reputation, could swallow that. It would've looked too self-indulgent, too narcissistic for the front office to officially condone that much TV time. So as a compromise, Torborg received a package with WFAN.

The contract, estimated to be worth in excess of fifty thousand dollars, called for him to be on the air for ten to fifteen minutes with Mike and the Mad Dog during drive time every afternoon, and then do a postgame show minutes after the last out. In some ballparks, the WFAN technicians couldn't hook up the proper equipment in the manager's office, so Torborg did the show right from the dugout. No other manager had a deal like this, but the drawbacks would become obvious: Mike Francesa and Chris Russo, the afternoon-show hosts, weren't club broadcasters lobbing soft questions, as was typical of shows other managers around the league participated in. Instead they asked Torborg tough questions, especially as the Mets began to falter in midsummer, and Torborg had to do more bobbing and weaving than he had ever imagined. Moreover, it was obvious within a few weeks that he wasn't on the air to entertain or offer insights to fans, because his answers were painfully and repetitively superfluous and one-dimensional. It wasn't yet May and on-air callers were asking Francesa and Russo why this silly charade was being broadcast not only live at 3:10 in the afternoon, but again on tape at 5:10. The answer was simple enough: WFAN was bound by its contract to Torborg. But why was Torborg torturing himself and the listeners like this? Why else but the cash?

Ditto for his postgame show: If he took losses as hard as it seemed early in the season, why would he put himself through the agony of having to answer questions on the air in addition to his press conference? Club broadcasters Bob Murphy and Gary Cohen weren't as tough on him as Francesa and

Russo, but there were cases after tough losses where Torborg was clearly annoyed by certain questions. Torborg would later tell reporters that one reason he persisted with the shows was that he hadn't anticipated such a disastrous season. But again, it seemed the bottom line was a desire to cash in—never mind that he had one of the most lucrative managerial contracts in baseball, a four-year deal worth $1.9 million.

In any case, his postgame show called for him to be on the air five to eight minutes after the game, depending on various factors. That left the beat guys with two choices: wait the twenty minutes after a game to talk to him, or hustle to the dugout and squeeze in a few questions before the show began. On tight deadlines after night games, there really wasn't a choice, and besides, the manager's tone or comments often became the starting point for a story angle to be pursued in the locker room.

On this day in Houston, there were still fans hanging over the dugout, trying to listen in on the postgame press conference. Torborg, meanwhile, was affecting the Stare. That's what the beat guys called it: that arms-crossed, jaws-tight, eyes-fixed, I'm-pissed, don't-fuck-with-me expression which seemed glued on after every loss. His answers, often short and terse, reflected the Stare. All of which would have been easier to accept if reporters didn't quickly notice that he seemed to have no such trouble completing sentences and giving more noteworthy answers moments later when he put on his headset and answered questions on his radio show. It wasn't long before the print guys were wondering how much of the Stare was contrived, while beginning to resent Torborg for his radio fixation.

In any case, this indeed had been a tough loss to swallow. Throwing errors by Dave Magadan and Willie Randolph in the seventh inning had opened the door to four runs by the Astros. But there had been a critical moment of decision: Right-handed reliever Wally Whitehurst had been left in to pitch to left-handed power hitter Eric Anthony with the bases loaded, and Anthony had lined a two-run single to right, all while

·

left-hander Paul Gibson was warming up in the bullpen. So the logical question to ask Torborg was: "Did you consider using Gibson in that situation?" The answer was: "Of course I did," and how a manager would answer such a question would tell a lot about him. It had to be asked, if only so the manager could explain his thinking. That's the reporter's job. But an insecure manager takes questions like that personally, not only as media second-guessing but as a threat. Billy Martin's pat answer—with voice raised, neck veins standing at attention—would be "Because I'm the fucking manager, that's why!" Davey Johnson would often just grin at a tough question, pause, and say, "You don't know shit about baseball, now do you? Because if you did, you wouldn't be asking me that fucking question."

Torborg was polite, and always made sure to engage the guys on the beat in small talk. But this day he revealed a mean streak that took everyone by surprise. Until then Torborg had allowed and even encouraged the media portrait of himself as a tough guy, but a religious, caring, fatherly figure. Now this: Sexton asked, politely and cautiously, if Torborg regretted not using Gibson to pitch to the left-handed Anthony. It had to be asked—Sexton just happened to be the one on this day, but the question touched a nerve in Torborg. The words were barely out of Sexton's mouth when the manager whipped around to face Sexton and said, "You know, you've been sticking it up my fuckin' ass for weeks. I heard about you, I tried to give you a chance, I tried to be fair with you, but you're always looking for the fuckin' negative. I'm sick of your bullshit. Enough is enough."

The entire dugout was shocked. The beat guys hadn't heard Torborg utter so much as a "goddammit" through spring training and four weeks of the season, and now he was spewing profanities like Billy Martin. Sexton had gone pale, but he kept his composure, saying calmly, "Maybe we should talk about this later." That was the professional thing to do, in fairness to colleagues on deadline and in efforts to avoid any further embarrassment, because make no mistake: This blowout was any-

•

thing but private. A dozen or so fans, ignoring the commands of stadium security guards, were still hanging over the short dugout ledge, getting an earful of venom. But Torborg would have none of it.

"Yeah, later," Torborg exploded. "That's when you do your best fuckin' work. I know how you operate. You're nice down here, but then you go upstairs and stick it to me."

Obviously, Torborg was responding to more than just the question. This was a personal matter with Sexton. Actually, Torborg was going off for the entire organization, since the hierarchy regarded the *Times* man as an enemy. Sexton, the 145-pound beast. He would've been a beatnik in the fifties, a hippie in the sixties. In the nineties he was simply an enigma to the Mets: intelligent, witty, high-strung, moody, exceptionally gifted with the language, but above all, something of a counter-culturist who rebelled at authority figures. His appearance alone ensured distrust among the players: He was skinny and wore scholarly-looking eyeglasses—the picture of intellect. Actually a pretty good athlete, Sexton looked like he'd never worn a jockstrap in his life, and players judge everyone, especially reporters, by their athletic quotient. Even as players got to know him, he was viewed with the ultimate caution in the locker room by all but the rebels. They figured anyone who had no reservations about wearing wing tips with white socks and jeans was to be watched carefully. Indeed, Sexton cared nothing about how he dressed, deeming it a sign of materialism—he was forever wearing badly wrinkled shirts as if in some form of protest, standing out even among other rumpled reporters. Every beat writer had his own quirks, but the Mets ultimately wanted to know just one thing about the guy who sat in front of the computer screen: Is he with us or against us?

For the better part of three decades, the Mets could count on comfortable copy from the *Times*'s veteran baseball writer Joe Durso. He'd grown up with the Mets, had documented their miraculous rise in 1969, was there for the crash in the late seventies and early eighties, and again was witness to the re-

•

building of the great Mets teams in the mid-eighties. Durso had a nice way with words, and the front office was grateful he wanted no part of the tabloid wars that had consumed the Mets, starting in 1985. While the *Post* and the *Daily News* sought to outscoop each other, a mania that also infected *Newsday* as the Long Island paper tried to muscle its way into Manhattan, the *Times* could be counted on for its lofty, gentle prose, safely distant from the Strawberry-Hernandez hissing matches or the rest of the clubhouse madness. The *Times* didn't ask Durso to get down in the mud, and he didn't pretend to be interested. Once, a day after news broke of some clubhouse catastrophe, Durso walked into Davey Johnson's office and, with other reporters present, half-asked and half-commented, "Davey, the tabloids tell me your team is in disarray."

But in 1991 the *Times* decided it was time to play the tabloid game too, at least in its baseball coverage. Durso was given the horse-racing beat, which he enjoyed as an aside to baseball anyway, and in came the Gray Lady's revolutionary, Joe Sexton. Almost immediately he established that he'd be there, step for step, with the *Post* and the *News*, critiquing the Mets on a daily basis in ways the front office never expected from the *Times*. Harazin once said, "Every day when I get to the office, I spread out the *Post*, the *News*, and *Newsday* and I ask myself, 'Which one of these bastards am I going to read first?'" Suddenly, there was another face in the hostile crowd, one who made his presence felt.

In spring training of '91, Sexton, no more than three weeks into his first year on the beat, sent the Mets a warning of just how much the *Times*'s coverage had changed: In his first analysis of Buddy Harrelson's regime, Sexton asked out loud who was actually running the club, Harrelson or bench coach Doc Edwards? The front office—not to mention Harrelson—was outraged. Buddy was a New York favorite, the darling of the beloved '69 Mets. How dare Sexton suggest that? Soon after, the corporate Mets began freezing out Sexton. You could see it in Jay Horwitz, of all people. Horwitz was unfailingly gracious

•

toward the beat guys, even when the tabloids were slamming his ball club, but what he perceived as Sexton's unprovoked attack—"The season hasn't even started yet, Joe," he said in reference to the story—prompted a cold shoulder even from him. And that only intensified Sexton's determination to slug it out with the Mets. It wasn't long before the *Times* was officially placed on the Against Us list.

Obviously Torborg had been warned about Sexton. He'd been cool to the *Times* man all spring. Sexton's manner of asking questions didn't help, either. Torborg thought of himself as a man's man, a no-bullshit guy who loved to talk baseball. Here was this skinny intellectual who asked long, conditional questions, phrased ever so adroitly that he could put anyone—even Harazin the lawyer—into his trap in such a way the victim never knew what hit him.

So when Sexton asked that day about Gibson instead of Whitehurst . . . well, two years of organizational resentment suddenly rose to the surface in Torborg. Sexton held his ground while the other beat guys just stared at the floor. They knew this represented the first shot. Finally, after a few uncomfortable moments that seemed even longer, Torborg let the matter drop and everyone went about his business. But that night in the bar, the boys on the beat teased Sexton, asking if he'd need backup help the next day in Cincinnati, where the Mets were to begin a three-game series.

No one had a clue as to just how seriously Torborg was taking this fight. When the beat guys showed up at Riverfront Stadium, about 4:15 P.M., Torborg still had that hardened look and angry tone. He conducted an uncomfortable pregame Q&A with reporters, both sides trying to ignore the obvious tension. Then, as reporters got up to leave, Torborg asked Sexton, "Do you have a minute?" Everyone assumed he was going to apologize not for his anger but for embarrassing the reporter so publicly. It didn't seem to be Torborg's style. Once, in fact, he'd been shown up in a similar fashion in the Yankees clubhouse by Billy Martin, who thought his coach was spying on

•

him for George Steinbrenner, and Torborg later told reporters in private how embarrassed he'd been. "I'd never show someone up in front of people like that," he told them.

But to the astonishment of everyone, Torborg had no intention of apologizing to Sexton; instead, he was lacing on the gloves for Round Two. The door to the manager's office remained closed for thirty minutes while the six other beat guys, PR man Jay Horwitz, and a handful of players and coaches kept walking by, ears cocked to pick up the argument. Actually, that wasn't necessary; Torborg's voice boomed right

EL SID AND THE DOGHOUSE

—J.H.

ON THE BEAT, the push of the tabloid mentality often clashes with the pull of journalistic integrity. What's a story and what's not? What's fair and what's unfair? The tug of war is constant: It's easy enough at times to take a quote out of context, twist it just enough to warrant a back-page headline. You won't last long in the clubhouse making a practice of irresponsible reporting, but there are more subtle decisions to make on a day-to-day basis, and many of them are born out of desperation for a story.

Some days the dreaded early story falls in your lap. An injury, a trade, a major lineup change—they are gifts from the tabloid gods. But on many days you cast your line into the clubhouse and whatever you pull out is your story. Some days you pull out nothing and panic sets in; actually, spring training can be the worst time of all—six weeks of trying to find stories that matter even though the games don't.

Simply put, that's how Sid Fernandez became the subject of a classic *Post* back page—the day in spring training of '91 that we put Sid in the doghouse.

El Sid had reported some twenty pounds overweight to camp, and manager Buddy Harrelson was treading lightly on the subject, for fear of offending a pitcher sensitive about his ample physique. Stories had been written the first week of camp about Sid's ongoing battle of the bulge, with El Sid offering little more than his usual mumbling to reporters. Fernandez is a beat writer's nightmare, his interviews coming off like *Saturday Night Live* skits. After eight years in the big leagues, the kid from Hawaii is still totally inhibited in postgame interview situations, but in casual conversation he's friendly, communicative, easy to like, which is why I still feel somewhat guilty about the doghouse.

I was standing around the locker room

•

through the door and walls at times, a muffled echo throughout the clubhouse as he berated Sexton.

"You believe this shit?" one player said, listening by the door. "Think they might go at it?"

It was truly unprecedented. The Mets, New York's darlings for nearly a decade, romanced by every media outlet in town, were suddenly ready to throw punches. "If you go after me or my team, so help me, I'll drop you," Torborg shouted. At that point, the manager had apparently risen from his seat and was standing over Sexton. Was Torborg really ready to fight?

---

e morning, complaining of nothing to ite, shooting the breeze with Ed Chris- e, the beat guy for Westchester-Gannett wspapers, when El Sid lumbered by, oking as hefty as ever. Together we wan- red over and casually mentioned that arrelson had spoken of Sid's weight the evious afternoon after the workout. Har- lson had indeed offered a progress re- rt, saying Fernandez was still overweight t doing extra running to try to lighten his d.

We didn't make that clear to Sid and he dn't ask for details. All he had to hear was at his weight was a matter of public record ain and he was incensed. Quietly at his ker, Sid started blasting Harrelson—fuck- this, fuckin' that, fuckin' everything. In th, Fernandez was off base: If anything, arrelson had been too easy on him about e extra weight, but this was no time to ason with him.

Neither Christine nor I was taking notes d at this point we figured everything was f the record—just another player venting

some anger in private. Just to make sure I said, "Sid, you don't want this written, do you?"

"Fuck it," Sid said. "Go ahead and write it, I don't care. Write it. They treat me like a fuckin' dog around here. I'm sick and tired of it. Go ahead, write it—I don't give a fuck."

Sid went on for another couple of minutes and still we weren't taking notes, partly because we didn't want any of the other reporters to notice. In fact, we changed the subject fairly quickly, figuring Sid had said plenty already, and then left Fernandez to drown his anger in the heavy-metal music that is always pouring through the headphones of his portable stereo. Minutes later Christine and I huddled outside the locker room.

"What do you think?" I asked. "Do we write it?"

Christine didn't hesitate. "He said to write it, didn't he?"

"Yeah, but you know he'll kill us if we write it."

•

133

No manager had ever crossed that line in New York—not even Billy Martin, who hated Henry Hecht from the *Post* so much in the late seventies it made him shake—but the standard rule on the beat was if someone was ready to go to fists, you defended yourself.

For Sexton this was as close as his anti-establishment ways had ever come to causing himself personal harm. He wasn't meanspirited, just forever rebellious. When he'd get on the beat guys' nerves, they'd threaten to lock him in a room somewhere with Dr. Lans and let the club shrink look deep into

---

EL SID AND THE DOGHOUSE

(continued)

"Fuck it. He said to write it. He said it twice. I'm writing it."

Of course, it was easy for Christine to be so cavalier. He knew damn well Fernandez wouldn't see his story, not in Florida, where the *Post*, the *Times*, and the *Daily News* were the only New York papers available. But I agreed that Sid had given his permission, even if it was in a moment of rage, and it did end the day's search for a story.

When I called the office to tell the assistant sports editor, Dick Klayman, what I'd be writing, I knew I was in trouble. At the mention of "They treat me like a dog," Klayman practically choked on his coffee. "He said what? Did he really?"

It was a made-to-order tabloid story and I knew it was headed for the back page. Only I didn't know that our sports editor, Bob Decker, a former minor league pitcher who could now give El Sid a run for his money in the heavyweight department himself, pounced on the story. He ordered a full back-page cartoon drawn by the graphics department, depicting poor Sid peering out from inside a doghouse. On the doghouse a sign read EL SID, and in front was a bowl labeled EL GRUB. The headline was—what else?—THEY TREAT ME LIKE A DOG.

The cartoon was funny, all right, but it wasn't hard to understand why Fernandez would fail to see the humor. The New York papers are sold a day late in Florida, but in the case of something like this, PR director Jay Horwitz hears about it from the New York office and has copies faxed to him. So when I arrived at the ballpark that morning Jay came scurrying over in his panic mode and said, "Sid's not happy."

I sort of gulped, envisioning all 240 pounds of an angry Fernandez waiting at his locker with the big hunting knife he carries around.

"He says that stuff was off the record," Horwitz said.

"Hey, Jay, he said to go ahead and write it."

•

Sexton's subconscious, see if he could get a handle on the guy.

Surely his background was grist for a case study in non-comformity. Sexton had grown up in Brooklyn, attended a Jesuit high school in Manhattan, then meandered through his college years. He spent a year in Ireland at the School of Irish Studies—"as a failed poet," he says wryly—between stints at the University of Colorado and the University of Wisconsin, from which Sexton finally graduated. It took six years in all because there were leaves of absence, one spent hitchhiking around the country, another spent working as a gandy dancer

---

'Well, I'm just telling you what he said. I ⊔ldn't go looking for him."

⊓hat might have been good advice, ex-
⊨t you couldn't hide from anyone in the
⊫ll spring-training clubhouse if your life
⊨ended on it. At the time, I wasn't sure if
⊧e did, but I felt I had to make an attempt
⊧alk to Fernandez about it. I grabbed
⊧istine for support and we headed for El
⊧'s locker, where he was sitting, as usual,
⊓ headphones on.

⊍When he saw us coming, he took off the
⊧dphones and very evenly said, "Get the
⊧< out of here, Harper, before I kill you."

'But, Sid," I said, "you told us to write

⊰id was in no mood to debate. Perhaps
⊨id he was about to lose his temper and
⊩ngle me, he got up and stormed off to
⊧trainer's room. I did my best to avoid
⊧ssing paths with him the rest of the day
' worried that I had a long-term problem.
⊧to my astonishment, only a couple of
⊧s later Fernandez walked up to me while
⊧s interviewing another player, gave me

the finger, and said, "Fuck you, you little fuckin' asshole."

Believe it or not, that was a good sign. Sid did this on a fairly regular basis with the guys he liked when he was in a good mood—it was his way of saying hello. Sid was smiling when he delivered his message, and I assumed it was his way of saying he'd forgiven or forgotten. Either way, I was off the hook. I thought about pursuing the question of whether he'd actually given permission to write the story, but figured it was best to drop it. Sid seemed to want it that way.

He did bring it up once, though, in a conversation with Dan Castellano of the *Newark Star-Ledger*. "The thing I really don't understand," Sid said, "is why would Harper draw that picture of me like that for the paper?"

Yes, it seemed that El Sid actually thought I'd done the artwork as well as the story. I can only imagine how he thinks the paper is edited, printed, and delivered. But in any case, I wasn't about to ask.

•

•

on the Union Pacific railroad. After graduating, Sexton got his first newspaper job as the lone white reporter on the newly founded *City Sun*, a black weekly in Brooklyn that has been a force in city politics since it began publishing in 1984. He moved on to work for the *Syracuse Post-Standard* for a couple of years before getting married and moving back to Brooklyn, working briefly at the *Bergen Record* before taking a part-time job at the *Times* that became full-time in 1990. By then Sexton had yet to own a single credit card, refusing to be sucked into any such establishment behavior, but in '92, tired of hassles with hotels and rental cars, he relented and sold out at age thirty to the almighty plastic. In college and beyond, meanwhile, Sexton had been a hard drinker, hard enough so that upon getting married and having a daughter in 1988 he decided to give up alcohol altogether. Now he drank nonalcoholic beers in the bars after games, a man consumed with his job and dedicated to his family.

As such, he was ready to do battle with Torborg, and came back at the manager with his own defiant reply: "I have a wife and two kids—this is my job. You're not gonna intimidate me or tell me what to write." They kept going at it, bits and pieces filtering through to the locker-room audience. It went on so long that the other writers started to wonder if Torborg was doing this for his players' benefit. When the door finally opened, Sexton emerged pale, shaken, but still standing. Torborg's face had that flushed look, as if he'd just run a couple of miles; he was clearly drained. Whatever he'd set out to do, it didn't appear as if he'd enjoyed it.

Whether the manager was delivering a message or just venting his own anger, battle lines had been drawn. But Sexton, true to his word, was determined not to be intimidated. And three weeks later he proved it, writing a critical analysis of the manager in his "Quarterly Report" on the Mets' season. It was nothing terribly harsh, making certain points about Torborg's in-game style, but it was enough to show he wasn't backing down, enough to piss Torborg off royally again. One

•

word did it: Sexton wrote that Torborg had been "block-headed" in his handling of bullpen roles. He could have said "inflexible" and Torborg probably never would have flinched. "Blockheaded" made Torborg crazy. Sexton later said he used it as a way to be light-hearted with his criticism, but the manager didn't see the humor. He even privately told a couple of other writers, "He's trying to make me look like a fool." The day it ran in the paper, Torborg was a guest speaker at a "Women in Sports" luncheon, and so was the *Times*'s sports editor, Neil Amdur. Torborg sought out Amdur and ranted and raved about Sexton for ten minutes, demanding that the sports editor do something about him. When it came time to speak to the group, Torborg was still consumed with thoughts of Sexton and turned his speech into a diatribe on fairness in the media. Amdur called Sexton at home and told him Torborg was furious, putting enough fear into Sexton that he called a couple of the beat guys that day and asked if they thought he would be in any danger at the ballpark that night. "What if he takes a swing at me?" Sexton asked.

This was not what Fred Wilpon or Al Harazin had had in mind when they hired Torborg over coach Mike Cubbage, a highly qualified candidate. The Mets saw Torborg as a man capable of handling the media problems that had buried his predecessor, Buddy Harrelson, and they were also afraid to take a chance on Cubbage, another guy who'd never managed in the big leagues. Harrelson had proven just what a gamble it could be, a New York hero who turned into the biggest public-relations blunder the Mets would make in the Frank Cashen regime.

Over the years Harrelson had built a reputation as a tough little bastard, forever remembered as the guy who fought with Pete Rose at second base during the '73 playoffs. As a coach he became Davey Johnson's right-hand man, a street-smart baseball guy to whom both players and reporters went for advice and insights about the game. He was well liked by everyone, still adored by the public as the fiery little shortstop on that

•

miracle '69 team. What no could have known was how insecure and paranoid he would be once he sat in the manager's seat. He was an instant sensation when he replaced Davey on May 30, 1990, getting much credit for inspiring a month of excellent baseball, but the pressures of pennant-race baseball revealed his shortcomings, and as the Mets began to fade, Harrelson was swallowed up by the job.

The press was no longer a friend but an objective observer. Buddy couldn't comprehend that when reporters questioned his strategy decisions, they weren't challenging him on any personal level but doing the job of the baseball writer. It took Davey Johnson some six years to lose control of the clubhouse, but from the start Harrelson was at a loss as to how to deal with the media-related issues that affected his ball club. He called team meetings to urge caution with the press, openly telling his players the writers were the enemy, even going so far as to tell them to lie about certain subjects—anything to keep the scrutinizing eye of the media away from the inner workings of the team. After Harrelson and Dave Cone engaged in a shoving match in the dugout in Cincinnati in 1991, an exchange that was prompted by Cone's anger with bench coach Doc Edwards, the manager asked Cone to lie for him. "Let's say it was a miscommunication," Harrelson said to Cone. "We don't have to tell them what happened—they'll only blow it up into something we'll all regret." Cone refused, saying he wouldn't be caught in a lie, it wasn't his way, and went on to admit to his own role in the affair that night.

"Buddy was obsessed with you guys," another Met told reporters after Harrelson was fired. "You guys drove him fucking crazy." Harrelson plain fired himself with a series of decisions that demonstrated his failure to grasp the scope of the job: He washed his hands of the Gregg Jefferies problem, refusing to get involved after Jefferies completely alienated teammates with his open letter to fans; he refused to reprimand Vince Coleman in any way after Coleman humiliated coach Mike Cubbage on the field with a vulgar display of temper

•

during batting practice one day; and, rather than go himself, he sent pitching coach Mel Stottlemyre to make a pitching change late in the season after the Mets had collapsed, admitting he didn't want to be booed.

Harrelson came apart so completely that Cashen took the painful step of firing the most loyal of Met players and employees a week before the end of the '91 season. That meant two dismissals in less than two seasons, an unprecedented level of turbulence at Shea. Harrelson never understood what had happened. To this day he blames the press corps for his demise, and that's sad. Management knew better. Even his favorite players knew. The one Met whom Harrelson had managed during his two-year stint in the low minors was Kevin Elster, but not long after the firing, when Elster was asked what kind of manager Harrelson had been, he pawed at the floor with his foot and said, "Well, Buddy was the best coach I ever had. Still is."

How, exactly, had Buddy failed? What, exactly, constitutes good managing? At the college level, and even in the minor leagues, a good manager teaches his players. He explains strategy, offers tips on turning the double play, suggests different batting stances. But once a player reaches the major league level, he isn't expected to need instruction, and rarely wants it. To such players, a manager has to be more like an airline pilot, guiding the plane and, while being responsible for them, essentially leaving the passengers alone. The most successful managers in the game, at least since big-money contracts created a more equal footing for players, have given their teams plenty of room to breathe, much the way Davey Johnson operated in the mid-eighties. Discipline has to be a product of a certain attitude and chemistry—a pact dedicated to the common goal of winning; discipline can't be forced on big leaguers anymore, not with all the money and freedom the game now provides. In an ideal setting, the honor system works: The manager treats his players like adults; the players respond by winning. That's all managers really care about—winning, and keeping their jobs. But for the honor system to succeed, a manager has to

•

have the respect of the clubhouse, and that means he must speak the same language as his players. He must argue with umpires, occasionally make sure he gets angry enough to get thrown out of a game, as well as throw a clubhouse temper tantrum when the mood strikes. He'll go to the back of the plane just to shoot the bull with the renegades, but not stay too long. And sometimes it doesn't hurt to go to war with the press, all in the name of protecting your boys.

The sharp manager knows when to leave a young pitcher in a tight spot, knowing it's important to build the kid's confidence. But he also knows when to pull a kid out of a game when he's ahead, just so his ego will soar, regardless of the outcome. A savvy manager will never admit to being jealous about a player's money or stardom. At the same time, though, a manager's presence simply can't be diminished in his clubhouse. Once the off-the-record complaints start showing up in the paper, it's the beginning of the end. It's a fine line between maintaining control and giving players their freedom, as Davey Johnson can attest. Imposing fines or dress codes won't necessarily do it. Ultimately, managers retain control on the strength of their personality and their handling of games themselves.

That's what players really respect in a manager: his ability to manage. As much as the Mets liked Davey in his best years, there was always a feeling among them that Whitey Herzog was the difference when the Cardinals beat them at the wire for National League East titles in '85 and '87. Darryl Strawberry finally said so publicly in an *Esquire* magazine article in the spring of '88: Whitey was a better on-field manager. That indictment hurt and angered Johnson, but he never really did dispute it. There was a dangerous, reckless feel to the way Whitey managed his Cardinals in 1985 and 1987, sort of the way Jim Leyland does it in Pittsburgh, where he's earned the title as the game's finest manager.

It isn't just Leyland's strategic skill that wins respect, or even his definable qualities—it's the feel he has for people, the

•

140

sense that he doesn't care about image, doesn't worry about how to form a well-polished answer. He's got a rapport with players that can't be faked or copied. Few managers have it, which is why managers are hired and fired so often. The job is more difficult than ever because of the power that players wield in the form of huge guaranteed contracts, so the new trend in baseball is hiring younger, hipper managers like Dusty Baker, Buck Showalter, Jim Riggleman, Tony Pérez, Felipe Alou, Johnny Oates, Butch Hobson, and Kevin Kennedy. They've all come up through the coaching and minor league managing ranks and for the most part can relate to the modern player.

The old-school Sparky Anderson types who rarely communicate with players are a dying breed. Some, like Lou Piniella, Jim Fregosi, Tommy Lasorda, and Jeff Torborg, still try to rule by the force of personality and/or reputation, but more typical these days are the '92 World Series managers, Cito Gaston and Bobby Cox—managers not unlike Davey Johnson—who ask little of their players other than an honest effort every night. Others, like Joe Torre, Buck Rodgers, and Art Howe, fall generally into that category, while Tony LaRussa has carved out a reputation as a genius—and influenced many others—with his intellectual approach to managing.

In the end, what counts most is whether a manager can consistently get his team to play hard for him, and nobody does that better than Leyland. His players know they live in a simple universe: Bust ass, and the manager is an ally; cross him, and the wrath comes down, without regard to how it looks, sounds, or feels in the press. That's what Barry Bonds learned about Leyland in spring training of 1991. The two went face-to-face after Bonds, in the wake of a stinging loss in salary arbitration, lashed out at coach Bill Virdon on a practice field. Although Leyland was on the field in full view of teammates, writers, and TV cameras, he engaged Bonds in a vicious argument, not caring who heard, just so Bonds would understand he would not take control of the Pirates' camp with anger over his contract or anything else.

•

The two soon made up, and to this day Bonds calls Leyland "the best manager I ever played for, or ever will play for." It was another example of Leyland going against conventional wisdom, and ultimately that's what Bonds respected: Leyland's boldness. By contrast, Buddy Harrelson's refusal to get involved in Vince Coleman's tirade against Mike Cubbage let everyone know he didn't understand what the job was all about. It was equally obvious in the dugout, where he was unwilling to listen to his baseball instincts, not even after four decades in the game. It's like a veteran Met once said of Harrelson: "Right until the last second, whether he was making a pitching change or sending up a pinch hitter, there he'd be with those fucking reports in the dugout, going over the numbers, like he didn't trust himself. It was kind of sad, really."

MAY 15. LOS ANGELES. METS 4, DODGERS 1.

FOR FIVE INNINGS the Mets saw their blueprint come to life against the beautiful backdrop of Dodger Stadium and the breathtaking view of the mountains beyond the outfield wall. Bret Saberhagen was in top form, had been for five straight brilliant starts. On this night he struck out eight Dodgers in five innings, absolutely devastating Eric Davis with fastballs, fanning him twice. Pitching was beginning to push the Mets toward the top. This win raised their record to 21–16. They were three games behind the Pirates, in third place, but no one was worried. Or were they? The telltale signs of an offense spinning its wheels were there for all to see, with Bobby Bonilla and Howard Johnson both off to terrible starts.

Bonilla was hitting .240 with three home runs and looking more and more vulnerable to the same off-speed pitches that were turning HoJo's bat to putty. One Mets pitcher shook his head, surprised because Bonilla had always looked like a better hitter, capable of adjustments, as a Pirate. "I wouldn't throw that guy a fastball the rest of the season. Bobby's so . . . man, you can see him going crazy up there, like HoJo, especially when he gets behind in the count." Bonilla, who'd started the season so full of hope, seemed a little lost in the clubhouse. On the road he often took in a movie and dinner with Jay Horwitz and trainer Steve Garland. Nothing wrong with it necessarily, but it was odd that Bonilla, a city kid, hadn't gravitated toward the Mets' inner circle—the streetwise, beer-drinking, we're-bad core of veterans ever hoping to rekindle the spirit of the eighties. Once practically a majority, the circle's population had shrunk to a minority in the clubhouse now. Elster was gone, his shoulder having lasted just a week before it was clear he needed major surgery, and Mr. Cool had been replaced by Dick Schofield, a nice guy who was so quiet and cautious that he'd have been delighted if reporters never asked him a question.

So now Cone and Franco were the only real holdovers. They were joined in '92 by Saberhagen, whose star status gave the group a much-needed shot of prestige, and Paul Gibson, the journeyman reliever who had a sharp, wry wit and quickly became friendly with Franco. That was the extent of it, though the circle extended at times to include Mackey Sasser, Dave Gallagher, young left-hander Pete Schourek, Daryl Boston, and Dwight Gooden. Occasionally Bonilla would join the boys at the bar for a beer as well, but he kept his distance from both the inner circle and the more recently formed black social club, which included Vince Coleman, Anthony Young, Gooden, Boston, and to some degree Eddie Murray and Willie Randolph. Murray was something of a loner, while Randolph was an ambassador of goodwill, floating easily among the various cliques. There were the more laid-back beer drinkers, guys like Wally Whitehurst, Jeff Innis, Dave Magadan, Charlie O'Brien, Todd Hundley, and Dick Schofield, who kept a low profile when they went out and wanted no part of any rebel behavior. And there were the religious guys like Howard Johnson, Bill Pecota, and Tim Burke, who did little more socially than read the Bible together.

More than ever, the ball club was fragmented and needed

•

a galvanizing force beyond Franco's humor. Was Bonilla the man? The coming weeks would indicate otherwise, as the Mets searched for someone to resurrect the soul of Keith Hernandez, the last true leader the Mets had had. HoJo didn't have the personality for the role, and five weeks into the season he was looking helpless at the plate. The Mets had built the offensive potential of this team on their belief that Bonilla and HoJo would deliver a minimum of fifty home runs and 225 RBIs, so by now concern was beginning to grow. Pitching, of course, was designed to rescue the Mets from their flaws, and Saberhagen's hot pitching after a slow start reinforced their faith.

Doc Gooden might still have been the spiritual ace of the staff, and David Cone might have had a deeper arsenal, but no one threw harder or more impressively when healthy than Saberhagen. Fact is, in his first spring as a Met he'd inspired the kind of reverence among hitters that had once been the property of Gooden. "I've never seen a starting pitcher throw that hard," Dave Magadan said one day. "He could win fifteen games a year just throwing his fastball." With that in mind, it hardly seemed fair that Saberhagen had an effective change-up as well. Chico Walker, picked up on waivers from the Cubs in May, was left speechless upon seeing Saberhagen up close in a simulated game one day at Shea. "You mean he's got a change-up?" Walker said to no one in particular, watching from behind the batting cage after Daryl Boston had swung about a day early on a pitch. "How does he ever lose?"

He didn't just throw, either. Saberhagen was so precise with his fastball that Gooden, after seeing him pitch, said with open awe, "Even when my shoulder was at its strongest, I didn't have control like that." Indeed, it was more than just the radar gun shrieking at ninety-five miles per hour that made you appreciate Saberhagen. It was watching Todd Hundley set up on the last, imperceptible edge of the outside corner that left you wondering how anyone ever hit Saberhagen hard. As Hundley said, "When Sabes is hitting his spots, all you have to do is put the glove there and you don't have to move. It's fun."

•

He was a treat to watch, a box-office draw. Already he'd brought some electricity back to Shea, having strung together twenty-six straight scoreless innings, and the Mets were starting to feel as invincible behind him as they once had behind Gooden. In many ways, Saberhagen seemed to be the cure for all that ailed the Mets. Like Cone, he'd learned to drink beer and enjoy big-league life at the hand of the master, George Brett, and to the Mets he brought both a sense of humor and a purposeful work ethic befitting a two-time Cy Young Award winner. He wasn't a rebel but he was the kind of player who could thrive in New York, it seemed, because he wasn't afraid to speak his mind. Ask most players if they have something to prove to the team that traded them and you get a long-winded answer that essentially says, "I'd love to say yes but I'm scared to death I may need a job someday and I don't want anybody mad at me." Saberhagen, on the other hand, merely smiled and said of the Royals: "Sure, I want to stick it up their ass."

It was Saberhagen's greatness, more than anything else, that convinced most of the beat writers to overlook the obvious flaws they'd seen in March and pick the Mets anyway to win the NL East. He had looked that good in spring training, obviously blessed with every gift from the baseball gods.

But he'd been nagged by injuries over the years, and now, on May 15, Saberhagen was struck by a mysterious injury and had to be yanked after the fifth inning against the Dodgers. The injury was announced in the press box as stiffness in his right index finger, nothing major.

"He'll be day-to-day" was the manufactured prognosis delivered by Horwitz, the PR man. That drew a big laugh on press row because "day-to-day" was the medical Band-Aid used to cover every injury known to man. Vince Coleman's hamstring is barking again? Day-to-day. Doc's rotator cuff torn? Day-to-day. Dude's been shot behind the counter at the liquor store? Send him to the Mets' training room—he'll be day-to-day.

So who could've known Saberhagen's day-to-day progno-

•

sis would become a sixty-six-day journey into a gloomy tunnel. The tendon sheath was inflamed, doctors said, at which point Saberhagen looked at them and asked what, exactly, that meant. The doctors hid behind their MRIs—soft tissue X rays, a phenomenon of the nineties that is as much a staple of the sports jargon these days as RBIs—and thickly worded diagnoses, but as the days passed, the truth was they didn't know.

The May 15 injury would end up taking him on a tour of the dark side, effectively ruining his season. Little did anyone know the Mets would travel the same road.

TOP FIVE BAD-GUY METS, ALL-TIME

1. Jesse Orosco
2. Eddie Murray
3. George Foster
4. Dave Kingman
5. Vince Coleman

·

JUNE

JUNE 4. PITTSBURGH. PIRATES 7, METS 2.

A T 1 A. M. T H E Clark Bar was still alive. Only a few blocks from Three Rivers Stadium and partly owned by Pirates catcher Mike LaValliere, this was the gathering spot for fans, players, and writers. On this night, Bobby Bonilla was working the room like he was running for office, occasionally going behind the bar himself to take orders. Bonilla sent a round of beers to a table of New York writers, his voice thundering across the room: "Don't thank me, thank the New York Mets." It'd been a cruel night for Bonilla, his first time in Pittsburgh as an ex-Buc, but there was no sign of it now. Instead, he was mingling with everyone, old and new teammates, friends, fans, even the writers, with whom he'd begun to skirmish in recent days. Something about these familiar surroundings softened Bonilla. Or was he just trying to flee the feelings brought on by this night?

Bonilla had been welcomed back not as a favorite son, but as some kind of greed-mongering traitor. He'd gone 0-for-4 at the plate in a 7–2 loss while the Pirates fans delighted in booing him—the noise level inside the park was awful—and even throwing objects at him in right field. When a golf ball hit him in the back of the head in the eighth inning, Bonilla stopped the game to put on a batting helmet for protection. Oh, the Pirates fans loved that, relishing every moment of Bonilla's retreat. Bonilla wasn't injured, but he was terribly hurt. After all, he had stood in right field a year earlier and watched the same fans

•

welcome back Sid Bream, another free-agent defector, with a standing ovation. How was this different? Like Bream, Bonilla had been extremely popular in Pittsburgh, perhaps the most popular of all the Pirates. Bonilla didn't want to believe race was a factor, and very possibly it wasn't. Pittsburgh had fielded baseball's most racially integrated teams in the seventies and eighties, and fans had had no problem accepting the likes of Roberto Clemente and Dave Parker as their heroes. Still, in his declining years, and when he was implicated in the city's infamous drug trials, Parker became a target: Batteries rained down on him as he stood, angry and bewildered, in right field.

Since then, Pirates fans had embraced Bonilla and Barry Bonds. But now what divided them was money. At least that's what Bonilla told himself. Bream had signed with the Braves for $6 million while Bonilla had turned down $24 million from the Bucs to eventually sign with the Mets for $29 million.

"B-i-i-i-i-g difference," Bonilla said in the locker room that night. "It's the money, no doubt about it. I understand."

Sensitive as he was, Bonilla didn't really understand. He couldn't quite fathom how much resentment big money stirred in fans, especially blue-collar types in Pittsburgh. Nor would Bonilla understand how the great plan to charm the city of New York could blow up on him. Where did it all go wrong? Basically, Bonilla was a nice guy who wanted to be liked by everybody, but as the days passed, the beat guys found more and more similarities between Bonilla and Jeff Torborg. The manager, as was clear from his explosion at the *Times* a month earlier, was consumed by image: Torborg read everything, heard everything that was said, uncomfortable with criticism.

Similarly, Bonilla was far more calculating than anyone initially believed and badly misjudged how sophisticated New Yorkers were. He thought he could seduce everyone with his smile and his "aw shucks" selflessness. The climate in New York was perfect for him, too: The press, many of whom had publicly urged the Mets to sign Bonilla and brighten the Mets'

•

dreary clubhouse, wanted to believe he was some modern-day
Lou Gehrig. But there was a troubling undercurrent out of
Pittsburgh during his last year, one that whispered Bobby Bo
wasn't quite as genuine as his smile. Bonilla was said to be
increasingly obsessed with money. At least once he'd humiliated Pirates manager Jim Leyland, a man Bonilla greatly admired, over that very issue. In the spring of '91, with
negotiations on a multiyear contract stalled, Bonilla went to
Leyland and asked him if he would speak to management on his
behalf. According to people in the Pirates organization, Bonilla
told Leyland he'd sign if the Pirates would offer him $16.5
million over four years. Leyland, sensing the market would
only go higher, pleaded with team president Carl Barger to
make the offer. In a matter of days, Barger agreed, but Bonilla,
through his agent Dennis Gilbert, rejected the offer. Feeling
betrayed, Leyland vowed never to get involved in a contract
matter again.

While New York wanted to embrace Bonilla as a local
hero coming back to his roots, right from the start he started
telling white lies. When Bonilla's bat failed him, his white lies
caught up with him. On the very first night Bonilla signed with
the Mets, in fact, he told a silly, image-conscious fib that in
many ways set the tone for his tumultuous year.

Gilbert, who had earned the nickname Bugsy among writers for his John Gotti–like suits and facial features, had
squeezed Bonilla's free-agent courtship for all it was worth,
stretching out the decision-making process for over five weeks.
Reporters in the cities involved had tracked him on their own
radar network as he and Bonilla toured the country throughout
November. After Thanksgiving Gilbert began circling the
country again, this time by phone from his home in Southern
California. As he moved from team to team, discussing offers,
asking certain teams to raise their offers, reporters passed him
along in the manner of air-traffic controllers, keeping him on
the screen at all times.

With whom was he talking? What was the latest offer?

•

Gilbert wasn't saying much, but there was usually someone from one of the teams who was willing to whisper to the beat guys in a given city. And writers kept each other informed. On Sunday night, December 1, some twenty-four hours before Bonilla signed, word came from Chicago that Gilbert was negotiating intensely with the White Sox, apparently close to a deal. Bonilla himself told Jim Leyland that night by phone that he was leaning hard toward the Sox. And the next morning, in a phone conversation with Jeff Torborg, Bonilla left the Mets' manager with the distinct impression he wouldn't be signing with the Mets. "It sounded like we'd lost him," Torborg would admit later. Monday afternoon, however, White Sox owner Jerry Reinsdorf stopped short of meeting Gilbert's demand for $28 million over five years. By late afternoon, word circulated that the White Sox were out. What next? The Angels were willing to pay the price, but Bonilla didn't really want to go west. New York or Philly? It was about 5 P.M. when Gilbert called Phillies GM Lee Thomas and whispered to him, "Bobby's decided that Philadelphia is his first choice. If you meet his price right now, he's yours."

People close to Bonilla would say later that he'd decided Philly was a nice alternative to New York. It was close to home without the family hassles and overwhelming media, plus he had once played under manager Jim Fregosi and was friendly with several of the Phillies players. The price: $28 million. The Phillies had offered $25 million in earlier meetings in November. Thomas told Gilbert he needed time to discuss the price with the Phillies' ownership. In the meantime, the Phillies writers, through their own back channels, heard about the new development and passed along the information on the telephone network. Ninety minutes later *Philadelphia Daily News* beat writer Paul Hagen reached Lee Thomas on his car phone as he returned home from his office. "We could have had him," Thomas said. "But we're not going that high for Bobby Bonilla."

Gilbert didn't mention that when he placed his next phone

•

call to Al Harazin. Not that it would have mattered. Harazin, still in his office at six-thirty, was anxiously awaiting a response from Gilbert. The Mets' GM was desperate to sign Bonilla, flex some muscle as a rookie executive, and perhaps gather enough ammunition to make a mega-trade for the likes of Bret Saberhagen. For that you couldn't fault Harazin. But Thomas and the Phillies were right, too: The price was outrageous for a player of such limited skills. After all, for all the size and strength Bonilla brought to the plate, he was not a pure power hitter, and his below-average speed made him a liability on the bases as well as in the outfield. In short, he was nowhere near the complete player that his teammate Barry Bonds was, and by no means was he a franchise player. Bonilla just happened to emerge as the leading free agent at a time when the market was exploding.

Of course, Bonilla knew money was no deterrent to the Mets, who were buying into the smile, overpaying for what they thought would be a man who'd return some heart and soul to a team that had gained a reputation as a bunch of spoiled brats. After Gilbert told Harazin that Bonilla was his if they could agree on a price, they negotiated for four solid hours, while reporters buried Jay Horwitz under an avalanche of phone calls, asking for the freshest developments. Finally, Harazin constructed a $29 million package, which consisted of $27.5 million in base salary and another $1.5 million in guaranteed endorsement income. Harazin called it a "creative structuring" of the contract. Gilbert called it $29 million, and at 11 P.M. the deal was done.

At 11:45 the Mets hooked Bonilla, at home in Bradenton, Florida, into a conference call with the beat writers of the teams with which Bonilla had been negotiating. The first question was obvious enough: Why the Mets? Bonilla didn't hesitate. "New York was in my heart all the way," he said, launching into a speech about what a dream come true it was to be coming back to his hometown. Under the cover of anonymity, writers everywhere rolled their eyes. Not that anyone

•

had a problem with Bonilla awarding himself to the highest bidder: Athletes are trained that way—to be the best in everything. But why couldn't he be honest enough to admit it? The New York press corps began preparing for the battles to come.

The press was sympathetic to Bonilla early in the season, because of the treatment he received at Shea. Even the most cynical of reporters was stunned at how quickly the fans turned on him, booing him two weeks into the season when he was popping up with runners on base. More than anything, it was an indication of the resentment that baseball's huge salaries had created among a population mired in a depressed economy. Bonilla, as the highest-paid player in baseball, was the obvious target for that frustration, even anger.

For weeks, Bonilla handled his angst well. Though he was stung—his self-image was still of a New York kid who had risen from the hard streets of the Bronx to become a star, a hero for the masses—he put on his happy face, refusing to let the hurt show. As his early-season slump slogged into May, he put in extra hours at the batting cage, stood at his locker and withstood all the questions—and hence received warm and generous press coverage from reporters who focused on his work ethic and hustle. Soon enough, however, his failures in the home ballpark began to wear on him.

By late May he was still hitting only .130 at Shea, and the boos were growing louder, meaner. After a loss Bonilla was flip when asked about the boos, saying he didn't play for the fans anyway, so who cared? The comment was thoughtless, and it sounded callous when it was played on WFAN radio. A couple of days later, May 30, Bonilla was desperate and took hitting coach Tom McCraw's suggestion that he wear earplugs at the plate. It was an unorthodox approach, but Bonilla believed the plugs would allow for better concentration. The artificial quiet didn't help, though, as Bonilla went 0-for-4 in a 6–1 loss to the Braves. And when a TV camera picked up the earplugs during the game, even zooming in for close-ups while Bonilla was hitting, a story was born.

•

Was Bonilla wearing the plugs to escape the booing? He said no, and, given how image-conscious he was, it was hard to believe otherwise. He would've surely considered how that looked: "Bonilla on the run from fan abuse . . . film at eleven." Of course, it would've helped his case if he had removed the earplugs while playing right field. But he claimed they had to be fitted just right, which is why he didn't dare disturb them between at-bats. So the earplugs quickly became an issue in the newspapers and on radio talk shows, and continued to be the next day, when the Mets were rained out.

Bonilla seemed shocked at the frenzy over the earplugs, though he was more amused than outraged by it. Certainly, as an isolated incident, it shouldn't have inflamed the press corps, and, in retrospect, the press's reaction was far too harsh. What the Mets community should have seen was Bonilla, in his own way, bleeding, increasingly overwhelmed. But the climate in the clubhouse didn't allow for much com-passion, and part of the fault rested with Bonilla. Over and over after signing with the Mets he'd chuckled at questions about dealing with the media, saying he'd grown up reading the New York papers and therefore understood the way the game was played. Only he didn't, not even remotely. It isn't a smile and a personal hello that tames the fearsome New York press, at least not the foot soldiers on the beat. These are the guys who live with a team, day in and day out from February to October: The beat reporter sees all, knows all, doesn't care about an athlete's manners. It's a ballplayer's honesty, a will-ingness to take the heat at critical moments, that wins the hearts and minds of the guys who ask the questions. As harsh as baseball writers can be on players, they're close enough to know how difficult it is to succeed in an endless season.

But, regrettably, those considerations were sadly lacking when it came to Bonilla. Reporters found themselves playing the no-win game of Gotcha with Bonilla: If he wasn't going to be honest, then the press corps unconsciously became his moral watchdog, made sure to catch his every fib. Thus the earplugs

•

incident, harmless and pathetic by itself, became a catalyst for the exploration of a larger issue, which was: Can Bonilla give it to us straight or not?

Truth is, baseball writers know the sport is lent to agony: In no other pastime does failure become such an integral and public element. The best hitters in the game fail at least twice as often as they succeed, and that ensures a more adversarial relationship between players and writers—much more so than in basketball or football. Always, it seems, there are crucial at-bats that become pop-ups, ones that demand interrogation in day-to-day game coverage. Is it any wonder that writers are chummier with pitchers than with hitters? Sooner or later, though, players of every position have to absorb in-print or on-air criticism, and in the case of the hypersensitive, under-achieving Mets, that led to tense postgame questioning. And that was when you found out who was who and what was what.

It's easy for a player to face the mob in front of his locker after a game-winning home run. The real barometer is how he reacts after striking out with the bases loaded to end a one-run game. It's a fascinating study in human behavior, and for the baseball writers it divides the world into two distinct catego-ries: the good guys and the bad guys. Unfortunately, the bad guys now seem to outnumber the good guys in the game, and the ratio seems to worsen every year. Any beat guy can name the pioneers of the antipress army in the last decade: John Denny, John Tudor, Dave Kingman, Lonnie Smith, and the architect of "No comment," Steve Carlton, who was legendary for never speaking to the reporters during most of his playing career, only resuming interviews when he was trying desper-ately to hang on at the end, moving from team to team in the late eighties. It is that kind of hypocrisy that irks writers: If you take a stand on principle as Carlton supposedly had, refus-ing to talk at all, how can you suddenly reverse field when you need the press on your side?

That's why writers appreciate the good guys so thor-oughly. Among the forces of good have been Andre Dawson,

Bob Ojeda, Steve Garvey, Don Baylor, Tim Teufel, Dave Righetti. And then there is Dave Cone, the all-time good guy, a player whose own interest in sportswriting as a high school student forged a sense of obligation to the press he'd never forgotten. On the New York media's scorecards, a player was awarded one or two games a year when he was forgiven for hiding out from an interview: We assumed everyone was going to have moments when it was psychologically impossible to face the public. Inevitably, even the best of them pulled a no-show. But not Cone. Never did he duck out after a bad game, not even that infamous night in Atlanta when he made a fool of himself, arguing with an umpire over a call at first base, the ball deep in his hand, while two runners scored. As the Mets went on to lose, the debate in the press box raged: Would Cone slide into a waiting cab as the last out was made? Players who'd been removed for a pinch hitter or pitching change were required to remain in the clubhouse until the game was over, but nothing required them to stay until the media arrived, usually within five to ten minutes.

But there was Cone, sitting at his locker, as the media entered the clubhouse. And as usual, he made no excuses, shifted no blame, took the responsibility for what he called "vapor lock." He spoke for a solid fifteen minutes, even managed some self-deprecatory humor, accepted reporters' thanks for his being there, and then went out and got drunk.

Cone's intelligence and analytical eye, not to mention his candor, made him the rarest of Mets in 1992. There were still a few good guys, but the number was dwindling fast. Dave Magadan ranked close to Cone, ever gracious and accommodating no matter what the circumstances, and honest enough to shoulder the blame when at fault. In fact, if Magadan had any fault at all as a major leaguer, it was that he lacked some of the meanness that, somehow, makes good players great. Darryl Strawberry once said Magadan had "too much sugar in his blood." He meant that Magadan was too gentle of a player, and in retrospect, the Mets may have felt the same

•

way. Except for 1990, the year he batted .328 and nearly won the National League's batting title, the organization never seemed too impressed with Magadan.

His below-average speed and lack of power were flaws, no question, but back in 1987, when Magadan was a rookie, then-VP Joe McIlvaine would lean toward a reporter's ear and whisper that the kid was certain to be "a future batting champion." Ah, if only Magadan could've hit more doubles, driven in more runs, crushed an occasional ball five hundred feet. His curse was to have followed Keith Hernandez at first base, and in 1990, even with Magadan's gorgeous batting average, Hernandez's ghost was everywhere at Shea.

Magadan played first base well enough, and he got all the proper base hits at the right time. Still, the Mets never seemed to forgive him for not being Mex, a spiritual leader, an on-field general, a guy whom McIlvaine would say, "we all wanted to be next to us in the trenches." The Mets watched Magadan drive National League pitchers crazy all that summer, slapping those base hits over shortstop, never chasing a fastball even an inch or two off the plate. And yet, when Magadan slumped in 1991, playing with torn cartilage in both shoulders, it was as if 1990 never existed.

"That was really the turnaround year. All the doubts that I'd made disappear in 1990 came right back in 1991, and to be honest, it was my fault," Magadan said after signing a free-agent deal in December '92 with the expansion Florida Marlins. "By the time the '92 season started, I felt the Mets didn't even remember the '90 season anymore. It was like it happened five or ten years ago."

Magadan's fate had turned so bleak by '92 that he was on the bench in the first month of the season, beaten out by Bill Pecota. He eventually won his job back, but was still unable to re-create the magic of '90. Although his average climbed over .300 again, Magadan still wasn't Hernandez, and it was obvious to the front office he would never be. Magadan sensed his career in New York drifting away, although he never quarreled

•

with the front office or Jeff Torborg. Instead, a dreamy calm came over him: Night after night, he would be at his locker, patiently explaining to reporters why the Mets were so awful. And then he would finish dressing, go home, and come a day closer to his liberation from Shea. Even in his funniest, wittiest moments, there was a sadness about Magadan that never went away.

Dwight Gooden shared in that depression, but for a different reason. Unlike Magadan, who at least had the rescue of free agency waiting in the off-season, Doc was stuck in New York. Still, he remained professional in defeat, having learned better than anyone that a newspaper might seem like a monstrous, impersonal product, but behind the bylines were people. Reporters had good days and bad days in their personal lives like anyone else, and couldn't help but be influenced by a player's behavior. The beat writers took pride in their objectivity, but at the very least they tended to give the stand-up guys the benefit of the doubt in print, especially on a team like the '92 Mets. Ah, the '92 Mets: Except for Cone and Magadan and Gooden, you needed a subpoena to get players out of the trainer's room to answer questions after a loss.

Most of the time, Jay Horwitz was forced to act as go-between. The PR man would have to manufacture horrible, empty excuses for his players, embarrassed at the whole process. Reporters would vent their frustration at Horwitz—in vain, of course—as Jay would mumble hopelessly, "He just doesn't want to talk. What can I do? I can't force him."

Among the exceptions was the unlikely Tim Burke, a reliever making $2 million who couldn't get anyone out. He bought himself some rope by showing class, answering all the tough questions with grace and perspective on nights when he'd been totally humiliated. Even sportswriters have compassion: It just has to be earned.

Some players just didn't understand, though. Frank Viola was a classic example. It used to infuriate him that, in his eyes, the beat writers treated Dwight Gooden like royalty, while

•

flogging Viola at every opportunity. "You guys are a joke," Viola once said to a couple of writers. "You guys kiss Doc's ass, you never go after him no matter how bad he's doing, but you're always on my ass." As a Met for two-plus years, Viola created a love-hate relationship with the press. The dossier? Nice guy, but the definition of a front-runner: as accommodating and quotable as any writer could ever ask when he was pitching well, but one of the all-time sore losers when the fates weren't kind. Viola was so sensitive that when he pitched on the road, win or lose, he had his wife read him every game story in the New York papers over the phone the next morning. He was quick to blame others, and teammates rode him unmercifully for being a whiner, sometimes in fun and sometimes not. After a loss in Cincinnati in 1990, when Viola fled the locker room rather than face the media, Bobby Ojeda feigned shock. "You mean V ain't here for you guys? If he'd won, he would've been here until four in the morning."

Viola could be nasty when he did take questions on a bad day. Had he re-signed with the Mets in '92 he would've had plenty of company, considering Murray and Coleman's contempt for the press. Reporters came to dread any need for communicating with them. In the rare cases when it was unavoidable, the press corps would act as one, debating in unison whether to give Murray or Coleman the satisfaction of saying no to an interview request.

"Why should we talk to that fucking guy?" was the usual rallying cry after Murray had won a game with a key base hit, or if Coleman had been involved in a decisive baserunning decision. Writing a good game story requires a central theme— an "angle"—and if Murray was the angle . . . well . . . More often than not, a morbid professionalism took hold: If we stay away, he's won. The reporters would trudge over to Murray's or Coleman's locker, bracing for the worst, and usually got it.

Yet, the most uncomfortable postgame task of all could be interviewing Howard Johnson after a tough loss. High-strung and terribly insecure, HoJo was a nice man turned werewolf by

•

repeated failure in critical situations. He couldn't own up to them, not publicly anyway. In the eighties he was combative in difficult postgame settings, regularly challenging reporters who questioned him about a costly error or a strikeout. Then, in the nineties, after finding God, he became less combative, but no more forthcoming. HoJo, in fact, was lucky that Bonilla was the focus of attention early in '92, because he was off to a miserable start himself. By late May he was slumping worse than Bonilla, staring at the floor, muttering one- or two-word answers to reporters or occasionally telling them flatly, "I'm not talking about my hitting." But then, Johnson wasn't the one wearing earplugs, so he was getting off easy by comparison.

Caught off guard as he seemed by the entire earplugs controversy, Bonilla dismissed the criticism, insisting he would continue to wear the earplugs. But he thought better of it by the next night, hitting a grand slam that sparked a 14–1 victory over the Giants. In fact, Bonilla went 3-for-3 with six RBIs. The boos melted away into curtain calls: The Shea drought was over and the timing seemed to be perfect. Bonilla was finally finding his muscles as the Mets flew into Pittsburgh for the first meeting of the season with the Eastern Division–leading Pirates. So the Mets saw the first night, when the Bucs hammered Doc Gooden en route to a 7–2 win, as merely the first shot fired in a war that would be decided when the Pirates came to Shea Stadium on the final weekend of the season. By Sunday, however, the Mets were beginning to wonder. Bonilla was in *their* dugout now, and yet the Pirates won three of four in the series, once again establishing their superiority.

It was disheartening for the Mets, and Bonilla hadn't improved the mood when he invited Barry Bonds into the clubhouse for a visit after the Mets were shut out 3–0 Sunday afternoon. It looked bad, Bonilla and Bonds joking around in the far corner of the locker room while the Mets dressed for a flight to Montreal. Cone liked Bonilla, but raised an eyebrow when reporters looked to him for reaction. Gooden didn't like it either, giving Bonilla a look of disdain. Only a few weeks

•

earlier, a similar incident in St. Louis had led to a fight between Cardinals Todd Worrell and Pedro Guerrero. Worrell objected when Guerrero invited Cubs outfielder Sammy Sosa into the clubhouse after a Cardinals loss, and fists flew. Now the question hung in the air for an awkward moment: Would anyone challenge Bonilla on this breach of conduct? Wally Backman sure would've told them both to kiss his ass and get the hell out of the clubhouse. Same for Ray Knight.

One reason Jeff Torborg had been hired was for his fire and brimstone as well as the attaché case and family philosophy. He was old school, and this episode went against everything he preached as a hard-line, us-against-the-world disciplinarian. Torborg was filling his plate at the postgame food spread when Bonds sauntered in, walking the length of the clubhouse with Bonilla, but the manager pretended not to notice. Finally a couple of beat guys approached Torborg, asking if he had a problem with it. The manager fidgeted and said no.

"Heck, I played with his daddy," Torborg said, referring to Bobby Bonds. "I don't worry about stuff like that. You compete on the field, not off it."

Still, it was Torborg who insisted the players walk the straight and narrow. It was Torborg who was fanatical about preparation and attitude and all the other intangibles. It was Torborg who talked tough with his team about how he wouldn't tolerate players going to the press with complaints or anonymous sniping.

He'd already made an example of Mackey Sasser, the unhappiest Met. The manager had called Sasser into his office a few days earlier, after his number three catcher was quoted as saying he wanted to be traded. Torborg was furious with Sasser for making his feelings public. It wouldn't be the last time Sasser spoke up or the last time they argued in Torborg's office.

Sasser couldn't understand Torborg's refusal to use his lethal line-drive bat at least as an attempt to jump-start the ever-stagnating offense. Torborg, a good-field, no-hit catcher himself, wanted a polished receiver behind the plate at all costs.

•

If he said it once, he said it a hundred times during the '92 season: "I always go back to the '65 Dodgers, the year we won the pennant with a .245 team batting average. Pitching and defense has to be your constant."

Fair enough. Sasser, a converted infielder, was mediocre behind the plate, and though he'd largely overcome his problems throwing back to the pitcher, he carried a stigma because of it.

Except Sasser was sure it was more than that. As he would say after the Mets let him go in December, deciding not to tender him a contract: "Jeff wants to have control of everything. That's why he had such a tough time—it can't be that way in New York, especially with a veteran team. I don't feel he knows how to handle pro ballplayers. I think he thought I was too independent."

Independent or unbridled? In short, Sasser was a free spirit who spoke his mind and kept late hours. He was one of the Smithers graduates among the Mets, who led the league in rehab for a while, sending Gooden, Strawberry, outfielder Mark Carreon, and reliever Jeff Musselman within a four-year period. Like all but Gooden's, Sasser's stint was labeled alcohol rehab. It's the safest and least painful announcement to make, which doesn't mean it's true. Unless a player is publicly caught involved with drugs, as Gooden was, ball clubs don't want the mess of explaining a drug problem to the media.

After his rehab, Sasser would offer vague explanations, hinting that alcohol hadn't been the root of his problem, though he would never be more specific. He clearly didn't feel he had a drinking problem, because he went back to having a few beers in the bar at night.

A good ol' boy from the South, Sasser didn't take life or himself too seriously. He loved his job, grateful for his privileged status as a big leaguer and determined to enjoy it. He approached hitting the same way. The Hacker, he called himself proudly. He didn't worry about technique. "I just go up there hacking," he'd say in his twang. "I was born to hit."

•

He could hit, all right. He hit .307, highest among major league catchers in 1990, the one year the Mets allowed him to be number one catcher. For a while that year, in fact, he was playing like an All-Star, throwing out runners at second base and hitting .336 at midseason. But the Sunday before the All-Star break, he sprained his ankle badly in a collision with Braves third baseman Jim Presley.

Sasser was never the same that year, or since. But he was

JUST A LONELY COWBOY
—B.K.

THE PHONE RANG at about nine o'clock on a Friday night in June '92. I was enjoying a night off from the Mets, watching a movie at home. I picked up the phone and heard a man screaming at me in Japanese.

"What? Who is this?" I asked stupidly.

There were a few more seconds of Japanese and I was ready to hang up when I heard "Fucking Klapisch, I should've remembered you don't speak the language. When are you going to admit I'm smarter than you?"

It was Davey Johnson.

He was calling from Florida, calling for no real reason, just to talk. We remembered the old days at Shea, noting how awful the '92 Mets had become both to cover and to watch on TV. I didn't ask Davey if he was having any luck finding another job in baseball. The hurt in his voice told me enough. The years blurred, one after the next, and the major league's greatest mystery remained unanswered: Why wouldn't anyone hire Davey?

One baseball executive says the Mets blacklisted Johnson back in 1990, and depending on whom you asked, Davey was: (a) a womanizer, (b) a heavy drinker, or (c) a poor disciplinarian. True, he had his faults, but none was severe enough to keep him away from baseball. The real problem was that Davey was just too tough for management to handle, a perfect renegade manager for a renegade team. Whether he drank or ran around . . . funny how that didn't matter much when the Mets won. Yet here on the phone was the manager of baseball's winningest team from 1984 to 1990, jobless, abandoned by both leagues because he had balls.

Johnson's finest moment as Mets manager came in September 1989, when he caught Kevin McReynolds and Darryl Strawberry in the clubhouse at Wrigley while the Mets were rallying against the Cubs. Neither player had expected to bat in the ninth inning, so when their turns came in the batting order, the Mets having scored run after run, McReynolds and Strawberry had to scurry to the dugout. Players said

•

a surprisingly agile athlete, considering his roly-poly shape, and he'd proved in '91 that he could be a valuable utility outfielder as well as a backup catcher.

And when Torborg was still refusing to play him by August '92, when all three of the regular Met outfielders were on the disabled list, Sasser spoke out again: "It's ridiculous," he said. "We've got five guys hitting about .200 in there, and I can't get in the lineup."

arryl was already undressed, and was so anicked when throwing on his uniform that e was still virtually naked at the plate: no •ck, no protective cup, and no stirrups, nly the batting-practice socks with the stir-ups painted on.

Of course, Strawberry struck out to end e game, and Davey was furious, fining oth players on the spot. Johnson wouldn't t either back in the lineup until they paid e five hundred dollars. McReynolds an-ily slapped the money on Johnson's desk e next day, but Strawberry, out of princi-e mostly, said the money could wait until ter the game.

Tempers flared in a pregame team meet-g, and the manager and his right fielder ere face-to-face, ready to throw punches. ad it not been for Ron Darling literally div-g in between the two, well, who knew? e team vowed to keep the incident a se-et, but the room was still full of tension hen the doors opened. The beat guys ensed a crisis, and one by one, each guy ent to his particular source. Soon enough, e story got out.

I asked Johnson a few nights later if he as worried about fighting a younger,

stronger, bigger athlete. Johnson just laughed. "You mean was I worried about getting my ass kicked? To be honest with ya, I would've been more worried about taking on K Mac," Davey said. "He never says a fuckin' word. Those are the guys that'll always beat the shit out of you, the quiet ones. Straw? All the talking he was doing, I knew he wouldn't do a thing."

Johnson let his starting pitchers and reserve players congregate in the trainer's room and lounge area if they weren't in the game. One afternoon in '88 Darling looked into the dugout between pitches, and "the only people I saw were Mookie, Teufel, [trainer] Steve Garland, and a couple of coaches." The back room was full of Mets, who were eating, watching TV, or sometimes just sleeping during a particularly long, dull game. In those days, Buddy Harrelson's primary duty as Johnson's lieutenant was to periodically roust the Mets out of the lounge.

Of course, all this outraged Frank Cashen, but since Davey's outlaws were winning, what could the GM do? For seven years, Johnson operated by the softest code known to baseball: Win . . . and what-

165

That was in Pittsburgh too. By then Torborg insisted he'd stopped reading newspaper clips on the road, yet the next day in Chicago, he called Sasser into his office again, infuriated by the quote. "We went at it pretty good," Sasser would say after the season. "He said he'd been protecting my ass all year, not telling the press that I was hurt and out of shape. I said he was full of shit—my injuries weren't enough to keep me out of the lineup. I don't know why he didn't like me. I never had a

---

JUST A LONELY COWBOY

(continued)

ever else you do, don't get caught. By 1990, though, the Mets had begun their descent, and in the process, the front office had grown tired of Davey. The honor system collapsed, and Johnson lost control of the clubhouse. Players mutinied against him, even though they didn't know how much they'd miss Davey in years to come.

After a bitter loss in San Francisco in May '90, only two weeks before he was fired, Davey was harshly criticized by his players for not bringing in a right-hander to face Gary Carter. Kid, having moved on to the Giants, beat Bobby Ojeda with an opposite-field double, and the Mets went crazy in anger when they saw Carter on second base, pumping his fists.

Later that night, after hours of hard drinking, a cab full of Mets pulled up in front of the team's hotel. There, a homeless man was begging for food. One of the veteran Mets stopped, sized up the beggar, and said, "See, Davey, I told you ya should've brought in the right-hander." His teammates roared with sadistic laughter, hardly

aware that Johnson's subsequent firing—along with Darryl's departure—would sever the Mets' last ties to the eighties.

Johnson returned to Shea for the first time in the summer of '92, introduced at Old-Timer's Day to a standing ovation. For all the terrific seasons the Mets had enjoyed with Johnson, the front office had ignored him for two years, not once inviting him back. When Davey finally arrived, he looked grayer, a little fleshier in the face, cheerful but still a little sad about having been away from baseball so long.

Maybe it was the friendly crowd that filled Davey with nostalgia. He'd promised never to walk into the Mets' clubhouse again, but he did, looking for a piece of his past. Almost immediately, Davey found Dwight Gooden, and the two men embraced.

"Doc, it's been a long time, hasn't it?" Davey said. Gooden didn't say a word. Couldn't, actually. For a moment, it looked like Gooden's eyes were moistening. Then he turned away. It was probably just the light.

•

•

166

problem with a manager in my life—I'll give a guy everything I've got. But we went nose-to-nose that day. That's as close as I've ever come to taking a swing at a manger."

Word of the heated exchange spread quickly in the clubhouse. Again the message from the manager was clear: Speak up and you'll hear from me.

So now some of his players were wondering just what this manager was all about. He talked like a tough guy but wouldn't argue with umpires and was willing to let Barry Bonds flaunt the Pirates' dominance over the Mets in their own clubhouse. Meanwhile, as the players packed their shoulder bags, many checked to make sure their flasks were filled, accustomed by now to bringing their own vodka and whiskey to pour into their soft drinks on the plane.

So when the Mets proceeded to lose seven of their next nine games, including a three-game sweep by the Pirates at Shea, the manager's popularity rating plummeted even further. A mutiny? Not quite, not yet. But when you asked about in-game strategy, you sensed a change in temperature in the strained smiles, in the unwillingness of nearly every player to discuss Torborg on the record. Just as they waited for Howard Johnson, the Mets clubhouse kept waiting and waiting for Torborg to have a hot streak. So far, it hadn't arrived.

JUNE 15. NEW YORK. EXPOS 4, METS 1.

DISCONTENT HAD TURNED to open crisis at Shea. Anthony Young was outpitched by Montreal's Mark Gardner, handing the Mets their fifth straight loss. Seven games out of first place, the Mets were no longer part of the Pirates' universe. Instead, the Expos were threatening to drop the Mets all the way into last place. In many respects, this was the date in 1992 when the first real cracks in the organization's armor began to show. How shall we count the ways?

Even before the day started, there was angst in the air. In his daily report on WFAN, Torborg had mistakenly blurted

•

out that John Franco had been suffering from a tender left
elbow, and that was the reason, in a game against the Pirates
two nights before, the manager had asked Wally Whitehurst to
preserve a 2–1 lead in the eighth inning. When Barry Bonds led
off with a home run against Whitehurst, he tied the game and
put the Mets in position to lose yet another heartbreaker to the
Bucs. As a result, the planet turned its eyes to Torborg and
asked: Where was Franco?

Torborg huffed and puffed about not wanting to use his
closer in the eighth inning or a tied game. That had been standard managerial strategy since Dennis Eckersley came along to
redefine the role of a closer for the Oakland A's. The textbook
said it was the safest bet a manager could make: Let your closer
protect a lead for one inning only, and that's it; trot him out
there two innings at a time, and come August, your closer's arm
has been nuked. Even worse, in Torborg's mind, was using a
closer in a tied game. What happened in extra innings? Who
was the savior in the fourteenth? Trouble was, the Mets
weren't getting too many fourteenth innings in June. They
weren't even getting to the ninth inning with a lead. These
critical games were being decided in the seventh and eighth
innings, the Mets' bullpen unable to strike anyone out.

So while the pennant was evaporating before Torborg's
eyes, his best late-inning pitcher, John Franco, was watching
from the bullpen. The Franco-must-pitch army wondered out
loud: Why not use Franco now, while there's still hope, and
suffer the consequences later? Franco customarily was careful
with his answers, while managing to let reporters know he
wasn't happy with Torborg. "He makes the decisions, not me,"
Franco often said, indicating with a slight roll of his eyes that
his irritation was bubbling close to the surface.

On this day, though, Franco made no attempt to hide his
rage. Quite the contrary: He put on a show, taking a bat and
flinging it against the batting cage upon hearing of the manager's on-air pronouncement, then seeking out first Mel Stottlemyre and then Torborg, going face-to-face with each and
gesturing wildly, his every move saying: You fucked me.

•

Indeed, Torborg couldn't back off from his comments fast enough. The manager admitted, "My big mouth just let it slip" that Franco's elbow was tender. Torborg apologized to his reliever, told reporters it was a regrettable mistake, and promised not to use his afternoon spot with Mike Francesa and Chris Russo as a launching pad for news anymore. That wasn't the first time Torborg had broken a story about his own team on WFAN, and it wouldn't be the last. The guys on the beat had started listening to the manager's show every day just so they'd know what story needed to be pursued. Players were locked on to 660 AM, too; that's how they found out who was in the lineup that night. All this from a manager who'd vowed in spring training to preserve the "family"—to keep the outsiders out and make sure the clubhouse was never again split open by the press, by the questions, by the anonymous quotes, by the infighting that had ultimately crushed Buddy Harrelson.

But by June, Torborg was finding out just how impossible it was to manage the news in New York. You can't stop players from talking to the press, can't control what's written, can't maintain an us-against-them, bunker-down philosophy. Doesn't work in New York, where seven papers—the *News*, the *Post, Newsday*, the *Times*, the *Newark Star-Ledger*, the *Bergen Record*, and Gannett-Westchester—cover the Mets as if they were baseball's White House. "The Magnificent Seven" Harrelson used to bitterly call the beat guys. No one in the press corps pretended national security was at stake in the Mets clubhouse, but the competition for stories was fierce. And so, as the manager, if you'd made a spring-training promise to "be there for you guys every day," then you'd better be good to your word.

In a way, the same went for Bonilla. "Just get the facts, and then I don't care what you write," he'd said to reporters in March. Those were sweet words. But then the media boycott, the boos at Shea, and the earplugs had constructed a wall between Bonilla and the press. And when Bonilla waved at Expo John Wetteland's third-strike fastball in the eighth in-

•

ning this night at Shea, something finally snapped inside Bobby Bo.

The Mets, trailing only 2–1, actually had a rally going in the eighth inning, starting with Dave Magadan's leadoff walk against Mark Gardner. That's when Wetteland arrived, and so went the Mets' miniature attack. First, pinch runner Bill Pecota was thrown out trying to steal second base by Gary Carter, of all people. Carter, who'd lost most of his arm strength by 1989, who'd once represented all that was good and warm and lovable about the late-eighties Mets, who now seemed to enjoy a private last laugh on the Mets' front office, asking a New York reporter later that '92 summer, "What's it like covering a disaster?"

Carter somehow found the fury in his arm to easily nail Pecota, and Expos manager Felipe Alou called it "the biggest play of the year so far." There would be many more bright moments for the Expos, who would spend the rest of the season challenging the Pirates—all the way to the final week of September—and shaming the Mets. So this was only the start: Once Carter had disposed of Pecota, Wetteland blew away Eddie Murray with three straight fastballs. That was out number two. Finally, Bonilla. Wetteland brought in his fastball somewhere in the low nineties, which, on some days, was good enough to beat even a terrific fastball hitter, even if he was looking for it. By mid-June, Bonilla was seeing a ton of change-ups, having yet to prove he could adjust to them with any regularity, but Wetteland had no time or use for finesse. He went one-on-one with Bonilla, power pitcher vs. power hitter. Wetteland threw a two-strike heater, Bonilla swung, and a moment later Bonilla was calmly removing his helmet, handing it to the bat boy, and walking out to right field.

He'd lost this war to Wetteland, and the noise inside Shea Stadium was awful. Actually, the fans were more than just loud; they were angry. Here it was, mid-June, and the Mets were letting it slip away, their $29 million savior still hitting only .204 at home and a soft .272 overall. So when Marquis

•

Grissom slapped a two-run double to left-center in the ninth inning off Wally Whitehurst, giving the Expos a 4–1 lead, you could feel the ballpark go cold. Men scooped up their coats, women reached for their pocketbooks. The traffic jam was inside the ballpark, as the exit ramps were suddenly choked with the disgusted.

After the game, the clubhouse had that quiet, hostile feel to it. The tone was set by Bobby Bo himself, who for the first time all season, blew off the press. "Not tonight," he said icily. "I've been too good to you guys."

"Tomorrow, Bobby?" some radio guy asked timidly.

"Maybe," Bonilla said haughtily. "Depends what kind of mood I'm in."

It wasn't anything the boys on the beat weren't used to, being frozen out, even for one night. Little by little, the Mets were becoming the old Yankees, the original press haters. Billy Martin had been the leader, a virtual dictator, even after he'd been humbled so many times by George Steinbrenner. Norman MacLean, then of United Press International, once walked into Martin's office and asked for a few minutes' time.

"Get lost, Norman," Billy said pleasantly.

"Just a quick couple of sentences," MacLean persisted.

"Norman, get the fuck out of here," Billy said, his face darkening.

"Look, all I need is three sentences," MacLean said, panicking.

Softening, Martin smiled and said, "Okay. You want three sentences? Turn on your tape recorder." When MacLean obliged, Martin leaned into the microphone and said, "Fuck you. You're an asshole. Get out of here." Billy leaned back in his chair and said, "How's that, Norman?"

Over the years, players have found it easier to walk away from reporters than answer tough or embarrassing questions. And why not? They know virtually every beat guy will be there the next day. Tabloid wars what they are, no one can afford to miss a group interview with, say, Darryl Strawberry or Dwight

•

Gooden. Maury Allen of the old *Post*, who engaged in a cold war with Mickey Mantle that spanned several years, claimed he never got beat on a story, despite his lack of access to the Mick. But that could never happen in the overheated newspaper climate of the eighties and nineties, where sometimes even a quote could be enough to justify a 100-point headline. If you missed the quote, you missed the story. If you missed the story, you deprived your paper of the chance to work its headline magic. And without that headline, your paper died on the stands, creeping one day closer to extinction.

This cold-blooded equation explains why the whole point of baseball coverage is access—private access. In the mid-eighties, whichever reporter was closest to Keith Hernandez usually prospered. Hernandez was intelligent, witty, charismatic, and understood the media game better than any Met or Yankee. If he thought Strawberry was being lazy, he'd pull a reporter aside and go off the record with him. Actually, Hernandez was the original "One Met said . . ."—that anonymous source, which was later a vehicle for Wally Backman, Bob Ojeda, Ron Darling, Kevin Elster, and Dave Cone. Hernandez was the master, though, sometimes talking to you as if he were two people.

You'd ask a question about Straw or Davey, and Hernandez, seated at his locker, legs crossed, cigarette glowing between his fingers, would ask, "Are we on or off the record?" If you said you needed something for attribution, Hernandez would give you a careful answer. That task completed, he'd say, "Now this didn't come from me, but . . ." That meant you were allowed to use the ensuing quote, but only anonymously. And usually you'd get to the truth of the original question. Sometimes Hernandez would switch between on-the-record Hernandez and "One Met" so quickly, it was difficult to tell which person you were talking to. But the rule, at least until 1989, was if you didn't cross Hernandez, he'd help you enormously.

Of course, that also depended on what paper you worked

for and how he felt about you that particular week. Mex could play the *Post* against the *News*, and turn the *News* against *Newsday*, all by one whispered comment. "Come see me," Hernandez would coo in your ear as he walked to his locker. That meant you were in his inner circle for that day and a nugget of information would soon work its way into your notebook. Not many Mets ever blew off the press in those days—partly because they won so many games and had no reason to quarrel with reporters. But a good part of the pleasant karma came from Hernandez, who set the tone in the clubhouse; even if Hernandez didn't like you, he spoke to you—he respected the job of the press and was wise enough not to fight it.

Not so with the '92 Mets, as evidenced by Bonilla's ice-cold response after the loss to the Expos. Was it the fans who had so enraged Bobby? Was it the mere sight of the reporters, who wanted to know not so much about that eighth-inning strikeout against Wetteland, but about what virus had infected the Mets' season? Here it was, the sixty-second game of the year, and the preseason expectations had faded. This team didn't look like it was going to win the East. For the first time that theory was gaining strength—and not just among the press. It'd been a month since Saberhagen's injury and he was still on the DL. Clearly, the absence of offense was more than some early-season funk. Players were wondering how so much on-paper talent could look so bad on the field. Even the front office was nervous. Attendance was down, and Al Harazin could offer only his hollow speculation that poor weather, the presence of both the Rangers and the Knicks in their respective playoffs—thus keeping fans at home watching TV—and a nationwide recession were biting deep into the Mets' gate.

But the truth was the Mets were playing lousy baseball, and they had no one to keep the public's interest while the bad innings blurred along. There weren't even any interesting side shows anymore. What hurt the front office more than the won-lost record was that the fans had apparently stopped caring.

•

JUNE 18. NEW YORK. CARDINALS 8, METS 3.

T HE MOOD IN the clubhouse was ugly. Less than twenty-four hours earlier, the Mets had been smothered by the Expos' Dennis Martinez, swallowing a 5–2 loss that had dropped them eight games out—the team's deepest deficit of the season. Only 20,269 had showed up at the ballpark the previous night, and what they saw was more of the same bloodless baseball the Mets had been playing since the start of their decline in 1991. What exactly was missing from these Mets? They themselves were unsure, which is why immediately after the game, the players held a private, no-press, no-coaches, no-execs meeting. That didn't affect Torborg much: His door was shut anyway, as he fulfilled his obligations to his postgame show. But Al Harazin was locked outside the clubhouse, pacing with obvious embarrassment for twenty-five minutes as the players dissected their own lethargy.

Inside, Howard Johnson took the floor and urged his teammates to "enjoy" the game a little more, forget the booing, ignore the tabloids, distance themselves from the beat reporters. "Let's go back to being a little arrogant. What happened to the curtain calls, anyway?" HoJo asked. Arrogance was no longer in Johnson's nature, not as a born-again, but this was his way of trying to lead, grasping for false personality traits from a colorless team. Indeed, Johnson was a victim of his own memory banks: What he didn't—or perhaps couldn't— understand was that Vince Coleman was not Lenny Dykstra and Bobby Bonilla wasn't Darryl Strawberry and Bret Saberhagen wasn't Ron Darling, at least not in terms of citywide charisma.

New Yorkers didn't respond to these Mets, simply because the '92 Mets enjoyed New York so little. One veteran Met said, "When I heard Howard giving his speech, I thought, 'Wow, he just doesn't get it. You just can't turn arrogance on and off like a switch. It's the chemistry of this team that's the problem.'"

•

Now that the front office's weeding-out process was nearly complete, some of the players were beginning to realize that the '92 Mets were like a baseball fillet: no backbone, no soul. Worse, these Mets didn't even like one another very much. Dwight Gooden said, "In the old days, you'd close your eyes, point your finger at any corner of the clubhouse, and when you opened them, there'd be a guy you could hang with. We were close, all of us. This team . . . I don't know. Soon as the game's over, everyone goes their own way."

Not only did those Mets like one another, but they trusted one another, and it showed on the field. Trust: like when a pop-up towered over the infield, Kevin Elster's eyes would be lifted toward the skies, and Wally Backman would be screaming in his ear.

"Catch it, you scumbag," Backman would say.

Elster, giggling now, would say, "Fuck you, man, you take it."

"Can't see it," Backman would say as the ball descended. "It's yours. It's your error, motherfucker."

This on-field chemistry persisted even as the roster slowly filled with men of lesser nerve. One day in 1990, Elster watched in sympathy as lefty Jeff Musselman was brought in to relieve David Cone, who'd left him with a one-run lead against the Reds. Elster saw the Harvard-educated lefty struggle with his composure, throwing pitch after pitch out of the strike zone, and he came over to the mound when he realized "the kid was hyperventilating on the mound. I really thought he was going to pass out."

Keith Hernandez used to be the infield's psychiatrist, trotting endlessly between first base and the mound to help out a pitcher in trouble. The classic example of Hernandez's leadership was in Game Six of the 1986 NLCS against the Astros. In the sixteenth inning, Jesse Orosco was faltering, trying to protect a 7–6 lead. The Astros had just rallied for two runs, and were threatening to tie the game.

With Kevin Bass at the plate, Hernandez approached the mound at the same time as Ray Knight. Orosco looked into

•

175

Hernandez's eyes and said, "I don't know if I can get this guy."

Hernandez shouted back over the roar of the Astrodome, "You can strike this motherfucker out, Jesse. Get him. Don't give in. Don't give up." Orosco found the inspiration to indeed blow away Bass, giving the Mets their first National League pennant since 1973.

After Hernandez left New York in 1989, it was Elster who became the in-game guru. Unlike Hernandez, who seemed to have a dossier on every hitter in the league, offering suggestions as to how to exploit their weaknesses, Elster relied on simpler ways of counseling his pitchers.

"Hey man, don't sweat," Elster breathed into Musselman's ear that afternoon at Shea. "Just get me a ground ball— I'll take care of you. Give me a little love, I'll handle the rest."

Now, two years later, the Mets uttered all the proper responses to Johnson's urgings. On the surface, at least, the meeting was a success. But to the handful of Mets who remembered what on-field magic was really like, calling a team meeting to re-create arrogance was a waste of time.

JUNE 19. NEW YORK. METS 4, CARDINALS 3.

THE CLOCK ON the clubhouse wall read four, the quietest moment of the day for most Mets. This was a time to open fan mail, glance through the newspapers, watch a little TV in the players' lounge, slap on the headsets and escape without being bothered. But on this day there was important business being conducted in the manager's office. There, Willie Randolph and Dave Cone had asked for a few minutes in private with Torborg.

Cone was there because, as the Mets' player representative, he spoke for the team in an official capacity. Randolph was there as the clubhouse's unofficial ambassador to Torborg, having done time with him in the Steinbrenner years. Despite their history, though, Randolph knew this subject would have to be handled carefully: Clubhouse discontent was growing

•

over Torborg's continuing refusal to allow alchohol on charter flights.

"You have a rule that makes us look like we're fuck-ups," Cone said cautiously. "At least that's the perception out there. You haven't even given us a chance to prove we can handle alcohol like adults. Right off the bat, you put us in a negative light."

Torborg heard them out patiently, probably not surprised by the message Cone and Randolph had brought. But the manager wouldn't relent. Instead, he repeated the philosophy introduced in the spring, and later enforced on that very first flight of the season back from Florida: "I've seen what drinking can do to a team. Every bad thing that's ever happened on a plane was the result of someone drinking too much." Torborg paused for a moment to lower his voice, even though no one else was in the room.

"Look, I know guys are sneaking booze on the plane," he said. "But I don't want to go ahead and say it's okay. I don't want to be sending up any red flags."

Randolph appealed again to Torborg, making the point that the Mets were not a young team in need of guidance like the White Sox, but a veteran group who took offense at such strict disciplinary measures. And while the inner circle might have dwindled to a minority, it still had influence in the clubhouse, a point that Cone tried to make as subtly as possible, noting that "a lot of guys just can't get used to this." But Torborg refused to loosen the grip, claiming, "I've never seen a renegade team that won." Cone's eyes widened. What about this very team under Davey Johnson? What about Jim Leyland, who gave his Pirates plenty of freedom as long as they put out on the field? And what would Torborg have called those Yankees teams of the late seventies, full of players ready and willing to fight the opponent, the manager, and the owner, not necessarily in that order? How, Cone wondered, could Torborg have clung so tightly to this rule, when even he realized it was being ignored?

•

And that wasn't the only quarrel the players had with the Torborg administration. There was grumbling about the need for daily meetings: pitchers' meetings, hitters' meetings, defensive meetings. Torborg had sold this idea to Harazin during his job interview, and the rookie GM had loved the sound of it. It was so . . . organized. For nearly a decade Davey Johnson had run an old-school National League clubhouse, where the lace-'em-up-and-kick-some-butt philosophy prevailed. Players weren't required to take batting practice if they didn't feel like it: Infield practice was usually attended by the Mets' bench players. If Keith Hernandez felt like taking a nap in the trainers' room right up until game time because he'd been out all night . . . well, Davey knew better than to demand that Mex take a few ground balls.

Trouble is, Frank Cashen absolutely hated that, especially when the Mets weren't required to be on the top step of the dugout during the national anthem. Cashen's love of order was passed on to Harazin, whose blood raced quickly through his veins when Torborg explained the level of preparedness the Mets would bring to each game. Torborg liked to say, "You can never be too ready," but he forgot one important factor: This was not some young team that needed—or even responded to—structure.

"You've got guys in here who are on their way to the Hall of Fame. Are you going to tell Eddie Murray how to get ready for a game?" Cone asked respectfully. The tedium of these endless meetings was leaving the Mets bored and worn out. Worse, they weren't having any real effect on the club, which was seven games out and five games under .500. One veteran said the rigid timetables, from batting practice to the various meetings between 4:15 and 6:50, were making him "claustrophobic." So Cone and Randolph had been sent to plead for at least one act of mercy from Torborg: Could he please, just for a while, ease up on the meetings?

Torborg might have been too firmly rooted in his beliefs, but he was no fool. He sensed that the complaints from Cone

•

and Randolph were real, that the clubhouse was starting to drift away from him. So while he wouldn't relent on the in-flight drinking—Torborg would never surrender on that point—he was at least willing to bend on the meetings. He walked out to the clubhouse and addressed the Mets as a group. Thus came the new order of the day: no more mandatory group sessions for the hitters to study scouting reports, although defensive meetings and pitchers-and-catchers strategy sessions would remain. A small victory had been won: Pregame time, at least partially, belonged to the players again.

JUNE 25. NEW YORK. CUBS 9, METS 2.

G REG MADDUX'S LINE drive one-hopped off Bobby Bonilla's glove, all the way to the wall, just another blemish on Anthony Young's awful seven-run first inning. Bonilla looked up at the Shea scoreboard and saw the insult: a large E-9 flashing, flashing, sneering at Bobby Bo, inciting the fans.

Bonilla shook his head in amazement. What was it about New York that made everyone on edge, even in their own ballpark? When he got to the dugout at inning's conclusion, Bonilla went right for the telephone and called the press box. He picked up the direct line, knowing his good friend Jay Horwitz would be on the other end.

"Jay, what're they flashing the E-9 in such big letters for?" Bonilla asked loudly. "Why are they doing that?" Horwitz stammered through his answer, telling Bonilla he would check on it. Loyal to the end, the PR director would never admit to his surprise. But it was the first time in his twelve years with the Mets that a player had ever called in the middle of a game to complain about an error.

At the time, none of the reporters in the press box were aware of the phone call. But the TV audience was: SportsChannel had followed Bobby Bo all the way to the home-plate corner of the dugout, right to the phone, and zoomed in close enough

•

to read Bonilla's lips. Virtually every Met either directly heard Bonilla shouting at Horwitz or heard about it through the grapevine.

"I couldn't believe my fucking ears," one veteran said. "We're getting our asses kicked, and Bobby's worried about the error? I started to wonder, 'What's he thinking about, anyway?'" Bonilla couldn't possibly have been concerned about another blemish on his defensive record, having once led the National League in errors as a third baseman. So what was the problem with one more in right field? But there was Bonilla, pushing past Torborg to get to the telephone. At first, the manager couldn't understand what Bonilla wanted either, as he watched him reach for the wall-mounted unit that had no dial. Normally, the only time the dugout bothered to call upstairs was when trainer Steve Garland needed to inform Horwitz about an injury. But Bonilla calling about an injury?

Torborg looked over his shoulder and his blood pressure rose. It didn't matter if Bonilla was earning $29 million or that he had been getting booed hard lately. This was ridiculous, and the manager finally snapped. "Forget the fuckin' error, forget the fuckin' official scorer. Get your fuckin' head in the game." This was said loud enough for everyone in the dugout to hear, but Bonilla finished his call to Horwitz and put the phone down.

It wasn't until after the game that everyone realized this was a public issue. Reporters were waiting in the clubhouse . . . waiting, waiting . . . no one in Pittsburgh had ever cared that much to wait an hour to talk to Bonilla. But the Magnificent Seven were too close to the fire to let the matter drop now. They had only one question: Why had Bonilla been on the phone?

Worse, Bonilla's timing was awful. A midweek afternoon game had brought out every columnist in town looking to write a leisurely baseball story. Now they had an explosive story on which to comment. For sixty minutes, Bonilla, Torborg, Harazin, and Horwitz remained behind the closed doors of the manager's office. The longer that they waited, the higher the

•

temperature rose in the clubhouse. Now it became a matter of macho pride: The longer Bonilla held out, the more resolute the beat guys became. Fuck deadline, fuck the game story—Bonilla would have to answer to this one. Finally, Bonilla emerged and hurled the greatest insult possible at the press.

With stunning calm, Bonilla said he'd called Horwitz to ask about his health. "I knew Jay had a cold and I didn't get a chance to see him before the game." Horwitz was forced to go along with this story—either that or lose his job. It wasn't the worst task Horwitz had ever been asked to swallow as PR director, and with glum resignation—not to mention a loyalty to Bonilla, who after all, was a Met—Horwitz acquiesced.

But the beat guys . . . well, they looked at one another in amazement. No words were necessary. One expression—from the *News* to the *Post* to *Newsday*—said it all: Did Bonilla expect anyone to believe he'd called Horwitz to check on a head cold? Compounding the lie was Torborg's insistence that he had "no idea" what Bonilla was saying on the phone. The manager conceded he'd seen Bonilla reach for the receiver, but didn't know what was being said. Not only did the beat guys take this story apart, but the city's heavyweights loaded up their rifles, too. Mike Lupica of the *News* and Tom Verducci of *Newsday* both flatly called Bonilla a liar and scorched Torborg for his complicity. Verducci asked out loud how New Yorkers could ever take Bonilla seriously again, knowing he was more interested in his individual scoring than his team's fate. Lupica called Bonilla a baby and a whiner.

If only Bonilla had told the truth. If only he'd emerged from Torborg's office and said he'd made a mistake, over-reacted, was stressed out by the Cubs' first-inning rally. Didn't he know better than to blur the truth? Didn't he know the futility of fighting not only the *Post*'s and the *News*'s and the *Times*'s foot soldiers, but Lupica and Verducci, too? One Met said it best, a day later. "Of all the shit Darryl pulled here over the years, he never, ever called the press box about an error. In-fucking-credible."

•

JUNE 26. ST. LOUIS. CARDINALS 4, METS 3.

IT WAS 8:30 P.M. when Mike Lupica found the light on his office answering machine flickering. Lupica had set up a work area in the basement of his New Canaan, Connecticut, home, so he was alone with his shock when he played back the message.

"Hello, Mike? This is Jeff Torborg. I wanted to get in touch with you. I wanted to explain what I meant about not knowing what Bobby was doing on the dugout phone yesterday."

Lupica's machine told him the call had been made at 7:00 P.M. Central Time, a half hour before the Mets were to begin a three-game series with the Cardinals at Busch Stadium.

The next day, there was another message on the machine. "Mike? Jeff again. I guess I'll try later on." This time Lupica heard the national anthem being played in the background, which meant Torborg was calling from the dugout, less than five minutes before the first pitch.

In all his years as a *Daily News* columnist, after all the fights he'd had with the sports world's biggest egos, Lupica had never gotten a telephone call like this. A manager calling to explain? At game time? Only now did Lupica realize how deeply wounded the entire Mets organization was. Every back page screamed about Bonilla's telephone call. WFAN was swamped with calls about it. And even the clubhouse was full of second-day gossip.

But while Torborg tried to effect damage control, Bonilla remained defiant, not caring if it cost him his status as team leader. The Mets didn't dislike Bobby Bo, but they realized he was waging a private war with New York and wanted no help from anyone else. So when reporters worked their source network the day after the incident to find out what exactly Bonilla had said on the phone, the Mets were ready to give him up. "He was screaming about the error," said one of the club's veterans.

•

Another said Torborg had indeed yelled at Bonilla, or as he put it, "Aired him right the fuck out in front of all of us." Incredibly, Bonilla stuck to his story, claiming the phone call had nothing to do with the error. Then he became testy, saying, "If that's sports news, then there's something wrong."

Bonilla went even further, claiming that the dugout and its equipment belonged to the players and team, not the manager, and if he wanted to use the phone, "then I'm going to." And, firing off a shot at his teammates—who, reporters informed him, had said he was complaining about the error—Bonilla said, "If players believe that about me, then I've got to question whether they want to win. They should worry about what we're doing on the field together, rather than what I'm doing personally."

Not far away, a small group of Mets stood, half-listening to Bonilla's group interview. One of them motioned to a reporter, asking what Bonilla had said. The newsman said Bonilla was still denying that the call was about the error. "Total bullshit," the veteran said, his voice tight with anger. "He ain't Straw. He ain't even close." In another corner of the clubhouse, Torborg was deep into spin control too, telling reporters that while he had been aware Bonilla was using the phone, he didn't listen to the dialogue and no such heated exchange had taken place between the manager and his right fielder. "Bobby asked me which phone [went to the press box]," Torborg said. "I said, 'What do you mean, which phone?' I said, 'Bleep the phone.' I was thinking about what we were going to do, down seven nothing. But then I don't know what Bobby said on the phone after that."

Torborg apologized to reporters for unwittingly misrepresenting the events in the dugout, saying, "I realize it looked like a cover-up. Bobby came off the field saying something about an error, and I said, 'What error?' Then he went to the phone. I knew Bobby was using the phone, I should've said so, and by not facing up to that, it looked like a major cover-up."

Too late, too late. If Torborg had looked closely, he

•

would've seen the *News, Post,* and *Times* guys all slightly shaking their heads—partly in disbelief, partly in disappointment over Torborg's lack of candor. Last-minute phone calls to Lupica weren't going to help, and glossy explanations to the beat reporters weren't going to do it, either. Of course, the Mets went out and got beat that night—Bonilla was 0-for-3 with two strikeouts—and now it was becoming obvious the path to the pennant race would be more like a long, flat road to nowhere.

THE METS' FIVE FAVORITE BARS
1. Clark Bar, Pittsburgh.
2. A.J.'s, St. Louis.
3. The Red Onion, San Diego.
4. Shenanigan's, Chicago.
5. Winston Churchill's, Montreal.

•

JULY

JULY 5. NEW YORK. ASTROS 2, METS 0.

THE FAN MAIL had been piling up for some time in Dave Cone's locker, which wasn't unusual at this time of year. Whatever inclination Cone had to answer his public had been dulled by the summer's growing heat and the Mets' lackluster play in June and July. Even though they were only six games out—certainly not a hopeless situation, even as a fifth-place team—the pennant race didn't have a healthy feel to it. What was going wrong at Shea? It'd been a long time since Cone had even tried to answer that question. Instead, he spent hours of empty pregame time smoking cigarettes, reminiscing about his friends from the old Mets teams, telling a confidant, "I just don't see myself fitting in here anymore."

It wasn't the first time Cone had uttered that thought, and it wouldn't be the last time either. His unhappiness wasn't related to the spring's controversies; incredibly, there was little fallout from the Gooden-Boston-Coleman rape case, and even less said about the indecent-exposure lawsuit that'd landed Cone's name in every tabloid headline and onto the *Post*'s Page Six. It wasn't bad publicity that infected Cone. It was the lifelessness at Shea that was slowly eating away at his soul.

It would have been like any other midsummer afternoon at Shea—sitting at his locker, waiting for another game—except now Jay Horwitz approached and asked for an unusual favor. "Coney, Fred Wilpon's outside. He'd like you to come out and sign some autographs for some kids," Horwitz said.

•

Cone nodded. Being pulled out of the clubhouse before a game was hardly out of the ordinary. In fact, it was one of Horwitz's more routine pregame responsibilities, to see that groups of young kids—usually orphaned or disadvantaged or handi-capped—were attended to by a generous Met.

Often all that was required was a few minutes' time—a few autographs, a few hellos. And it didn't really matter who Horwitz produced, or what the player had to say to the kids, who only cared about seeing a real live Met, in person, in his uniform. Just a few weeks later, in fact, a group of Hispanic kids from a local charity would pay a visit to the Mets. Horwitz and the club's community-relations office had arranged for the visit, but at the last minute, Horwitz realized there wasn't a single Met—besides Bonilla, who wasn't around—who could speak Spanish. After years of fighting a racist image, the Mets had somehow rid themselves of virtually all their Hispanic ballplayers. Not even Sid Fernandez, despite his Spanish-sounding surname, could speak a word of the language; he was Hawaiian and, further back, of Portuguese origin. Frantically, Horwitz went from locker to locker, asking any of the Mets if they could speak Spanish.

"I can say 'el pussy.' Would that help, Jay?" one of the veterans said, snickering. Horwitz had no time to laugh, though, with the kids waiting in the runway. Finally, Horwitz stumbled upon Chico Walker, who'd taken a year or two of Spanish in high school, remembered a little of it, and now volunteered for the assignment.

Walker stepped outside, saw the pack of glowing faces, and said, *"¿Qué tal?"* That was enough to send the kids spirits' soaring, and Horwitz's crisis was over.

There was no such problem getting an audience when Wilpon asked, though. Not even the most rebellious Met would dare turn down such a simple request from the man who ulti-mately would fill their coffers with millions of Mets dollars. So when Horwitz asked Cone for a minute of his time, the pitcher said yes without hesitation. But as he headed for the door, Cone wondered, "Why me?"

•

Of course, he was one of the Mets' brightest points in a dull season. But Bonilla, even with the booing, was still more popular with the fans on a one-to-one basis. The same was true for Howard Johnson, especially with the kids. Despite all his successes, Cone could never escape the feeling that the front office was out to get him. Nothing overt had been said, but the climate had changed ever since Cone had rejected management's four-year offer for $16.8 million. Cone thought of himself as a $5 million-a-year pitcher and had decided to gamble on his ability to have a big year and reap the benefit as a free agent. He knew he'd anger Harazin by taking the Mets to arbitration, but he was determined to prove that his '91 season had been better than either his 14-14 record indicated or the club was willing to grant in negotiations. He won his case, earning a $4.25 million salary for '92, and though he knew there would be some hard feelings, Cone at least thought there'd still be a dialogue. But the ensuing months had produced a chill that, in retrospect, Cone realized he should've expected.

After all, he was an inner-circle Met, one of the original wild-siders. There had been safety in numbers back in the eighties, but by July 1992, Cone looked around and realized he was alone. Going into the season, only Cone and Elster were left from the old days, and Elster was gone because of shoulder surgery—at home in California, hardly even keeping in touch with his teammates anymore.

Yet, even with Cone stripped of his former comrades, the front office was still resentful of him. He was dangerous in every respect, too close to the reporters, too close to the remaining renegades, too unpredictable on the mound. If Cone had any on-field flaw, it was his own intensity. At the first hint of trouble, he would rush his delivery, overthrow the fastball, choke the slider, bounce the splitter in the dirt. That was the only obstacle between Cone and perennial twenty-win seasons, that panic which seemed to engulf him once or twice a game.

Teammates could see it coming, too: Cone's eyes would get wide, crazy. Reporters called it the "Marty Feldman look," one that Cone himself acknowledged was impossible not to

•

laugh at. The tortured side was never so evident on the field as that 1990 night in Atlanta when he argued with first-base ump Charlie Williams, allowing the Braves runners to score. But the off-the-field devil consumed Cone later that evening, when he stepped into Flamingo Joe's, a popular bar near the Mets' hotel. Cone burst through the doors, obviously drunk, and found a group of New York writers in the corner, pulling hard on long-necked Coronas. Within moments of Cone's arrival, the waitress delivered a fresh round to the media's table. The reporters glanced over their shoulders, only to see Cone across the room, pounding his chest, shouting, "Retaliate!" The writers sent back a shot of 150-proof rum, which Cone downed instantly. Seconds later, he rushed out the door in a panic, barely making it to the sidewalk before throwing up. But he calmly returned to thank the writers and begin some serious drinking.

Mets management was well aware how hard Cone lived the nightlife. Al Harazin didn't have to spy on his players, at least not directly: Word filtered back easily enough about who stayed in their hotel rooms and who didn't. The information could flow through a number of channels. A coach would serve as the eyes and ears of the organization, or perhaps the traveling secretary. Even the public would turn into informants, often calling the club or writing letters to complain about a player's behavior the previous night in a bar. Most Mets assumed that anything they did in public was sooner or later bound to find its way into management's dossier. And the late-nighters were getting easier and easier to identify, unlike the old days, when the bite-to-eat-and-back-to-the-room-to-call-home Mets were such a minority. Mookie Wilson belonged to that small army. Mookie was such a kind and religious man, he not only refused to chase women, teammates remember him for not even looking at them. One Met recalled a slow moment in 1986, as the team bus was caught in traffic on its way to Wrigley Field. Suddenly a beautiful woman appeared beside the bus. "Mookie, man, look at that," the Met said, nudging

•

Wilson in the ribs. To his astonishment, not only did Wilson refuse to turn his head, he even changed the subject.

The front office, in its obsession to cleanse the Mets, would've gladly accepted a team of Mookie Wilsons. But the Mets gave him away in August '89, trading him to the Blue Jays for reliever Jeff Musselman. Despite Wilson's gentle personality and extraordinary athletic skills, the front office was sure Wilson would never be better than an undisciplined free-swinger, striking out too often for a leadoff man, prone to long, severe slumps, and since Wilson would become a free agent at the end of '89, they preferred to trade him.

Ironically, two months earlier the Mets had traded Lenny Dykstra because they weren't willing to turn center field over to him on an everyday basis, yet they still dealt Mookie away even after getting a close look at Juan Samuel's incompetence in center. It made no sense, and the fact that Wilson had a fine year with the Blue Jays in 1990 spoke volumes about the Mets' error in judgment. But, of course, that wasn't the first time they'd erred.

Now the question was: Would they allow their personal feelings about Cone to influence their baseball judgment—as they had with Darryl Strawberry? In late June '92, Cone was the cover story of *The Sporting News,* and in it there were anonymous quotes from a source within the Mets management. Defiantly, almost with hostility, the source wondered if Cone would ever break through and be a consistent eighteen- to twenty-game winner.

Infuriated, Cone pulled a reporter aside, produced the article, which had been sitting in his locker, and said, "Look at this shit. Read it." Before the newsman even had a chance to digest a few paragraphs, Cone hissed, "You believe that? These are the guys who've been telling us how much they hate the 'One Met' thing, and now they go anonymous to rip me? What kind of bullshit is that?"

Cone had a hunch it was VP Gerry Hunsicker, because ever since the contract talks had broken off in March, the VP

●

had been cool toward his pitcher—almost as if Hunsicker had taken the rejection of the $16.8 million personally. Finally, what was once unthinkable was a point of open discussion for Cone now: a possible trade, perhaps to a pennant contender before the September postseason-eligibility deadline.

Why not? The Mets had traded every other player who'd gotten in the front office's way. Cone was so sure his days were numbered he asked a reporter to probe Hunsicker. "See what he says," Cone said. And the answer came back just as Cone expected. Hunsicker said it was "very possible" the Mets would trade their once-untouchable righty, in the event they'd fallen out of the race and concluded it'd be too costly to re-sign Cone as a free agent that winter.

All of these thoughts were racing through Cone's mind now as he approached the door of the clubhouse. The kids' requests for autographs would be simple and honest. But what did Wilpon want? When Cone reached the group, he smiled tentatively at Wilpon, shaking his hand. The gathering was comprised of friends of the owner and their kids, and after greeting Cone Wilpon addressed them. "This is David Cone, one of our best pitchers," he said. Cone warmed to the moment, wondering if he'd read too much into Wilpon's request. A moment later, however, his worst suspicions were realized.

"Dave has a wonderful girlfriend," the owner said, turning to look directly into Cone's eyes. "We're trying to get him married." Wilpon's point was lost on the kids, of course, but Cone got it immediately. He felt he'd been set up, especially when one of the kids gently asked, "Are you really getting married, Mr. Cone?" Cone tried to laugh off his answer, but it was obvious Wilpon had used the moment to issue a warning: Settle down, get married, get with the program.

All at once, it hit Cone that Jeff Torborg and Al Harazin's desire to cleanse the Mets came from a much higher source. It was Wilpon. "He was the trigger guy all along," Cone said later that season. Now, more than ever, Cone recognized the Mets for what they were: an organization committed to enforcing

•

rules. Those who did wrong would suffer for their sins. Operating in the largest, most liberal city in the country, the Mets had somehow managed to become one of baseball's most conservative organizations. That's what finally turned Cone against the Mets: not their on-field decline, but what was happening in the clubhouse, and, ultimately, his own refusal to conform. Get married? Because Fred Wilpon suggested it? At that moment, Cone wished he could convene the old tribunal—Darryl, Mex, Lenny, Ronnie, Ellie, Bobby O—so everyone could have a good laugh.

JULY 6. ATLANTA. METS 3, BRAVES 1.

THE ANNOUNCEMENT CAME over the wire early in the afternoon, so by the time the Mets arrived at Atlanta–Fulton County Stadium, the clubhouse was full of the depressing news: Commissioner Fay Vincent had ordered the National League's realignment, forcing the Braves and Reds into the Eastern Division. Not only would the Mets have to spend the rest of the decade fighting the Pirates and the upstart Expos, but now they had to deal with the West's bullies, too.

The commissioner's edict would be rescinded following his own ouster later in the season, but at the moment the prospect of facing Steve Avery and Tom Glavine eighteen times a year instead of twelve made the Mets swallow hard. How could they ever hope for a resurrection? Even Jeff Torborg couldn't put a friendly spin on the news. "Holy shit," he said, running a hand through his hair. "This is going to make it tougher than ever."

Torborg had no choice but to stick it out for the three more years on his contract, but for free-agents-in-waiting like Dave Cone and Dave Magadan, there was at least the possibility of escape. And in Cone's case, it was more than just a possibility: It seemed almost a certainty now. "No question that has to affect the way you think about the future of this club," Cone said. Privately, Cone asked, "Why the fuck would I want to stay here now?"

•

It was a fair and reasonable question, and not even a 3–1 win over Atlanta helped matters much. If anything, the battle Cone waged to stay close after Deion Sanders's leadoff homer in the first inning said everything about his distrust of the bullpen and his own team's offense. He walked seven Braves in seven innings. He also struck out nine, which means he came nearly as close as baseball allows to taking on the opposition all by himself. As Cone later described it, "I pitched around everyone in the lineup. I didn't want to make a mistake with anyone, like it was the seventh game of the World Series." Cone got lucky, though: the Mets tied the score at 1–1 on Magadan's infield single, and after Cone was through, the Mets went ahead in the eighth. Daryl Boston's home run off Marvin Freeman gave Cone a 3–1 win, upped his record to 7–4, and lowered his ERA to 2.65. But did it make Cone any friendlier toward the Mets?

For the next ten days, Cone let the issue remain dormant in his mind. Then came a fateful start against the Giants. In a 1–0 win, Cone threw 166 pitches, an outrageous request of any arm, even a healthy one. After the game, the press wondered whose idea it was to allow a pitcher to risk so much, still remembering how Doc Gooden's '91 season was ruined not long after Buddy Harrelson let him throw 150 pitches in the raw of an April drizzle.

At first, Cone said, "It was my idea. I didn't want to come out of the game," and Torborg was more than happy to let him assume the responsibility, saying, "We kept asking him every inning, and every inning Dave said he was fine. He was throwing hard, his mechanics looked great. We didn't see any reason to take him out." But as the weeks progressed, Cone's arm paid the surcharge for those 166 pitches. In the next four starts, Cone allowed fifteen earned runs, his fastball suffering the most.

By mid-August Cone was privately wondering how Torborg could've allowed him to throw 166 pitches. "I told him I was fine, that's true, but no manager should let a guy stay out

•

there that long," Cone said. He questioned Torborg's managerial instincts, even his competence, and in his most irrational moments, Cone half-wondered if management wasn't out to simply ruin his arm and strip him of all his free-agent appeal.

The point was academic after the season, as soon as Cone signed a three-year, $18 million pact with the Royals—$9 million of which was delivered up front. Still, Cone was astonished to hear at the winter meetings in Louisville, Kentucky, that members of the Mets' hierarchy were whispering he might not be worth the investment.

After he signed with the Royals, Cone was seated for dinner with his agent at a Louisville restaurant, not far from where the Mets' executives were dining. It wasn't long before Cone saw Harazin heading for the men's room, with Cone's table directly in his path. As Cone saw it, Harazin navigated all the way around the other side of room, just to avoid his former pitcher. On his return from the bathroom, Harazin either made a wrong turn or said the hell with it, because he walked right past Cone's table. But rather than offer congratulations or even a simple hello, Harazin didn't so much as acknowledge Cone.

Cone said, "Nice talking to you, Al," while Harazin was still in earshot. Cone knew it might be the last time he'd ever get close enough to his former boss to let him know he felt insulted.

JULY 8. ATLANTA. BRAVES 2, METS 1.

C AN ONE INNING, all by itself, rob a team of its self-respect? That was the question the media was left asking after a devastating Mets loss to the Braves, in which they had the bases loaded with no one out in the ninth, only to fail against former teammate Alejandro Peña.

Incredibly, the Mets melted in just five pitches after Todd Hundley's leadoff single in the ninth off Kent Mercker and back-to-back walks to Bill Pecota and Daryl Boston. That's

•

when Peña arrived, and as one Met said, "If Al had fallen behind in the count—even one-and-oh—to HoJo, I guarantee you he chokes." But Johnson swung at the first pitch, popping out pathetically. Four pitches later, Peña beat Willie Randolph with an inside-corner fastball, getting him to bounce to Terry Pendleton at third, a perfect 5–4–3 double play that left the Mets ruined.

Gerry Hunsicker was to call this "the most crushing loss of the year." And it made for a miserable clubhouse. Rage was everywhere in the room—players' eyes wouldn't meet reporters', food was left untouched, the showers seemed to last forever—as the press searched for professional ways to conduct their interviews. How does one ask a player why he failed? It's the most elementary problem that faces a sportswriter, one that has no real solution. You get better at asking the tough questions as the years pass, but for those first few moments at a player's locker, everyone clearing his throat, staring at the ground, the discomfort is a terrible thing. It doesn't matter if you're a ten-year veteran or a guy in his first year on the beat, the opening question is always the hardest.

Some players make it easy. Guys like Dave Cone and Willie Randolph know exactly why a reporter is at his locker—not to embarrass him or make the hurt any worse, but simply for an analysis. The real professionals begin talking without being asked a question. But baseball is full of touchy, hypersensitive players and managers who lash out at reporters as a way of coping with their own frustration.

Perhaps the player with the worst demeanor in the last decade was the Cardinals' John Tudor, who hated reporters and any question they asked. No matter how you asked, how neutrally or professionally you phrased it, Tudor would roll his eyes and say, "What kind of fucking question is that?" The Mets have had their share of strange and bad guys over the years—Dave Kingman, George Foster, Jesse Orosco, Juan Samuel—although in the years they were winning, the front office would lean on the hostile players to cooperate. Usually, though, once a player hated the press, there was little one could do to change his mind. While playing for the A's, Kingman once presented Susan Fornoff of the *Sacramento Bee* with a nicely wrapped box. She opened it up to find a dead rat. Foster, now coaching high school baseball in Connecticut, was one of the most uncooperative Mets of the early eighties. And Orosco probably had the worst grasp of what the media's job was, consistently refusing to answer questions after a blown save.

When he did grant time, Orosco was so distrustful of reporters, he'd try to read their notebooks as the interview was taking place. That meant reading upside down, or at least trying to. No one was ever sure if Orosco was successful, but just to make sure he wasn't getting away with this breach of conduct, one reporter calmly scribbled "fuck you" in the middle of his notes while speaking to Jesse. Orosco, as always, had twisted his head grotesquely in an attempt to steal a peek at the notebook. Whether or not he deciphered the message, no one will ever know. Orosco never said a word about it.

By 1992, the entire clubhouse was so decidedly anti-press that management gave up trying to enforce détente. It was common now for most Mets to behave as HoJo did after that disastrous ninth inning in Atlanta. He was in a strange, far-away mood, answering questions as woodenly as possible. "We did the best we could. We just didn't get the job done." He buttoned his shirt in a hurry and left for the team bus. In the manager's office, Jeff Torborg worked on a couple of slices of pizza, seemingly oblivious to the state of his locker room. "We've had so much garbage dumped on us this year," Torborg said between bites, "we'll bounce back."

Many in the press corps later felt that the Mets had finally accepted their fate on July 8. Even the umpiring crew seemed to think so. Only a day before, Bobby Bonilla had been ejected by Harry Wendelstedt for arguing a fourth-inning called strike. That prompted a stunning explosion from Bonilla, who had to be restrained by Jeff Torborg. The exchange of words between Bonilla and Wendelstedt was so heated, the beat writers felt it

•

merited a follow-up, so after the game the *News, Post, Newsday,* the *Times,* and *USA Today* went looking for Wendelstedt.

Visiting an umpires' dressing room is a roulette game. Some umps enjoy being interviewed, even if it means answering a tedious question about a rule interpretation. But other umps resent reporters just as intensely as the players do. In fact, *Newsday*'s Tom Verducci and American League ump Rich

---

SOURCES, FRIENDS, AND ENEMIES

—J.H.

IT IS THE BEAT writer's ultimate and constant dilemma: Where do you draw the line in relationships with players? It's not hard to become friendly with many of them, especially when they're young and impressionable. You stroke their egos in print and in person, and the invisible barrier disappears quickly. It can be unhealthy as well as unethical, but then, the demands of tabloid reporting usually supersede the laws of journalism. If you're not close enough to be able to count on certain players for inside information when necessary, you'll get blown off the beat in New York.

Then, too, you can't help getting to know players on a personal level, and for all of the spoiled millionaires, some are just good people. Reporters are paid to be objective, but sometimes you're torn. How do you ever write harshly about a player who goes out of his way to befriend your son, as Keith Miller did with my son Matt during the lockout in the spring of 1990? I liked Miller anyway—he had the hustling, love-to-play style

you hope for in a major leaguer. But when he called Matt, then five years old, over to play catch a few times during the public-park workouts that spring, his name became Saint Keith in our household.

As a reporter you generally try to avoid mixing business with the public adulation that surrounds ballplayers. Often friends can't understand why I politely say no to requests to get autographs, but there's nothing more unprofessional than a sportswriter whipping out a baseball in the locker room and asking Doc Gooden for his signature. In fact, if I've got my family with me on a road trip somewhere, I tend to dive behind a plant or something if Matt and his brother, Chris, spot a player in the hotel lobby and go scurrying off for an autograph.

With Miller it was different. I'd become fairly close to other players at times, but you always worry about compromising yourself, knowing that sooner or later the job may come first. It happened with Frank Viola: He was a great guy when he wasn't losing one-

•

Garcia had to be separated one day in 1990 following an aggressive question from Verducci. Yet, the Mets' beat guys sensed they'd have a comfortable audience with Wendelstedt, simply because of an encounter they'd had with him in 1991 in St. Louis.

Wendelstedt and shortstop Kevin Elster had engaged in a vicious flurry of personal insults that day, after Elster had

games, and I'd played golf with him once twice, had a beer with him here and there. in '91 he started going bad, started king out on the beat guys after losses in while he was publicly criticizing teamtes for not being willing to stand up and e the heat that summer. So I wrote a colon saying that good old Frankie V. ought practice what he preached; it wasn't peral, but Viola was offended by it, and, in a her heated discussion, he accused me of kstabbing him. Eventually he got over it, we never played five-dollar Nassaus on links again.

Of course, I didn't have to write the colon, but I thought it was important. That's ere your integrity is on the line: All reportare influenced to some degree by relanships in the clubhouse, but if you let em dictate too much of what you do or n't write, you're a fraud. Klapisch and I jue about this all the time. He's more ined to cultivate sources and write sympatically when they make excuses for poor rformance. Let the reader decide, he ys: "My job is to report, not make judgnts about what they say." My feeling is t the readers look to the beat writer

for perspective as well as information, and if you're quoting some guy who complains about his "role" or whatever every time he goes 0-for-4 or gives up a critical hit, you've got to write it in the context that it deserves.

That's what makes player-reporter relationships so volatile. Sooner or later, the worm turns on everyone. Nothing is more difficult than writing about the decline of greatness. Ballplayers are always the last to know when they're slipping anyway, but it's especially painful for a superstar to admit— or be told by the same reporters who have been filling his scrapbook for years. Even Gary Carter, Kid Sunshine, became bitter toward the beat writers in '88 and '89, his last two years with the Mets, sure that he'd become the target of some conspiracy to run him out of town. But even more awkward for the New York press was a similar decline by Keith Hernandez in those same two years.

Hernandez had been celebrated and even fawned over by the beat guys for his keen insights about the game, which he shared freely on the record, and his informed opinions about the club, most of which he whispered selectively off the re-

•

taken too long to get in the batter's box. Wendelstedt instructed Cardinals pitcher Rheal Cormier to hurry up and throw the ball, and when Elster protested, he was immediately ejected. After the game, Elster insisted that Wendelstedt had made the speed-up command because "he's too fucking fat and couldn't take the heat. He just wanted to get out of there, that fat fuck." Reporters went to the umpires' dressing room, figur-

---

SOURCES, FRIENDS, AND ENEMIES
(continued)

cord. Night in and night out, Hernandez was the first stop in the clubhouse after a game. He'd always give you something to work with: like the time in '88 when he was officially divorced in the afternoon, then went out that night and hit two home runs, including a ninth-inning game-winner. "I should get divorced every day," he said, taking a swig of beer. "I'd be in the Hall of Fame. Of course, I'd be broke, too."

That was Mex, as teammates called him. Reporters couldn't get enough of him, and he loved working them, playing the role of the thinking man's ballplayer. But his whisperings took on a nasty edge when injuries threatened his status as King Keith. Teammates began to keep their distance, and interviews at his locker got tense, especially when Hernandez realized management was going to cut him loose. He was also bitter that reporters, in his mind, turned on him after all he'd done for them.

That's the sad truth about the job, though: You report what you see and hear, no matter how cruel, and try not to let rela-

tionships interfere. That was my dilemm during the opening week of the 1990 se son, when Miller, whom the Mets had d cided to shift from second base to cent field, was running circles around fly bal This was only a few weeks after he become my son's idol. As delicately as po sible, I wrote that maybe Miller in cent field wasn't such a great idea. He took t heat, didn't complain, eventually went ba to being a utility player, and we remain close. He continued to be a pal to my so even taking him to breakfast one morning Chicago.

When Miller was finally traded after t '91 season, I was saddened but a tad r lieved, too. His personality lit up the clu house, and all the beat guys would mis him. But I no longer had to worry about du destroying our friendship. Matt, of cours had no such concerns. Crushed by t news of the trade, he decided that I w somehow responsible. Proving just ho dicey reporter-player relationships can b then, my own son wouldn't talk to the pre for two solid days.

•

ing to get the standard no-comment. Instead, when informed of Elster's remarks, Wendelstedt chuckled and called the short-stop "an alibi artist . . . it's about time people know the truth about him. I'm tired of his excuses." The epithets went so far beyond the usual player-umpire hostility that National League president Bill White investigated the incident, questioning both Wendelstedt and Elster.

The umpire was just as candid now about Bonilla. In fact, Wendelstedt seemed to be waiting for reporters in his club-house, quick to explain that Bonilla prolonged the argument at home plate, and charging that Bonilla "wanted to be ejected."

It was eerily similar to the Elster incident. Bonilla, as Elster had, strayed nearly fifty feet from the batter's box after a called strike. Once again, Wendelstedt ordered a hurry-up pitch, this time from Steve Avery, and when Bonilla said something in return, the verbal war exploded.

According to Wendelstedt, the right fielder said, "Don't look at me, you can't look at me." The umpire shook his head and said now, "I didn't realize His Holiness had risen to that level. I don't eject guys for nothing. It appeared to me he wanted to be ejected. I believe in giving players ample time to have their say, but I'm not going to put up with that nonsense. Bobby Bonilla has always been a gentleman, and I like him as a person. But he kept the argument going. He's under a lot of pressure. I think it's got his goat."

More important than the argument itself was Torborg's response. Charging out of the dugout, the manager went after Bonilla, not Wendelstedt, and appeared to be shouting directly in his right fielder's face. Teammates later said Torborg was heard screaming, "Get your head in the fucking game!" For weeks, Bonilla had been quarreling with umpires, convinced he was getting squeezed on corner strikes. Bonilla had even con-fided to teammates that he believed a league-wide umpires' conspiracy might be operating against him, punishing him on every close pitch.

Now it was learned that on the day he had called the press

•

box to complain about his error flashing on the scoreboard, umpire Joe West's crew had presented Bonilla with a mock document, certifying Bonilla as a "Grade-A Asshole."

Those who know West say it was his way of trying to lighten Bonilla's burden, just a little jock humor between athletes. Standing at six-one, 280 pounds, West was a former college quarterback, setting conference records in the seventies while at Elon College in North Carolina, leading the school to three conference championships between 1971 and 1973. In 1986, West was elected to Elon's Hall of Fame.

Even at age forty, West retained his athletic grace, or at least his strength. Once during a bench-clearing brawl between the Mets and Phillies, West—seeking to break up the fight—picked up pitcher Dennis Cook and threw him to the ground so forcefully, so effortlessly, members of both teams froze in shock. West was just as big as Bonilla, maybe just as strong. So West considered the certificate a joke between equals, an umpire's way of saying, "Smile, man." Because, in truth, most National League umpires liked Bonilla, at least when he was with the Pirates. They were sorry to see him undergo a change since coming to the Mets, so tense, so defensive.

But Bonilla and the Mets didn't see the humor in it, alerting the National League to West's prank. In the meantime, the certificate ended up in Eddie Murray's locker, proudly displayed on the top shelf.

JULY 10. HOUSTON. METS 7, ASTROS 6.

C *R I S I S* N O L O N G E R described the Mets' state. They were bumping along now at the same level of mediocrity, interesting only for their apparent fatal attraction to controversy. On this day the manager shocked his team by moving Howard Johnson to left field to make room for a kid center fielder named Patrick Howell—known mostly to veterans for having struck out in a spring-training game against Clint Hurdle, the Tidewater manager. Howell, nervous and wildly ex-

•

cited, had just arrived from Triple A to take John Franco's roster spot after the lefty had been placed on the DL. Torborg cast aside all logical arguments about how to use Howell and decided to be bold: With Vince Coleman still hurt, why not use Howell in center field, bat him leadoff? The new look may have been worth a try, but again Torborg handled the politics poorly. Again, he created his own news leak on his afternoon radio spot. Since they were on the road, the Mets didn't actually hear Torborg breaking the code of confidentiality, but the beat reporters heard about it from WFAN reporter Steve Levy upon arriving at the Astrodome at 4:30 P.M. It was impossible to ask Torborg for an explanation since he was meeting with Frank Cashen, so the beat guys started for Howard Johnson's locker.

It wasn't exactly a stampede: Beat guys don't move that way. Only TV and radio people rush, slaves to deadline, looking like sheep. "Fuckin' vultures" was the oft-heard comment from players as the harried microphones scurried by. The beat guys considered themselves far more hip: The news didn't happen unless they were there to report it, so why hurry? But even moving at their leisurely pace across the room, they were intercepted by a frantic Jay Horwitz. "He doesn't know yet," Horwitz said of HoJo, his face panicked. No doubt he was worried that HoJo would require immediate, round-the-clock psychological care when he heard the news. It'd been that kind of season for HoJo; his psyche, ever fragile, was more vulnerable than usual.

So the press corps went into a holding pattern: nothing to do but try to look busy. This is when reporters make their rounds, try to nurture relationships with certain players—"clients" is the phrase of choice—and maybe uncover some nugget of information along the way. Most every writer develops friendly, trusting relationships with at least a few different players to whom they can then go for information, a decent quote, or just small talk. Sometimes a writer wins favor with a player by writing glowingly about him, or sometimes, as in the

•

case of Ed Christine and Randy Myers, a common interest becomes a bond.

There have been other famed alliances: Harper and Keith Miller, Klapisch and Ron Darling, Noble and Keith Hernandez, but no player and writer have ever been as close as Myers, the Mets' left-handed closer in the late eighties, and Christine, the beat writer from the Westchester-Rockland branch of the Gannett national newspaper chain. Myers was hardly a typical major leaguer: Having grown up in rural Vancouver, Washington, he disdained the excesses big leaguers flaunted. He wore flannel shirts, bragged that he bought his required road-trip neckties in Woolworth's, and pocketed most of his meal money on the road by eating at McDonald's. He was no hick, though. Myers became a regular at New York nightspots like the China Club, and, as one of the few single Mets in the late eighties, seemed to know half the women in the city. But Myers reveled in the image he created as a headstrong mountain man who refused to conform to baseball customs. He was different. He might be the only player in major league history to ever stage a spring-training holdout so that he could finish coaching a girls' basketball team at home in Washington. (Myers's iconoclasm finally did him in when he exhausted the Mets' patience by ignoring warnings to curb his in-season weight-lifting regimen; he was traded to Cincinnati soon thereafter.)

Above all, Myers was notorious for his fanatical interest in the military, specifically its weaponry. He wore camouflage fatigues around the clubhouse, kept his locker stocked with *Soldier of Fortune* magazines and other military paraphernalia, and soon became known as "Rambo" to his teammates. While Myers got along well with his teammates, he wasn't close to anyone. But when he heard that Christine, who arrived on the beat as a midseason replacement in 1988, had voluntarily served two tours in Vietnam as a marine, the two struck up an instant friendship.

Myers wouldn't explain his fascination with the military,

•

except to say his father had served his country. It was hard to decide which Myers admired more: his father or his automatic weapons. The lefty had a gun collection at home and was always on the lookout for more.

Myers was twenty-six, Christine forty-one, yet they were a perfect match: both loud, both crazy, both in pursuit of a good time. The bond was their passion for combat. Christine insisted that the firefights his marine unit engaged in were the best times of his life. When drinking, he would go even further, admitting to a brief deployment in the CIA, working well above the DMZ into North Vietnam. The next day, Christine would disavow any such talk. True or not, Myers was in awe, always wishing he could've served, too. Suffice it to say they didn't talk baseball nearly as much as, say, the methodology of enemy torture. Harper once walked into a conversation Myers and Christine were having about the techniques involved in popping a human eye out of its socket. "It's not hard at all," Christine was saying, as Myers nodded earnestly. They were always out together for beers. Had Christine not been married, their carousing might've reached toxic levels. As it was, they became legendary during spring training in 1989 for the number of nights spent in a beach bar called Mr. Laffs. They even roomed together that spring, renting a house on the beach and hosting their share of *Animal House*-type parties. Myers was advised—even warned—more than once by teammates and front-office underlings to cool his association with Christine, and of course that only fueled the friendship.

Myers had a grudge with the Mets brass: He'd pitched for the club during the '86 season, going up and down between New York and Tidewater, but he was left off the postseason roster and then passed over for a championship ring. It was a snub that Myers would never forget. After a game, he would spot Christine across the locker room interviewing a player and yell loud enough for teammates and front-office personnel to hear, "Scratch [his own nickname for Christine], where we going for beers tonight?"

•

It wasn't the most professional relationship for a beat writer, either, but Christine wasn't trying to make a name for himself in the industry. Or, as he would say virtually every day on the job, "I just don't give a shit." He worked the beat, but he didn't have that tabloid pressure to produce provocative stories every day. Nor did Christine have the patience to endure Eddie Murray–type mood swings. No wonder Christine had bounced around in the business, working for several newspapers: Once you'd commanded men in actual combat, as Christine had in Vietnam, it was difficult to take seriously the nightly pursuit of excuse-making ballplayers.

Defiant as he was, though, Christine never had a serious run-in with a ballplayer. No doubt it would've been different if his stories were included in the daily clips that circulated in the Met clubhouse—photocopied and overnight-mailed from Shea to the club every day they were on the road. The clips included stories from only the four New York dailies, so Christine's caustic humor mostly went unnoticed. He dubbed Howard Johnson "Howard Scissorhands" for his unsteadiness at third base, and over the years ridiculed the likes of Kevin McReynolds and Gregg Jefferies and Vince Coleman and Eddie Murray with more regularity than anyone else on the beat. Of course, Christine knew they rarely, if ever, saw his paper, and though he'd never admit it, that gave Christine a certain amount of freedom to swing the hatchet.

Still, word spread around the locker room of his past, and players gave Christine his space. He wasn't shy about announcing his willingness to rumble, anytime, anywhere. And even though he wasn't physically imposing—maybe five-ten, 180 pounds—he had thick forearms that served as a reminder of his marine training. Players weren't sure what to make of him. More than one would occasionally nod toward Christine across the locker room and ask another reporter, "He really that tough?" Nobody ever tried him, although Gregg Jefferies, of all people, came close. Late in the '91 season, there was much speculation about Jefferies's future as a Met—he would be traded in a few months—and the subject was becoming a

•

source of irritation to him. When Christine, speaking with Jefferies at his locker one day, asked him if he'd be willing to play the outfield in the event the Mets made such a request, Jefferies snapped.

"That's a stupid fucking question," he said.

"Well," Christine shot back, "then I guess I asked the right person."

"What do you want me to say, that I won't play the outfield?"

"You can say whatever you want—I'm just asking the question."

"All right, I'm not gonna play the outfield. I don't want to play the outfield. But if you write that, I'll have to hook you."

With that, Jefferies turned to his locker. Christine, thrilled at the opening, actually stepped into Jefferies's cubicle and turned back toward the player so he could be face-to-face with him.

"You're gonna what?" Christine asked quietly.

"I'll hook you," Jefferies said, employing the baseball slang of the day, meaning he'd throw a punch at the marine.

"Well, why don't you just do it right now," Christine said, his face only inches from Jefferies.

"You'd love that, wouldn't you," Jefferies replied, lowering his voice, beginning to look uncomfortable.

"I'm not the one making the threats. You want to go, let's go."

Jefferies didn't want any part of this confrontation. His mouth had gotten away from him, that's all, so finally he just turned and walked away from Christine, muttering to himself as he escaped to the trainer's room. Christine didn't go looking for fights, but he couldn't let some twenty-four-year-old threaten him. Later that day, Jefferies apologized and Christine shook his hand. The press corps kept waiting to see if Christine would ever have to provide an answer to the question "He that tough?" But it never came to that.

Through it all, Christine was only marking time. His wife

•

Pam's father was a publisher of several small newspapers and Christine knew eventually he and Pam, a respected newspaper editor, were going to buy and operate a newspaper themselves. They did just that in the winter of '93, moving to Danville, Pennsylvania, to run the *Danville News*. So Christine was in it for laughs mostly, and he had a lot of them with Myers.

In December 1989, when the Mets were frantically trying to locate Myers to tell him he'd been traded to the Reds for John Franco, Christine was the one who broke the news. Word of the trade had filtered to the press room during baseball's winter meetings in Nashville. Myers was in Arizona for a Players Association meeting, and Christine had him on the phone instantly, telling him of the deal. Myers was hurt. He'd been in the Mets' organization for six years and didn't want to leave, and especially didn't want to give Joe McIlvaine the pleasure of delivering the news.

"Should I tell them where you are?" Christine asked.

"Go ahead," Myers said, "but they won't be able to reach me for a couple of hours. I'm going to go lift."

That was Myers. Right to the end as a Met, he did it his way.

Torborg, however, demanded conformity. Players were much more careful choosing their words with reporters now, especially when conversation drifted into off-the-record areas. Some players were paranoid, sure that Torborg had spies in the locker room reporting back to him. Actually, Torborg's security network wasn't that advanced, although even the middle-of-the-road Mets knew Torborg was especially close to the coaches he'd brought from the American League, Barry Foote, Dave LaRoche, and John Stephenson. Players were always a little more cautious around Torborg's lieutenants, so for reporters, making rounds in the clubhouse wasn't nearly as productive anymore. Still, it was part of the job.

* * *

Now, finally, on this July afternoon, Torborg emerged from his office. Rather than speak to HoJo privately, he simply pulled

•

Johnson aside in the clubhouse and, with reporters watching, informed him of the switch to left field. The conversation was short and uneventful, but it left HoJo stunned. Anyone could've read the pain on his face: Why me? Why is it always me?

In many ways, HoJo was a tormented man, his All-Star ability often in conflict with his insecurities. He could never seem to truly escape his past. Sparky Anderson labeled Johnson a basket case after his rookie season with the Detroit Tigers, benching him in the '84 postseason. Anderson was convinced Johnson was too uptight to cope with October's pressure. When Johnson blossomed as a power hitter with the Mets, three different managers—Whitey Herzog, Roger Craig, and Buck Rodgers—humiliated him by repeatedly asking to have his bat examined for cork. Johnson would shake his head every time the bat was X-rayed. It seemed to him that he'd never earn the respect he sought. As far back as high school in Clearwater, Florida, where he was a three-sport star, Johnson remembered people doubting him. In fact, HoJo told a story about a high school football coach who questioned his decision to pursue a baseball career, signing his senior yearbook with this chilly farewell: "Hope you don't regret your decision."

HoJo's response to all this was, in a word, confusion. How was he supposed to act? He didn't know. Basically a shy, soft-spoken man, HoJo tried rebelling at first. As a Met, he figured that maybe if he was loud and brash and intimidating enough, he'd make the talk about being a nervous player disappear. So his first few years in New York, he had an opinion about most anyone or anything, though it seemed forced. When Ray Knight left, HoJo publicly snubbed Dave Magadan, saying the impressive neophyte could wait his turn. "I'm the third baseman here, not him," Johnson told reporters in the spring of '87. And when Magadan was sidelined because of a problem with the lymph nodes under his arm, briefly triggering a cancer scare, HoJo was less than sympathetic. "I can't worry about him," he said. "I've got a job to win."

But insults seemed to follow HoJo. In 1987, after Cardinals righty Danny Cox hit Johnson in the ribs with a fastball,

•

HoJo made the proclamation that "the next person who comes inside on me is going to have to pay." In response, the six-foot-three-inch, 230-pound Cox just laughed. "Every morning I hear chirping birds outside my window, and I just heard another one today: Howard Johnson."

Still, the National League could barely contain HoJo that year, as he hit thirty-six home runs with ninety-nine RBIs. Then, in 1988, his numbers collapsed, and Sparky's words became like an eerie prophecy: During the playoffs against the Dodgers, Johnson went 1-for-18 and struck out helplessly against Orel Hershiser to end Game Seven. Joe McIlvaine spent the winter trying to trade HoJo to the Mariners as part of a package for pitcher Mark Langston, and, indeed, HoJo's career with the Mets would've been over had Seattle not backed out of the deal.

By the spring of '89 HoJo was spiritually defeated. He was so hurt by what he considered to be a public rejection, he wouldn't even make eye contact with reporters anymore. Then, suddenly, he couldn't throw. Rehabbing from arthroscopic surgery, Johnson ran into a psychological wall that made it impossible for him to reach first base accurately, not even getting within ten feet of Keith Hernandez. Poor HoJo: He'd take bags of balls onto the field after exhibition games and lob them against the backstop, as if trying to relearn the elements of throwing. He answered questions in such a robotic state the press corps seriously wondered if his sanity was slipping away. "Norman," someone in the press room dubbed him that spring. Norman, as in Bates.

Johnson was bound to snap sooner or later, and he finally did with Harper, over an anonymous quote in the *Post*. HoJo had made three throwing errors on the first five ground balls he fielded in the '89 season, and when the third one cost the Mets a game, Harper quoted a teammate saying anonymously, "I hope Howard gets straightened out, but how long can we keep him in there like this?" A day later HoJo cornered Harper in the clubhouse and threatened, "You do it again and I'm going

•

to beat the shit out of you. Klapisch pulled that shit on me last year and I'm not going to put up with it this year." Johnson was so tense with anger, the muscles in his forearms were twitching. Harper tried to reason with him. Players have a right at times to be angry about anonymous quotes, but such quotes are often the only way for a reporter to accurately convey the sentiment in the clubhouse—especially when the room is full of fear of repercussion from the manager. In this case, the quote wasn't used maliciously, but to cement the Mets' concern about Johnson's throwing. HoJo didn't want to hear that, though, and he and Harper didn't resolve their differences that day. But a week later HoJo apologized, admitting he'd been horribly frustrated.

Soon enough, Johnson had conquered the throwing problem and went on to have his finest season, making the All-Star team along the way. Yet he wasn't at ease. He didn't have the assurance of an All-Star, still scarred, perhaps, by taunts from the past. He simply couldn't stand to take the blame for an error or a strikeout or a team slump. He wasn't meanspirited, just seemingly overcome by insecurity. He always seemed to think the press was out to embarrass him or his team. "You think it's over?" Johnson barked on more than one occasion when the press would ask about the Mets slipping out of another pennant race, his face ready to implode with tension. "You guys just want to bury us."

Finally, HoJo resolved his anger. Arrogance wasn't part of his real nature, so no one was terribly surprised when he showed up in the spring of 1991 a converted man, proudly calling himself a born-again Christian. The players were skeptical, however. They whispered it'd been his wife's doing, not HoJo's, and they snickered openly when he began writing biblical verses under his name when he autographed baseballs. "I'm going to sign mine with the month and year of my favorite *Playboy* playmate," Ron Darling said. Teammates had always respected HoJo for his work ethic and hustle—few, if any, of the Mets were in better shape or spent more time in the weight

•

room—but they just didn't know what to make of Johnson. He wanted to lead, especially with Darryl Strawberry departed, but born-again Christians are viewed with the ultimate cynicism in the locker room. HoJo had never been famous for carousing, but he could be found in the bar occasionally, having a few beers with the boys. Now his conversion seemed to put distance between himself and a sizable segment of the team.

Meanwhile, the Mets were crumbling in the most embarrassing manner in the summer of '91. They'd lost eleven straight to completely disappear from the pennant race and now, finally, in the second game of a doubleheader, they were beating up on Willie Fraser, the Cardinals' journeyman reliever. Kevin Elster hit a three-run homer to break up the game in the seventh inning, and Kevin McReynolds followed by going deep as well. With his next pitch, Fraser struck HoJo in the back with a fastball, about as blatant a retaliation as you'd ever see. The pitch practically screeched its taunt: *Fight me. I dare you.* Johnson reacted immediately, running three or four steps toward the mound. Then, suddenly, he stopped and merely gestured at Fraser, almost as if asking: Why? Both teams had responded to Johnson's charge, players scrambling to the top step of both dugouts. But when HoJo stopped, all movement seemed to stop, and as everyone paused, it seemed the hostility would dry up altogether. But then Rick Cerone, a tough, street-smart ex-Yankee, sprinted out of the dugout. Cerone understood the need for the Mets to show some backbone. He'd played on some of the hard-ass Yankees teams of Reggie and Billy and Piniella and Nettles and, in fact, had become a quasi-legend for cutting short a postgame lecture from George Steinbrenner following a loss in the '81 playoffs by blurting out, "Fuck you, George," in front of the whole team.

Now here he came, racing toward the mound, with both teams in pursuit. Cerone wasn't particularly big or strong, but he was so angry that when Pedro Guerrero stepped in front of him, Cerone bowled him over. He reached Fraser and connected with at least one good punch before disappearing in a

•

sea of players. "Had to do it," Cerone would say later. "Sometimes you just have to do it. We've just lost eleven games, we're finally winning one, and some guy is going to throw at our best player? You can't let that happen." Teammates were grateful. They didn't want to say so publicly, but they were embarrassed for HoJo. A few pulled reporters aside to ask, "Why did he stop?" Deep down, though, they knew, and soon enough HoJo confirmed their fears. "I thought about going after [Fraser]," Johnson said to reporters. "I probably would've in the past. But then I remembered, the Lord doesn't believe in violence." That may be an admirable credo, but it didn't sit well in the locker room. A few of Johnson's teammates rolled their eyes when his explanation was relayed; HoJo would never get their vote to lead them into battle.

Johnson was ever the good soldier, though. When his fielding at third base was becoming more of a liability that year, he finally agreed to move to the outfield. Johnson spent the month of September in right field, where he did a fair imitation of Darryl Strawberry, feeling his way along with every step.

Suffice to say, reporters were stunned in December '91 when Torborg suggested the possibility of making HoJo his center fielder. It wasn't a bad idea on paper, given Johnson's athletic ability and Vince Coleman's own inadequacies as a center fielder, but it was a terrible misjudgment in terms of psychology. Torborg didn't know any better; the blame belonged to Harazin. He should've recognized the potential for disaster. They say Jimmy Leyland's genius is putting his players in situations where they have the greatest chance of succeeding. Moving HoJo to center was quite the opposite. The press corps asked, nearly in one voice: Hasn't anyone been paying attention the last few years? You want the best out of HoJo, turn the lights down low and play meditation tapes. Do not—repeat *not*—dress him up and put him out in front to lead the band. Maybe it was coincidence that HoJo was having his worst year ever in '92, but chances are it wasn't. He was in denial practically from the moment spring training began, in-

•

sisting he felt like a natural in center field. He looked *unnatural,* often uncertain, but he was working hard, as always, at the new job. A week into the spring-training games, he declared the experiment over. "I consider myself the center fielder on this team now." He had that look—*that look*—like he was consumed with the idea of not failing, and most anyone who knew him could sense a problem.

Back in May, when the Mets had traveled to San Diego, Tim Teufel sought out his old friend. Teufel and Johnson were alike in many ways: small-egoed, family-oriented, nonpartici- pants in the Mets' nightlife. Teufel made small talk with HoJo at the batting cage during batting practice, chatting about the kids, the season, the old days at Shea. But even in the comfort of their nostalgia, Teufel sensed something odd about John- son's behavior. "I'd never seen Howard that tense," Teufel would say later, "like there was something on his mind the whole time." Teufel made a mental note to invite his friend to his home that weekend—"let him sit by the pool, relax, see what's going on." Teufel had become just another member of a growing army that was worried about HoJo.

Even the front office was wondering what to do about Johnson. By current market standards, the National League's home-run champion was grotesquely underpaid, only $2 mil- lion per. At one point during the winter, Al Harazin was ready to hand HoJo more cash, but Johnson called off the talks him- self and the GM soon disappeared in a frenzy of free-agent signings. By the time he finally took a breath, spring training had arrived. March turned to April, April to May, and now here it was midsummer, and Johnson still wasn't hitting.

Even so, by July 10, there had been no sign the club was ready to take drastic action. HoJo was in over his head in center field, but Torborg had stubbornly claimed there was no problem. Now, out of nowhere, Johnson was being moved for a kid who couldn't hit Triple-A pitching. And while the man- ager insisted the move wasn't permanent, no one believed him. Least of all HoJo, who handled the situation badly, too, com-

•

plaining to reporters for three straight days in Houston, even while continuing to kill the Mets with his anemic bat. Johnson had no right to complain, not while he was hitting .220 with six home runs. But then again, it was only natural for him to resent Torborg, the man who'd asked him to play center field in the first place. HoJo took plenty of heat in the papers for his reaction, and he returned from the All-Star break a broken man. "I feel like I'm on trial," Johnson said when reporters surrounded him the first day back. Quickly, he pledged his loyalty to the Mets, said he'd do whatever they asked, as always. He just didn't want to be viewed as a failure. His words sounded like a quiet plea to reporters. He never did go back to center field, nor did he regain his home-run stroke. Maybe it was the injuries. Maybe it was the way the planets were aligned in 1992. More likely it had a lot to do with what was going on inside HoJo's head.

FIVE WORST MISTAKES
BY FRANK CASHEN ADMINISTRATION
  1. Trading Lenny Dykstra.
  2. Letting Darryl Strawberry go.
  3. Letting Ray Knight go.
  4. Building around Gregg Jefferies.
  5. Signing Vince Coleman.

•

AUGUST

AUGUST 4. PITTSBURGH. PIRATES 3, METS 2
(twelve innings).

O N   A   S C A L E of one to ten, the Mets beat writers have always rated the city of Pittsburgh at the top of the chart. Look, the boys aren't hard to please: Give them a ballpark not too far from the hotel, a gym or a basketball court within walking distance, press-box food that won't destroy the intestines, and reasonable access to the clubhouse after the game, and they're happy.

There's a new wave of sportswriters in press boxes around the country. The old Oscar Madison image, once dead accurate, is largely dead. Where sportswriters once lived for the chance to eat huge meals in four-star restaurants and play late-night poker while drinking scotch, the younger generation is fitness-conscious and more attuned to the demands created by a sports-sophisticated society. For the most part they're writers and reporters first, fans of the game second.

They all have their favorite restaurants, but priorities are different now. Tighter deadlines have made access to clubhouses more critical, which is why writers dread night games at Wrigley Field. The old ballpark has no elevator from the top of the stadium, where the press box sits, to the bottom, where the locker rooms are. You have to fight your way through thousands of fans to get to the clubhouse. Candlestick Park requires a long, windy walk to a tiny elevator—poison for any writer on deadline. On all counts, though, Three Rivers Stadium is

•

heaven, even down to the little touches provided by the scoreboard.

The Pirates furnish the hippest music and wittiest scoreboard in the National League, primarily because of the way they use John Belushi on the Diamond Vision. About four years ago, Pirates officials, in all their hipness, snipped out segments of Belushi's hit movie *Animal House* and used them as a way to whip up their fans in the ninth inning. Belushi screams into the screen, "Let's do it!"—from a scene in *Animal House* where Belushi's entire frat has been thrown out of school by Dean Wormer. Belushi then looks into the camera and says, "It's not over until we say it's over." Incredibly, the entire ballpark has been trained to respond to Belushi, including the Pirates. Vice-president of media relations Rick Cerrone instructs the Diamond Vision operators to use the clip only in the ninth inning when the Pirates are behind by one run. So far, Belushi has batted over .500, more than once victimizing the Mets. (The closest the Mets ever came to being that street-smart was in 1988, when they used the Curly Shuffle on the scoreboard from the old Three Stooges series. But that gimmick died mysteriously in the nineties, replaced by the tired present-day rendition of "Let's go Mets.")

It would take a lot more than that to help the Mets in Three Rivers Stadium. How many times had the Mets marched into Pittsburgh, sure this would be the trip on which they'd find their muscle and reestablish their eighties dominance over the Pirates—only to be rudely reminded that they didn't have the defense, the offensive discipline, the overall savvy, or the late-inning nerve the Bucs did? It became terribly embarrassing to them; there were so many bloodstains on the Three Rivers Stadium carpet that the Mets recognized as their own. One of the worst examples of this was in September 1990.

Buddy Harrelson invited mutiny by allowing management to persuade him to start a frightened rookie, Julio Valera, over Ron Darling in a crucial pennant-race game. Valera lasted two innings, getting pounded for eight hits, as the Pirates com-

•

pleted a three-game sweep to move three and a half games ahead of the Mets. Afterward, John Franco was ready to explode at Harrelson, he was so angry. In fact, the manager's decision to call up Valera from Tidewater for the start had firmly convinced the inner-circle Mets that Harrelson was merely a front man for the brass, and this cost him whatever little respect he'd earned in the clubhouse since taking over for Davey Johnson. Harrelson was basically doomed as a manager from that point on. And for the Mets, it marked the end of the spell they'd held on New York during the mid-to-late eighties. The Mets would never really recover from that sweep in Pittsburgh, finishing a disappointing second place for a second straight year. Within weeks Darryl Strawberry was a Dodger, and, symbolically, the undressing of the '86 champs was complete. New York has been longing for a pennant race ever since.

There was more bloodshed in Pittsburgh on the night of August 16, 1991. Under Harrelson, the Mets had lost seven straight games, to fall ten and a half games out of first place, the first time in seven years they were out of contention for a division title. It'd happened with incredible swiftness, but now a three-game series in Pittsburgh gave the Mets a chance to regain pride, if nothing else. In the ballpark that Friday night were all the power brokers: Fred Wilpon, Frank Cashen, Al Harazin, and VP-treasurer Harry O'Shaughnessy, who'd flown in on Wilpon's private jet from an organizational meeting at Nelson Doubleday's summer retreat on Nantucket. By the seventh inning, the Mets had made five errors and fallen behind 8–0 en route to a humiliating 8–2 loss. Wilpon stormed out in disgust, taking Cashen and O'Shaughnessy back to New York on his plane and leaving behind the soon-to-be-GM Al Harazin to answer for the sewage.

In fact, people close to Cashen say he all but turned over the keys to the ball club that night, realizing the scope of the task ahead was too great for a sixty-four-year-old man. Five weeks later the Mets made it official: Cashen was stepping down, Harazin taking over as GM. But even as early as that

•

night in Pittsburgh, reporters sensed a coup in the making. The beat guys didn't want to bother with Harrelson—the story was bigger than that—but there was little choice, since Harazin was in the tiny visiting manager's office himself after the game. There were a few obligatory questions asked of Harrelson about the embarrassing events on the field, then an awkward silence set in. There was nothing more to ask the manager, but there was no way to begin asking Harazin questions about the state of the Mets—and Harrelson's future—as long as Buddy was sitting there. Finally, Ed Christine, who of all the writers was friendliest with Harrelson, made eye contact, and Buddy understood. "I guess you guys want to talk to Al," he said, rising from his chair and quietly walking out of the office. Even the writers who'd quarreled with Buddy during the summer had to feel sorry for the little manager: evicted from his own office, about to be dissected by his boss.

Harazin didn't say much other than to express the disappointment of the owners as well as the brass, but the evidence was clear: Harrelson might as well have turned out the lights when he left the office. He was a fired manager waiting for the pink slip.

Pittsburgh was no different for the Mets in 1992: It had become their official burial ground. By season's end they would lose eight of nine games there, making a total of twenty-one of twenty-seven during the Pirates' three-year reign as Eastern Division champs. This time it was beyond embarrassing. The Bucs were thoroughly vulnerable, a team without a bullpen or any real power other than what Barry Bonds supplied. Why was it that the Mets still couldn't beat them? Torborg was supposed to return the Mets to sound, fundamental baseball, but his team still didn't have a shred of on-field intuition.

Incredibly, though, since the division lacked anything resembling a powerhouse, a sliver of hope still remained in August: As poorly as they'd played, the Mets were only five and a half games out of first place and knew that a sweep of this two-game series could serve as a resurrection. And while the

•

Mets didn't bother with any false optimism—Bobby Bonilla (fractured rib) and Howard Johnson (fractured wrist) had just gone on the disabled list—everyone knew the team's moment had arrived. Even Jeff Torborg, who hadn't publicly deemed a specific game as important all year, admitted, "We've got to make a stand here." Al Harazin, sensing the urgency, decided he would inspire the Mets with a pregame pep talk.

In all his years as GM, Frank Cashen had had the sense to avoid any rah-rah speeches. It wasn't the little man's nature to make speeches, and he knew any attempt would be perceived as fake. By contrast, Harazin was a far better public speaker, and his decision to help the Mets might not have been a bad idea—except that Harazin wrote out his thoughts on index cards and relied heavily on them. If he wasn't reading his speech, he sure fooled the players. Worse, the GM quoted lines from a Broadway musical, something about overcoming obstacles, keeping the fight alive. Cone groaned, shot a Can-you-believe-this? glance at Franco, and rolled his eyes. Then he lit up a cigarette in the back of the room, hoping to anger Harazin. It was so like Harazin, Cone would say later, so like the corporate Mets of the nineties: a speech with all the right words and no soul. "If he'd spoken from his heart," Cone muttered, "we might've listened."

But no matter how badly Harazin had misplayed the moment, the Mets understood that this game represented their line in the sand. In the dugout, players said there was a do-or-die atmosphere. Taking their last real breath of 1992, the Mets played hard, too. Sid Fernandez and three relievers got them through eleven innings, tied 2–2. Jimmy Leyland had already used two of his best relievers, Stan Belinda and Bob Patterson, to keep the Bucs in the game. Torborg was now down to Franco, his closer, and two other pitchers, thirty-five-year-old journeyman Tom Filer and twenty-seven-year-old Mark Dewey, both recently called up from Tidewater. The manager's handbook said, Play it safe, don't go to your closer until you've got a lead to protect. The circumstances, however, screamed

•

for the manager to show some nerve: Why not summon Franco, extend the game as long as possible, give the Mets the best chance to win?

Ah, how different the summer of '92 might've turned out if Torborg had flirted with the wild side, just once. But as always, he was a connect-the-dots manager, his every move dictated by the numbers or conventional wisdom. The contrast to Leyland would become obvious in a game the following week at Shea. The Pirates manager, annoyed at the way his closer, Belinda, was pitching, yanked him with a 3-and-2 count on Chico Walker and the tying run at first base. Patterson got Walker to fly out and finished off the Mets for the win. Torborg wouldn't think of being so bold, so unorthodox. That's why now he brought in Filer to start the twelfth inning, and immediately Don Slaught was on third base, having singled, stolen second, and been sacrificed to third. At this point, Torborg did bring in Franco, who gave up a game-winning soft liner over the infield to Alex Cole.

Torborg was sitting in the same room that Harrelson had vacated a year earlier, bent over in a chair, staring at the floor, when the writers entered. Because the game had ended so suddenly, it'd taken some ten minutes for the press corps to complete and file their second-edition stories—to be rewritten with quotes for final edition—and get to the clubhouse. So Torborg had already finished his radio show. But there it was, for the first time since before the Bonilla phone call: the Stare. It seemed to pain Torborg to speak, but he made a point of saying how proud he was of the way his team had battled. When the questions about the use of Franco began, he stiffened, sensing an ambush. "There would've been nothing worse than for us to get a lead and not have John to close it out," he said defensively.

It was a terrific game story and easy to write—full of baseball detail and revolving around a singular decision that could be dissected and analyzed over and over in the newspa-

•

per. It was better yet when Franco disagreed with Torborg over the notion that his arm was still too tender to go more than an inning. "I would've never come back from the DL if I wasn't ready to pitch two innings," Franco said pointedly.

Soon enough the beat guys made the walk to the Clark Bar. Billy the bartender kept the kitchen open for the press corps' postmidnight arrivals and always had a hilarious story or two to tell. Rotund, pleasant, but street-smart, Billy saw and heard a lot, serving up beers to players from every team in the league. He judged the importance of a series differently than the Pirates did, ranking teams by how many of their players drank at his bar and how much money they spent. At the top of his party-hearty list were the Mets, Astros, and Phillies, although the Mets had begun to slip in recent years. Billy gave the New York writers high marks for attendance, and why not? It was a good chance to check the pulse of the ball club. Sooner or later the handful of Mets who still ran it hard at night would assemble, often ready and willing to toss the beat guys a bone of information or gossip. Nothing made them more talkative than disgust, and they were full of disgust on this night: disgusted with Harazin and his wooden speech, disgusted with Torborg and his push-button managing, and though they wouldn't admit it, disgusted with their inability to beat the Pirates . . . ever . . . when it mattered.

Interestingly, none of the Mets had yet grasped the possibility that they were being beaten by a superior team. That admission would've been too difficult to make, forced the Mets to rethink their own ability. For now, it was easier to direct their anger outward, especially when there were so many other easy targets. It wasn't just Torborg's putting the game in the hands of Tom Filer ahead of Franco that bothered the Mets. The players couldn't wait to pick the manager apart for bunting with Dave Magadan in the first inning, and then for pinch-running for Magadan at first base in the seventh inning, even though the go-ahead run was already at second. Naturally,

•

Magadan's spot in the lineup came up twice more, both times with runners on base. As a result, the emotional level—perhaps the alcohol level, too—was such that players were only too happy to sit down at the reporters' table and grill the press for a change, everyone chewing on zucchini sticks and washing them down with Coors.

"You believe he ran for Magadan there?" Or "What'd he say about Franco?" Then there was "Didn't he know Leyland would walk Murray if Magadan bunted?" The off-the-record mutiny continued all night. The Mets were growing weary of Torborg: For all his polish and righteousness, he wasn't really all that different from Buddy Harrelson. Certainly he didn't manage from the dugout with any more feel or vision, and both managers were slaves to numbers and the percentage decision. But unlike Harrelson, who managed with only a one-year contract, Torborg had a four-year deal. He wasn't going anywhere and the players knew it, so more than disgust, one could sense the resignation in the players who were sitting in the Clark Bar.

Torborg would take the stories the next day personally. TORBORG MANAGES TO LOSE sneered the back-page headline in the *Post*. Torborg would get word of the stories from his two college-age sons, who had called from back home in New Jersey, and he was incensed. More than anything, Torborg hated to have his image soiled in front of his family. For the first time since he'd blown up at the *Times*'s Joe Sexton, Torborg was cursing at the press like Tommy Lasorda: "You fuckin' guys are gonna have a fuckin' story every time I don't bring fuckin' Franco into the game now, right?"

It hardly mattered anymore. The Mets were finished. They would lose their next six games, eleven of their next twelve, and there would be still more humiliation to endure in Three Rivers Stadium, the Bucs sweeping a three-game series in late September to clinch the division title. Still, the Mets would remember August 4 as the night the fight went out of them for good.

•

AUGUST 6. CHICAGO. CUBS 5, METS 2.

T HE GAMES WERE turning into a blur now. The Mets came to the park, put on their uniforms, played another nine lethargic innings, and then went home. Of the first six Cubs Wally Whitehurst faced that day at Wrigley, five either drew a walk, got a hit, or drove in a run. The Mets were down 2–0 after that first inning, and, in reality, that was it for the night. The rest was watching the outgunned bullpen go through the motions of keeping the game close, although when it really counted, Lee Guetterman allowed Luis Sanchez an RBI double in the seventh, putting the Cubs ahead 5–1. The Mets had now dropped eight and a half games behind the Pirates. No one in the clubhouse really believed they could win the East anymore, so with fifty-six games to go, the problem became how to fill up the time.

The Mets weren't the only team facing this dilemma. After one hundred games, most pennant races have boiled down to two or three teams, meaning there are often three or four teams in each division serving time, waiting for the off-season to hurry up. Generally, teams that are the farthest out of the race arrive at the ballpark the latest, since being in the clubhouse reminds them of their own failure. For a 7:35 game, players are required to be in uniform by 4:45, with batting practice beginning at 5:10. At home, most players arrive between 3:00 and 4:00.

On the road, the deadline is measured by the team bus: It leaves the hotel three hours before game time, and if a player hasn't already taken a cab to the ballpark, he's expected to arrive with the bus. A winning team hardly ever uses the bus—most players are already in the clubhouse, cab after cab delivering them to early-afternoon card games or extra batting-practice sessions. But on teams that have fallen out of the race, the bus can get crowded in August, when no one feels like showing up until the last minute.

•

In-game activity can be a problem, too, especially for relief pitchers and bench players. More and more time is spent in the clubhouse during those meaningless August and September innings. In fact, during the Dodgers' last visit to Shea in 1992, an eventless night in late July, more than half of Tommy Lasorda's team was said to be in the clubhouse, ordering in sandwiches and washing them down with cold beers.

There are certain parks in the National League that are ideal for in-game meals: San Diego serves hot food on the premises. Wrigley is within walking distance of McDonald's; all it takes is a five-dollar tip to a clubhouse boy and a Big Mac can be delivered within minutes. Philly is famed for its ballpark cheese steaks. All these outlets serve bored players, often even the ones involved in pennant races. Not even the most disciplined player can watch nine innings a game, 162 games a year. Clubhouses are full of relief pitchers who have no responsibility before the fifth or sixth innings, or pinch-hitting specialists who aren't enlisted before the seventh inning. The dugout can be like a prison over the course of a summer. What else is there to do on a slow day except eat and watch TV?

One way the Mets filled August's infinity was their NFL rotisserie-league mock draft, which operated like any other fantasy league: The Mets would pick their players, set up pools, then see who brought in the most money. No one made much, really—not in relation to their yearly salaries—but the idea of professional baseball players turning to football as an escape said plenty about the Mets' season. The draft was such serious business for the Mets, Bobby Bonilla even flew in from New York, broken rib and all. Of course, he was scheduled to start taking batting practice around then, but the timing couldn't have been more perfect. As one of Bonilla's teammates said, seeing him burst through the doors of the Wrigley clubhouse in street clothes, "Bobby wasn't going to miss this."

If Bonilla was bored with the season, though, it wasn't hard to blame him. He was only as guilty as the rest of the Mets, unable to find a leader to energize them. Jeff Torborg

•

had long since given up trying to find the recipe. Mostly the manager was reduced to running a hand through his hair after all those losses, exhaling long and hard, and saying, "Boy, that really hurts. We're just not hitting the ball." Not once did Torborg call a team meeting or lash out at his players or attempt even a cosmetic solution like turning over a table in the middle of the clubhouse. For a manager who'd made no secret of a temper and flashes of violence in his past, Torborg was remarkably passive. And that's what made him such an enigma to his players. More than three quarters of the way through the season, the Mets still hadn't figured out their manager. Torborg seemed to have a strong personality, but he had yet to argue with an umpire. Torborg insisted that he hadn't been genuinely provoked all year; thus any show of anger would look manufactured. "And if you're just arguing to argue," he said, "then people will see right through that. There's no point in being phony."

Torborg was right in one sense, but the absence of a response from either him or the front office made the void in the clubhouse seem that much worse. In the lackluster 5–2 loss to the Cubs this night, Eddie Murray did hit a solo home run in the ninth inning, but all Murray's blast did was make the Mets realize they lacked a true cleanup hitter. Even though Murray was batting in the number four spot in Bonilla's absence and had a terrific-looking résumé—who could argue with four hundred career home runs and all those ninety-RBI seasons?—it was clear Murray wasn't the man to lead the Mets. He was too quiet, too self-contained, too full of repressed anger toward the world.

Even that was no crime. Murray was never any different, not in Baltimore, not in Los Angeles, so no one had a right to expect anything else from him in 1992. But every day that went by invoked the ghost of Darryl Strawberry. It was times like these—amid losing streaks in August—that had awakened Strawberry's ego. Darryl became the closest thing New York had seen to a true baseball entertainer since Reggie Jackson.

•

Just like Reggie, Straw had his biggest moments when it counted, when the world was watching—and a good percentage of it was rooting against him.

Strawberry could be loved and hated at the same time, both by fans and teammates. Truth was, that's what made Strawberry so unique as a hitter—the attention. He needed to be booed, needed to be ripped by Mike Lupica in the *News*, needed to rage at Keith Hernandez. It was what made Darryl feel alive. In that sense, there was no replacement for Straw at Shea: not Howard Johnson, not Eddie Murray, not Bobby Bonilla. None of them were as complex, as crazy, as conflicted as Darryl.

One day earlier in the summer, alone in the visitors' clubhouse at Shea, Strawberry had sat at his locker, full of regret. "I miss this place," he said. Strawberry had thought he was leaving the Mets to find peace, and to hurt Frank Cashen in the process, but Straw's only accomplishment had been to hurt himself. Strawberry had never been very good at dealing with the demons inside himself, which explains his sometimes-yes, sometimes-no conversion to born-again Christianity. One month in 1991 Darryl would have that religious, faraway look in his eyes, saying this world—its hostile fans, its tabloids, its small-minded obsession with sports—could no longer hurt him. In response, the Mets would roll their eyes, smile, and say, in Kevin Elster's words, "Just wait." And then, a few months later, word would trickle back through the National League's gossip network that Darryl had returned to the race of men, or at least the race of baseball players, which meant drinking, women, playing clubhouse politics.

That was one area in which Darryl excelled, polarizing the Mets like no other player. For the first five or six years at Shea, he was Keith Hernandez's disciple, swallowing Keith's behind-the-back insults without too much retaliation. But by 1989, when it was obvious Hernandez's career with the Mets would soon end, Strawberry emerged as the strongest personality in the clubhouse. Only, that designation carried its price. To be

•

led by Darryl meant one had to listen to his constant whining about Cashen and about his need for offensive support from the lineup ("I can't do it all by myself," he'd say). This became especially tiresome in 1990, Strawberry's last year in New York. It almost became an inside joke with the media: Need a story? Stoke up Darryl a little, ask him how he feels about Cashen, ask if he's serious about leaving New York. Ready, set, quote.

Teammates were bored with Darryl's threats, the press had memorized all his answers, and management had already made up its mind not to re-sign him. The four-year $15.5 million package they threw at him in November '90 was designed to fail: Cashen was well aware the Dodgers had offered more years (five) and more money ($20 million). So why did the Mets let Strawberry go?

Like all the wild-siders, Strawberry ran a hard nightlife, and as with many Mets in the mid-to-late eighties, the club had its worries about Darryl succumbing to cocaine in the way Dwight Gooden had. Drugs were so prevalent in baseball during that era, any player or pitcher undergoing a prolonged slump was suspect. It wasn't just Darryl. It was Hernandez and Darling and even the little tough guy Wally Backman who were targeted by the rumor machine. In fact, Backman came under direct interrogation from the Mets in 1988, probed by team psychiatrist Allan Lans. The way Lans went after him, Backman was sure someone had whispered an evil rumor in management's ear. And that someone, Backman was convinced, was Hernandez.

To this day, the genesis of their quarrel remains fuzzy, but late in 1988, Backman moved his locker all the way across the clubhouse, just to be away from Hernandez. Once they were neighbors, buddies who bummed cigarettes off each other. But now Backman moved next to Gary Carter—clean-cut and full of smiles and happiness, Backman's antithesis—just so, in his words, "Jefferies would have a space to put his stuff." No one, including Hernandez, believed that excuse: Backman loathed

•

Jefferies. Right after the season Backman was traded to the Twins, an indication, perhaps, of how powerful management's fear of cocaine scandal had become. Even the most subtle hint of drug use could be reason enough for a trade.

But even assuming Darryl had no nightlife problems, there were disturbing signs that money would've been an issue had he stayed at Shea in the nineties. Teammates say Strawberry was so strapped for cash that by 1989 he asked management for a portion of his 1990 salary—normally paid in biweekly installments only after opening day—up front because of a monstrous credit-card debt. It wasn't money he was spending on himself. Strawberry's family and an army of "friends" drained his finances—a problem that seemed to have resolved itself after his conversion to Christianity, although he would pledge 20 percent of his $20 million contract to a small church in Encino, California.

But Strawberry's greatest crime, at least in the eyes of management, was that he hated Gregg Jefferies so openly. In 1989, Jefferies was being groomed as the batting order's heir to Keith Hernandez—quick with the bat, plenty of RBIs, a hitting robot. Never mind that the front office had no idea how little respect Jefferies commanded in the clubhouse. To Frank Cashen and Joe McIlvaine, Jefferies was the player upon whom the Mets could build in the nineties. Strawberry must've sensed his time had come and gone as the most important cog in the Mets' machine, and for that he blamed Jefferies. He blamed the rookie for the way Davey Johnson treated Jefferies. He blamed Jefferies for being too sensitive, for overreacting at every strikeout, for his brooding on the field.

"Imagine if I pulled half the shit Jefferies did? Man, he doesn't know what real pressure is," Strawberry said a year after leaving the Mets. "He's just a baby." What irked Strawberry more than anything was the way Jefferies treated his own bats, a Japanese model he was being paid by the company to use. He would sit at his locker, polishing them with rubbing alcohol to remove marks made by batted balls and keep them shiny. And he would ask equipment manager Charlie Samuels

•

to pack them separately, away from the rest of the Mets' wood, so Jefferies's personal stock wouldn't chip. It was part of the egocentric behavior that eventually made Jefferies a pariah in the clubhouse. One day in Atlanta, Strawberry had seen enough. Moments after Jefferies had handed Samuels one of his bats, the second baseman rushed to make the team bus to the airport. Strawberry—still undressed, always one of the last on the bus—stormed across the room and shouted, "Gimme that bat, Charlie. Gimme the fucking thing."

Samuels was only too happy to oblige. He handed Strawberry Jefferies's prize possession. Darryl ceremoniously walked back across the room and dumped the bat in the trash. "Fuck that fucking bat. Fuck Jefferies," Strawberry mumbled, returning to his locker. Everyone in the clubhouse had, at one time or another, wished they could've defaced Jefferies's bats in some way. But only Strawberry had the balls to actually do it.

Later that same '89 season, Roger McDowell followed suit: He sawed Jefferies's bats in half, then taped them together to make them appear whole. In the middle of a subsequent game in St. Louis, Jefferies broke his favorite bat and returned to the dugout for a replacement. To his astonishment—and delight of the Mets—the new bat collapsed in the rookie's hands.

It was a brilliant gag on McDowell's part, but it was Strawberry who had fired the first shot.

No wonder Darryl's closest friends were the renegades, the Mets least liked by management. The public always assumed Straw's best pal on the team was Dwight Gooden, but that was far from the truth. The two were linked mostly because they were the Mets' only inner-city blacks. Doc was always much more shy, more modest than Darryl, not prone to the same mood swings. Gooden often told friends, "Darryl's a walking time bomb. Always has been." In fact, Gooden would often tease Straw with that indictment, walking by his locker and saying, "Hey Straw, you know what Dr. Lans said about you? He said you're a walking time bomb."

Darryl would just laugh, never bothering to argue with

•

Doc. As long as someone was paying attention to Darryl, he was pleased. Ron Darling used to say, "All D really wants is to be loved." There was a soft, gentle side to Strawberry few ever saw: He never turned down autograph requests from kids, and to this day—whether separated from his wife, Lisa, or trying one more time to make his marriage work—Strawberry has always worshiped his two children. Still, poor judgment could take Darryl to uncivilized lengths, such as the time the Mets decided to harass a female reporter at Wrigley Field.

Carrie Muskat, then a correspondent for UPI, was conducting herself professionally in the clubhouse one afternoon in 1990, when all of a sudden a bunch of players descended upon her. Through the years, the Mets have been generally fair with female reporters, but all it takes is one player to yell "cockwatcher," and she's doomed. "Cockwatcher" is a term to describe any female in the clubhouse—newspaper or radio reporter, TV person, camera operator—who, the players believe, likes to stare at naked men.

Ironically, it's the born-again Christians who find women's presence in the clubhouse so offensive. Of all the Mets who resented female reporters in recent years, it was Tommy Herr—a thoroughbred Bible-studier—who would be the first to sneer, "We got us a cockwatcher today," as soon as a woman approached with a microphone or notebook. Even the gentlest among Christian athletes, Dale Murphy, couldn't accept the idea of women invading the locker room, the final domain of male athletes.

Conversely, it was the wild-side Mets who—despite years of womanizing—welcomed women trying to do their job. Strawberry was rarely guilty of obstructing a female interviewer. In fact, he usually went out of his way to be polite, seeming to enjoy the attention he thought he was getting. But like most Mets, Darryl was just flattering himself, and in this case, Muskat was working the clubhouse like the rest of the press corps, asking questions of one player or another, taking notes, paying no attention to the other Mets, who were in

•

various states of undress. But that didn't matter to Strawberry, who was standing near Muskat, quite naked himself.

Straw took a dish of ice cream from the food table, returned to his locker, and began using various body parts to mix the ice cream with chocolate sauce. Muskat took one sideways glance at the prank and decided it was best to simply ignore Strawberry. But Darryl was having fun with the dessert: too much fun, in fact. Dave Cone came over and poured a cold beer on Strawberry, starting from the waist down, saying, "You need to cool off, partner."

The Mets were nearly delirious with laughter, wondering if they'd pushed Muskat's sensibilities to the outer limits. And they had: She angrily left the clubhouse, and soon after filed a letter of protest to the Mets. The club apologized on Darryl's behalf, but trying to get Straw to say "I'm sorry" was, in those days anyway, impossible. What else could the Mets do except wait for the man-child to grow up?

AUGUST 8. CHICAGO. CUBS 4, METS 3.

D AVE MAGADAN HAD never suffered a broken wrist in his life, but he knew instantly something terrible had happened between first and second base. Here it was, the fifth inning, and Magadan was about to be forced out at second by Kevin Bass's grounder. Ryne Sandberg fielded the ball cleanly and flipped to Luis Sanchez, who was ready to fire a strike to Mark Grace. Everyone at Wrigley Field was already scribbling 4–6–3 in their scorebooks: The heavy-legged Magadan had no chance to beat Sandberg's throw to Sanchez, and Bass had hit the ball too hard to avoid being doubled up.

Out of sheer reflex, Magadan raised both his hands as he started his slide, and at the next moment, he felt a sickening sensation in his left wrist. It was his bone shattering, making a sound Magadan likened to "eggshells cracking." He went down in an awful collapse, and, just by the way the trainers huddled around him, it was clear his season was over. The injuries were

•

coming at the Mets in a flurry now—fourteen players would spend time on the disabled list in '92—but Magadan's injury, coupled with Willie Randolph's four days later, wasn't just depressing; it left the Mets fielding something resembling a Triple-A lineup.

Like the Mets, the beat guys were having trouble with the idea that, for the second straight August, there'd be no pennant race to cover. In some respects that was fine: No race meant less interest in New York, fewer demands from the editors in the office, a quiet month before the postseason crush.

One of the suburban guys remembered calling his office during that road trip, offering his ideas for an early-edition story on Kevin Bass, detailing the possible angles to pursue about the outfielder the Mets had acquired from the Giants only a few days earlier.

The editor listened politely for a few moments, then finally cut off his reporter. "Look, whatever you wanna do is fine. Just keep it tight, will ya?" The newsman put the phone down, stunned by the revelation that, in his words, "No one gives a fuck about the Mets anymore. Not even my own paper."

It was true: At home, the Mets were lucky to draw even twenty thousand, as New York turned its attention to the upcoming football season. Trouble was, there were still seven weeks to go, and game stories were becoming impossible to produce. That's why losing Magadan hurt so much. He was one of the few good guys left from the eighties. Privately, the beat guys hoped the Mets would re-sign Magadan as a free agent, but his tenure with the club would clearly come to an end by September. That's when Magadan reported that his wrist had healed, but he was sitting at home alone in Tampa because the Mets never bothered to call. In fact, when a reporter informed Al Harazin of Magadan's recovery, the GM, eating lunch in the dining room at Wrigley, looked up from his plate and said simply, "Is that right?"

Magadan knew then that there'd be no returning to the

•

Mets in 1993. He doubted they'd even offer him a contract or pursue him as a free agent. And he was right: When Magadan signed a two-year deal in December with the Florida Marlins worth $1.4 million, he walked away from the Mets without ever having received a phone call. It was an inglorious end to a career that never was. As Magadan put it, "I never did have the success with the Mets I imagined I would. I always thought I'd have a longer, better career in New York than that."

And that regret is what led Magadan to an expansion team. He took the Marlins' offer, knowing full well he'd be part of a team that would lose close to one hundred games in 1993. To Magadan the wins and losses hardly mattered now. "I want to show some people, the Mets, actually, that I can still play. The Marlins were the only ones who guaranteed me everyday playing time. I had chances to be a DH or be a part-time player, but I want to play every day to prove the Mets wrong."

Willie Randolph's season was virtually ended as well when he joined Magadan on the disabled list, struck in the hand by a Bob Walk fastball, the bone splintering badly. By mid-August Randolph had lost much of his bat speed, not to mention life in his legs. He seemed more brittle than ever, although that was hardly his fault. At thirty-eight, the former Yankee was a perfect free-agent addition to the Mets, still capable of turning a fine double play, able to give the Mets an anchor in the number two spot, as long as he wasn't overused. But Jeff Torborg must've thought this was 1982, not 1992, because he forced Randolph to play every day, burning him out by mid-summer. The manager couldn't resist Willie's appeal: a loyal soldier, selfless behind Vince Coleman, and one of the most well-liked players in or out of the clubhouse.

Randolph kept a locker in the farthest corner of the Mets' home, away from the cold war the press and players waged with each other. He could be found, day after day, listening to his headphones or sharing a joke with Dwight Gooden or giving an honest, in-depth interview with just about any reporter who asked. Randolph didn't hold grudges, didn't bullshit anyone,

•

didn't need to have his ego massaged. Everyone in the club-house knew 1992 would be his first and last year with the Mets—maybe his last in baseball—so when he went down, holding his hand in pain after absorbing Walk's fastball, it seemed like a cruel joke from the baseball gods.

Bravely, Randolph stuck out the season, waiting through two months of rehab just to get his final at-bats for 1992. On October 4, the Mets' 162nd game, Randolph went 0-for-3 in a 2–0 loss to the Pirates. Afterward Randolph said it was all worth it: all the rehab, the days of endless bad baseball, all this when he could've easily gone home and collected the rest of his $800,000 salary. But he had wanted one more game, "just so my season wouldn't have to end this way. I wanted to give something back to all the people who've supported me over the years." The beat guys nodded to themselves, all of them thinking what a great job it would be, year after year, pennant race or not, if everyone in the game had the integrity of Willie Randolph.

AUGUST 23. SAN DIEGO. PADRES 4, METS 3.

THE GAMES FELT more awful each day, as the guys on the beat desperately sought ways to keep themselves interested. Historically, the second West Coast trip of the season had been the stepping stone to great September theater for the Mets, but all this trip offered was the daily chore of recalculating the already absurd math. At fourteen and a half games out, the Mets stood a reasonable chance of finishing last, or at least getting to ninety losses. The players themselves were beyond embarrassment—in fact, the Mets had long since switched to automatic pilot, distancing themselves from the day-to-day pain. Interestingly, that provided some short-term success, as the Mets went 5-4 on the Coast, then came home to sweep the Reds in a four-game series.

But that didn't make a dent in the public's—or the reporters'—perception of the Mets. More than ever, walking into the

•

clubhouse became an us-against-them venture, nobody having a pertinent question to ask anymore, no one really wanting to talk about the season. The search for story angles bordered on desperation, although two of the beat guys had the advantage of being newcomers.

In midsummer Mark Hermann had replaced Marty Noble for *Newsday*. Noble, a fifteen-year veteran, had been reassigned to cover the business end of baseball, although there were hard feelings with his superiors. Noble had been pressured from *Newsday* editors, he told coach Dave LaRoche, to "write trash, and I wasn't going to do that." Noble's writing had never revealed any real love for baseball, not in a purist's sense. When not delving into players' contracts and salaries, Noble seemed more interested in the Mets' personal behavior—their clothes, their eating habits, their friendships—than in fastballs and home runs. He devoted an entire daily story during spring training to the Mets players' different musical tastes, and later remarked to a colleague that he thought it was the best story he'd written all spring. When *Newsday* pushed him in another direction, Noble resisted, and the decision to make him a baseball-labor reporter was probably the best compromise possible. Indeed, Noble switched beats just in time, just as Fay Vincent was going down in an owners' mutiny.

For the *Newark Star-Ledger*, New Jersey's largest paper, Roger Farrell replaced Dan Castellano, a switch that wounded many of the players. Castellano would've been welcome in the Met clubhouse into the twenty-first century, but poor health had forced him back to the office in a copy-editing job. Danny was missed in the press box, too, but said one day over the phone, "You know something—I don't miss this shit at all." The beat had worn out even its most benevolent soul, and the remaining guys—Sexton from the *Times*, Christine from Gannett, as well as Harper and Klapisch—wondered how much more meaningless baseball they could swallow.

The beat guys barely worried about competing for stories anymore; the '92 Mets simply didn't generate any news. That

•

made it easier for the reporters to be friends, not having to worry if the guy you were sharing a beer with or playing three-on-three hoops with had an exclusive ready to go in the next day's paper. Five years earlier, in the Mets' prime, covering the club was as intense and competitive as any beat in professional sports. Even two years before, as the Mets' crash became real, the competitiveness still bordered on maniacal. After all, the disgraced Mets were just as entertaining as the prosperous Mets, outraging and fascinating the city at the same time. As a result, relationships on the beat were ever fragile, always vulnerable to the stress of competing for stories.

It was on the first West Coast trip of the '90 season when Howard Johnson, sensing a crisis during Davey Johnson's final days, and following a loss to the Padres, announced his intention to call a team meeting the next day in L.A.

Because of differing deadline requirements, Harper, Christine, and Steve Pate of the now-defunct *National* all had left the clubhouse and returned to the press box before HoJo had emerged from the shower and begun his interviews. Klapisch stayed long enough to get the story, as did Noble from *Newsday* and Mike Martinez from the *Times*. Things got sticky when Klapisch climbed into a rented car for the two-and-a-half-hour drive up to L.A. with the three reporters who didn't have the story. It was an awful moral dilemma for the *Daily News* veteran. As the radio blasted away, the four reporters unwound, mocking one another's papers, and then one another. Pate got it for a southern accent Christine liked to call "pure white trash." Christine was ribbed for his undying loyalty to the marine corps. In fact, that afternoon at San Diego's Jack Murphy Stadium, the Padres had invited a contingent of locally stationed sailors and marines to the ballpark. Klapisch asked Christine why the two groups were seated on opposite ends of the stadium.

"Why? I'll tell you why. Because anyone in the navy is scared shit of a marine," Christine said pointedly.

"That right?" Klapisch said. "I overheard a couple of

•

sailors talking in the bathroom. They said anytime they need a workout, they put a marine in the hospital."

"Listen, dickhead," Christine said, devouring the bait. "No fucking sailor stands a chance against a marine. Got that? One marine equals twenty fucking pussies from the navy."

That said, Christine leaned back in his seat, satisfied. "By the way," he added, "how many marines come from Columbia?"

"Not too many—you're right," Klapisch said. "We're too busy producing baseball stars: Lou Gehrig, Gene Larkin, Bob Klapisch."

Harper laughed out loud. "Yeah, right. Tell us the Ron Darling story again. You struck him out when he was at Yale, I know."

"Bullshit, man," Pate said (except it came out "Boool-sheeeet").

"Yeah, total bullshit," Christine said.

"Big fucking deal," Harper said. "Am I missing something? Is Darling in the big leagues for his pitching or his hitting?"

"Wait, wait," Klapisch said, looking at Harper in his rear-view mirror. "I have to hear this one more time. You can turn a better double play than Jefferies, right?"

"Don't insult me," Harper said with a certain disgust. "My six-year-old kid can turn a better double play than Jefferies."

For hours, the jokes flew, until Christine finally got around to asking if anything important had been said in the clubhouse after he'd gone upstairs.

Was Klapisch obligated to share the quotes? Professionally, no. Morally, maybe, because it wasn't the *News*'s story alone. The standard rule among reporters went like this: If you've got an exclusive, keep it to yourself. But if a colleague misses a quote because of deadline restraints and most of the competition is there to record it, then the struggling reporter gets help from the pack. This time, the cut went right down the

•

middle. Three papers had HoJo, three didn't. Now, full of guilt, Klapisch avoided the question and managed to change the subject without arousing suspicion.

Harper and Klapisch didn't speak for days after the *News* blew up the team-meeting story the next day, fully aware that the *Post* had missed out. In fact, some of the bad blood lingered into the next season.

But by 1992, the Mets had accomplished the near-impossible: They had dulled the press corps' cutthroat instincts. Thanks to numbingly bad baseball, the New York press corps had been bonded by indifference.

AUGUST 27. NEW YORK.

JAY HORWITZ STARTED making the phone calls at about 10 A.M., knowing he would be waking most of the beat writers from a dead sleep. This was a cruel trick, the morning after a West Coast trip, but Horwitz had no choice: Dave Cone had been traded. The words didn't register immediately for some of the writers, half comatose as they were. Most had taken red-eye flights home from San Francisco, touching down at LaGuardia or Newark at 7 A.M., getting home and falling into bed for some sleep after 8 A.M. For Mets writers, the red-eyes were not unlike postgame interviews with Eddie Murray. You went in expecting the worst and therefore rarely emerged disappointed: Surely the people who can sleep for an extended period in airplane seats are the same people who can eat a pizza with the works day after day and never gain a pound. So a veteran reporter plays it smart. He pulls out the laptop computer and writes the next day's story on the plane, thereby ensuring a few extra hours of sleep upon landing. At least a few of the beat guys had done so, and, ironically, Cone was the subject of the stories. A group of writers had cornered him the day before in San Francisco, partly because his impending free-agent status was the only remaining story of any real interest, and partly because August 31 was the cutoff date

•

for a player to be eligible for the postseason. If Cone was going to be traded, it would surely be in the next few days.

There was no sense among the writers, however, that he was about to be sent away. We had been scoffing at Cone's own suspicions, and two weeks earlier, Harazin had said flatly that he wasn't going to trade Cone, preferring to take his chances trying to re-sign him after the season. In addition, there hadn't been so much as a whisper around the league that the Mets were ready to trade Cone. If he was being shopped, word would've trickled out. Instead, the stories written on the plane home from San Francisco, the stories that suddenly became useless, said there was a growing likelihood Cone would sign elsewhere for 1993.

Off the record, Cone had told a few writers he'd heard through the grapevine that the Yankees and Phillies were both prepared to bid heavily for his services. In fact, Cone said he'd been openly recruited by Phillies players and even a couple of their coaches the last time the Mets had been in Philadelphia. Cone said he'd have no trouble playing for either of those teams, and admitted that the idea of moving across town was seductive. In addition, Cone said he'd received no indication the Mets would be willing to meet the market price to keep him. This was as forthright as Cone had been all year about the possibility of leaving, even off the record. And though the information couldn't be attributed to him, it could be cited in a story as coming from "a source." The source could be from anywhere one chose; as long as it didn't point to Cone, he didn't mind. In other words, it worked very neatly as an off-day story. Then the phone rang.

Cone was hurt by the trade. Deep down he wanted to be romanced by the Mets and paid handsomely to stay. He still loved New York. He and his girlfriend had an apartment on Manhattan's East Side, off Second Avenue. It was a rent-controlled bargain at seven hundred dollars a month, and Cone had his pick of dozens of restaurants and bars, all within walking distance. He didn't need money—he was careful with his finances, saying earlier in the summer he had nearly $4 million tucked away in conservative investment accounts—but at the same time, Cone was ready to demand top dollar. He had taken a huge gamble by turning down the guaranteed $16.8 million in January and he'd gone out and pitched well, almost single-handedly keeping the Mets at least within striking distance of the Pirates for most of the season.

Meanwhile, the market had inflated still further. Greg Maddux and Doug Drabek each had recently turned down five-year deals worth in excess of $25 million. The Mets knew it wouldn't be easy to re-sign Cone, and they used that as justification for the trade. They were right, but the Mets were making a huge public-relations blunder by dealing him without having so much as a token conversation with his agent.

It gave Cone an opening to bludgeon the club, and he was smart enough to take advantage. "How would they know they can't afford me?" Cone asked out loud. "They never even asked me what it would take." Cone played the moment perfectly, making himself available to the media all day. He took writers' calls, he went on WFAN with Mike and the Mad Dog, charming them for twenty minutes straight. Cone then put on a tie and jacket and took a cab over to Shea Stadium, where he did one-on-one interviews with every TV station in the city. Cone didn't exactly defame the Mets—he just did his best to make sure public sentiment was his.

Not that it was necessary. The outcry was deafening. No one but the rotisserie players in New York had ever heard of Jeff Kent, the infielder acquired in the trade, and the Mets could only call outfielder Ryan Thompson "a player to be named later" because they couldn't add him to the roster until September 1. The equation was appalling: two nobodies for a pitcher who was on his way to leading the league in strikeouts for the third straight time, a pitcher who hadn't missed a start since 1987, a pitcher who was 13-7 at the time of the trade. It was a difficult decision to defend, particularly by an organization that had thrown so much money at free agents Vince

Coleman, Eddie Murray, and Bobby Bonilla. And as recently as March, the Mets had made John Franco the highest-paid reliever in baseball.

It was impossible for New York's baseball community to digest. Fans screamed on WFAN all day. Writers, after researching the reports on Kent and Thompson, mostly came to the same conclusion: Both players were considered good prospects but neither was a true blue-chipper. The Mets were desperate for help at these positions because the upper levels of their farm system were virtually bare. But trading Cone to replenish the stock? It was a terribly high price to pay, especially considering Gooden, struggling in his first year back from shoulder surgery, was on his way to the first losing season of his career.

The beat writers felt no guilt in writing from Cone's corner. It would've been difficult to applaud any trade of Cone, but this was license to write punishingly. Most everyone did, too, with one exception. Mike Lupica shocked the city by defending the same Mets brass he had shredded with criticism in recent years. New York's most influential sports columnist, Lupica had scored another coup by going against public opinion and thereby placing himself in the middle of the controversy.

Lupica himself admitted he made up his mind about the Cone trade after listening to WFAN, hearing wave upon wave of callers who pleaded for Cone to come back. It was perfectly natural for Lupica to listen to WFAN to get a feel for the city's baseball pulse. The station had become such a force in the industry that it could influence the way stories were presented in the newspaper, particularly stories such as this, which broke early in the day, giving the radio station hours to discuss and dissect it. By the time a newspaper reaches the stands twenty-four hours later, most readers have already reached the saturation level and have one more reason not to buy it, no matter how outrageous or clever the headline.

The war to find such a fresh angle will ultimately decide

•

the tabloids' fate in New York. For decades, a newspaper represented the public's only conduit to the ball club. But then came television, and soon enough reporting the scores wasn't enough; it was old news. Then newspaper reporters trekked to the clubhouse, where postgame quotes became their staple. But soon WFAN and the ever-intrusive TV cameras launched an invasion there, too, and newspapers, in full retreat, were left with only one weapon: the exclusive news story, or, at the very least, a unique point of view.

Lupica had no trouble deciding which way the wind was blowing in the wake of the Cone trade. As he put it, "I heard this hysterical reaction on the radio, and I couldn't understand it. Dave Cone is a very fine pitcher, but he will never be a great pitcher. I told my friends that day, 'I thought the Mets traded Dave Cone, but apparently they just traded Tom Seaver.'"

As close as Lupica had become to Cone over the years, often relying on the pitcher for off-the-record information about the Mets, Lupica decided to side with the front office. Although he knew he would stand alone in this controversy—just as Dick Young had outraged an entire city by endorsing Tom Seaver's trade to the Reds in 1977—Lupica was sure he was right, sure that Cone wasn't coming back to the Mets as a free agent, and, as he put it, "I don't believe there's any nobility in begging." And Lupica had also gotten close enough to Fred Wilpon to understand ownership's feeling that it was throwing away huge sums of money.

At some point in August, as the Mets were becoming a laughingstock and tickets were going unsold at Shea, Wilpon notified Harazin that the vault was now locked. With more than $16 million worth of salaries on the disabled list, Wilpon had vowed to stop playing the fool to long-term contracts. He informed Harazin there would be no $25 million to sign Cone to a five-year contract. Harazin was never ordered to trade Cone, but a suddenly budget-conscious ownership began pushing him in that direction.

Even if Harazin's hand was forced, though, he played it

•

poorly. He never did shop Cone. He waited for offers, and when the Jays teased the Mets with the chance to pick up two prospects from a limited list, Harazin nearly jumped through his own flesh. Relying heavily on scout Paul Ricciarini, who had worked previously for Toronto and Triple-A manager Clint Hurdle, the Mets decided on Kent and Thompson in a matter of two days. Harazin still had four days before the roster deadline, but he had no intention of calling another contender to let them know Cone was available. What might the Orioles or Brewers have offered the Mets to both acquire Cone and prevent him from going to Toronto? The A's? All they did four days later was trade José Canseco. Even the Expos, an organization, like the Blue Jays, thick with prospects, might've been willing to deal for Cone in hopes of catching the Pirates. But Harazin wanted to do the deal quickly. He was worried that the media would pick up the scent if he began talking to other teams, and he feared the Blue Jays would be offended and pull back their offer. That's how paranoid Harazin had become, and his fear cost him a chance at a better deal for better players.

A more experienced GM would have dangled Cone and taken the deal to the eleventh hour, hoping at least one team would panic and raise its bid significantly. Instead, Harazin made the deal, stunning his fellow GMs and prompting both the Orioles and A's to call a day later with the same question: Why hadn't Harazin let them know Cone's right arm was available?

In any case, Cone was on his way to the World Series, his name now written alongside those of Mitchell, Backman, Dykstra, Ojeda, Darling, and other important Mets of the eighties who'd been traded, most with disappointing results for New York. Kent and Thompson, both of whom the Mets are hoping will be everyday players in '93, ultimately will decide the wisdom of this deal. But newspapers have no such patience. Instant judgments are the fuel of this industry, so for Harazin there was no escape. Lupica's endorsement saved him from a public flogging, but the GM was still wrapped up in the long,

•

mean tentacles of the second-guessers. Indeed, the man the tabloids had celebrated as a genius on the back page nine months earlier for acquiring Bret Saberhagen was now pictured on the front page of the *Post*—with a dunce cap superimposed on his head. It was that kind of year.

FIVE BEST METS MEMORIES OF THE EIGHTIES

1. Bill Buckner.
2. Game Six of the '86 NLCS against the Astros.
3. Darryl Strawberry's clock home run in 1985 in St. Louis.
4. Lenny Dykstra's home run in Game Three of the '86 NLCS.
5. The parachute that landed at Shea during Game Six of the '86 World Series.

SEPTEMBER

SEPTEMBER 1. NEW YORK. BRAVES 4, METS 1.

S O M U C H H A D turned out wrong for the Mets since 1986. So many decisions had exploded on them, so many graduates of Cashen Tech had turned up on the covers of magazines or on TV in October. Lenny Dykstra turned into an All-Star after the Mets traded him for Juan Samuel, a man who hated New York only slightly more than he hated center field. Kevin Mitchell won an MVP award and led the Giants to the World Series in 1989 after he was dealt for Kevin McReynolds. Rick Aguilera and Kevin Tapani became key members of the world champion Twins in 1991 after going there as part of the five-player package for Frank Viola. Viola: a pitcher whose second-half evaporations killed the Mets for two seasons. Wally Backman came back to play a significant role with the division-champion Pirates in 1990, two years after the Mets had traded him to the Twins for three minor league pitchers who never made it. Randy Myers won a world championship as a closer for the Reds in 1990 after he was traded for John Franco, whose awful September that year cost the Mets dearly. Al Peña turned into a late-inning savior for the Braves, pitching them into the World Series in 1991 only weeks after the Mets traded him for the immortal Tony Castillo. In October '92 Ron Darling would pitch the A's into the playoffs a year after the Mets traded him for Tim Burke, who may be long remembered as the worst pitcher to ever make $2 million a year. And finally, Dave Cone would pitch the Blue Jays to the

•

club's first world championship two months after he was traded for Jeff Kent and Ryan Thompson.

There were so many critical mistakes by the same management team, you often had to stop and ask: Were these the same men who'd rescued the Mets from the ash heap in 1980? What happened to the foresight, even the common sense? From ignoring the chemistry Ray Knight provided, to planning the future around Gregg Jefferies, to putting Buddy Harrelson in charge, to letting Darryl Strawberry leave, the Mets were a study in mismanagement. But this night provided a vivid reminder that the single worst decision made during the Mets' decline was signing Vince Coleman. When he openly confronted and then pushed Jeff Torborg on the field after the manager intervened in an argument, Coleman earned himself a two-game suspension, punctuating two years of injuries and hostility that had already made him an embarrassment to the Mets.

He had no business being a Met in the first place. Everyone in baseball knew that. Coleman personified the new breed of artificial-turf players, marginal major league hitters who could reach base chopping the ball off the carpet, becoming offensive forces on the strength of their awesome speed. Turf had given the game a face-lift in the last twenty years, putting a premium on speed, especially in the National League, where six stadiums were carpeted. Teams began tailoring rosters to fit their ballpark. Whitey Herzog made the Cardinals a powerhouse in the eighties, going to three World Series, by emphasizing speed and defense. Coleman became a huge factor, leading the league in stolen bases six straight years. But he owed his success to turf. Turned into a switch-hitter in the minors, he could chop the ball into the turf—especially when hitting left-handed—and outrun the play to first base often enough to make him dangerous. In 1987, Coleman struck out 126 times yet still managed to hit .289 and steal 109 bases. Basically, anytime Coleman made contact he created panic in the opposition. Against the Mets he always seemed to beat out an infield

•

chopper in the late innings, steal second and maybe third, too, then score on a sacrifice fly to tie or win a game. In fact, he stole 57 straight against the Mets, until Mackey Sasser finally threw him out in 1990 to end the streak.

Meanwhile, the Mets had been looking for a leadoff hitter since trading Dykstra in '89, and then when Strawberry left in November 1990, they were really panicked. Their answer was to replace power with speed. Ah, how smug the Mets had been for years: turning away from free agency, saying it contradicted their philosophy of drafting and developing talent. Only now, with their farm system near naked from trades and three to four years of bad drafts, the Mets were ready to embrace the new order of baseball: talent for cash.

What really hurt was Joe McIlvaine's sudden departure—a defection, really—to San Diego in September '90, leaving a huge void in the organization. McIlvaine, whose reputation as a smart operator was built mostly on the steal of Dave Cone from the Royals, had made some ill-conceived trades, but he knew talent. He'd been running the baseball end of the Mets' operation for a few years, with Cashen acting more and more as merely an adviser. Cashen never expected McIlvaine to leave, and the elderly GM wasn't prepared to assume the day-to-day responsibilities of working the phones, combing the league for players the Mets could acquire in trades. Al Harazin and Gerry Hunsicker took the reins by default. Hunsicker, a former minor league pitching coach, scout, and assistant GM with the Astros, had left baseball to work in investment banking for five years, then returned in '88, hired by the Mets as an elixir for the organization's minor league ailments. Now, following McIlvaine's departure, he began to emerge in the Mets' decision-making process.

With both Coleman and fellow Cardinals outfielder Willie McGee available as free agents, Hunsicker favored McGee, noting that he was a true .300-type line-drive hitter and not just a turf creation. Harazin and Cashen, however, were determined to fill the need for a pure leadoff hitter, regardless of the

•

obvious flaws in Coleman's game. They were aware also that Coleman wasn't exactly Gandhi. They knew that Whitey Herzog had kept his distance from Coleman, and that Herzog had ultimately resigned in disgust as manager of the Cardinals in 1990 in part because of his difficulties with Coleman. Nevertheless Harazin and Cashen flew to Chicago to have dinner with Coleman and his agent, Richie Bry. Coleman passed the polite-manners audition. Harazin said in a casual conversation to a reporter a few days later, referring to Dwight Gooden and Coleman, "They're both real gentlemen."

If that sounded like a white executive patronizing black ballplayers, well, it's probably not what Harazin intended. Much like Cashen, he had a sincere fondness for Gooden. The only time the press had observed genuine emotion from the ever-poised, ever-corporate Harazin was the day in the spring of 1991 that negotiations on a long-term contract with Gooden broke down. Gooden would rethink his self-imposed deadline and eventually sign a three-year extension worth a guaranteed $15.45 million, but that day it appeared he was on his way toward free agency. Harazin, his voice choked with emotion, called it "the most difficult day for me since I've been here."

Still, there could be no denying management's concern about the racial makeup of the Mets as they pursued Coleman. Outfielder Brett Butler would be available shortly as a new-look free agent, the result of a court ruling that had declared owners guilty of collusion during the late eighties, but with Strawberry gone, Gooden and Daryl Boston were the only blacks on the ball club. New York City was awash in racial violence, and baseball was being scrutinized for its racial policies in the wake of Dodger GM Al Campanis's infamous racist remarks on ABC's *Nightline*.

The Mets knew they had to bring more black players into the clubhouse in the nineties, both for image and on-field success. It wasn't the sole reason they signed Coleman—they could have pursued Willie McGee—but it was a consideration. And soon enough Coleman was a Met, even though no other

•

team aside from the Cardinals even made him an offer. Bry kept the Mets waiting, no doubt correctly reading their state of desperation. In truth, Coleman was just hoping to use the Mets' interest to coax more money out of the Cardinals. He and his wife and two sons had made St. Louis their home and really didn't want to leave, and Coleman was well aware that he wasn't likely to be as effective on grass. But the Cardinals wouldn't offer more than a three-year contract, so when the Mets agreed to go to four years at $11.95 million, Coleman was officially seduced.

On paper, the results spoke for themselves: For seven straight years the Mets had finished no worse than second place, always in a pennant race. With Coleman as the offensive catalyst, the Mets promptly finished fifth twice and were out of the race both times by August. He missed 180 games during those two seasons, all but a few because of injury, and earned the designation as the most antagonistic Met in the clubhouse since Dave Kingman. There was always an angry cloud around Coleman, one that never went away. He and the media were at odds from the start. Accustomed to dealing with a single beat writer from the only newspaper in St. Louis, Coleman had no patience for the army of New York reporters. "It's all I been doing since I signed is talkin' to the media," Coleman barked at Jay Horwitz the very first day he arrived at spring training. After much cajoling by Horwitz, Coleman agreed to speak with reporters that day, but he made it clear he didn't like it. When the injuries began, he got nastier. A question like "How's the leg, Vince?" more than once produced an answer like, "What the fuck's it matter to you?"

Coleman would spend his pregame hours with Daryl Boston. A reporter who ventured over was usually met with a hostile stare. Finally, an icy coexistence was forged between the beat guys and Coleman. He would answer the most necessary questions as long as you stayed away from his locker at all other times.

Coleman could be equally short with teammates, and his

•

obscenity-filled tirade directed at hitting instructor Mike Cubbage during batting practice in San Diego in 1991 was an example of just how hostile he could be. The incident was even more damaging to the Mets than it should have been because Buddy Harrelson refused to admonish his player. Coleman had lashed out at Cubbage in full view of teammates and early-arriving fans all because Cubbage told Coleman that his batting-practice group—the Mets, like most teams, hit in groups of four—wasn't due in the cage for another ten minutes. Cubbage was startled and offended by Coleman's language and how abusive he was: In essence Coleman told him to go fuck himself. But the coach restrained himself, reasoning it wasn't his place to pick a fight with a player. Indeed, coaches, most of whom earn between fifty and seventy thousand dollars a year, carry little weight with the ball clubs.

It's the manager's responsibility to demand respect for his coaches. When Coleman challenged Cubbage, he was issuing the same challenge to Harrelson. But Buddy wanted no part of negotiating a truce with Coleman: The situation was potentially too explosive. When the beat writers asked if he would order Coleman to apologize, Harrelson stared at his feet and said, "What if he says no? Then what do I do?" That was early August, and that was when all of New York knew Harrelson wouldn't be back in '92.

It was a seemingly kinder, gentler Coleman who came to spring training in 1992, wanting to establish a better relationship with the press. He was more cordial at times with reporters, but then he pulled a hamstring four days into the season. For the second straight year injuries ruined him, and he went back to being as nasty as he was miserable. No one accused Coleman of not wanting to play. Teammates said his effort to get in shape was honest enough, and between the lines Coleman played hard. But the injuries made him a target for ridicule. In his very first at-bat after coming back from the hamstring injury in '92, he pulled a rib-cage muscle striking out in Atlanta. "Feeling a little discomfort" became Coleman's catch-

·

phrase, uttered so many times the beat guys unconsciously began using it in on their own. "This fucking story," a reporter would say to an empty screen, "is giving me a little discomfort."

But as hostile as Coleman could be to the media, he always seemed to be laughing in the clubhouse with the few teammates he was close to. He'd be sitting with Daryl Boston and Anthony Young and Doc Gooden, and Coleman's laugh would pierce the clubhouse. Actually, it was more like a cackle, high-pitched and distinctive, crawling right under your skin. "It's like a goddamn toothache," one player said, listening to Coleman. "It never goes away." Torborg and his coaches didn't particularly care for it, especially since Coleman seemed to have no sense of clubhouse parliamentary procedure: He'd be on the DL, cackling away in a corner with Boston after the Mets had lost an extra-inning game. Torborg's face would be like a closed fist as he filled his plate at the food table, seemingly debating whether to personally silence Coleman for good.

Finally, on this night in September Coleman gave Torborg no choice. Thoroughly frustrated by his injuries, Coleman had been thrown out of a game in the first inning two nights earlier against the Braves, and now it happened again when he was called out on a check swing his second time up. By the time Torborg reached him, Coleman had already been ejected by umpire Gary Darling and was arguing wildly. Torborg, no small man, got in front of Coleman and pushed him away from Darling. Coleman expected Torborg to argue on his behalf, but the manager was tired of Coleman's antics and instead focused his attention solely on his player, giving him another push toward the dugout.

That was when Coleman exploded. "What the fuck you pushin' me for?" he yelled at Torborg, and gave a token push of his own before Bobby Bonilla grabbed him and hustled him off the field. Torborg was enraged but kept his composure on the field. As Coleman went into the clubhouse, Torborg walked back to the dugout. But then as play resumed, Torborg

•

marched the length of the dugout, turned, and sprinted up the runway for a clubhouse confrontation with Coleman.

People who saw it, and there were a few, said it was one of the most heated player-manager wars they'd ever witnessed anywhere in baseball. Torborg demanded an apology. Coleman told the manager, "Go fuck yourself," and accused Torborg of trying to show him up by refusing to argue with the umpire.

WHICH WAY TO COOPERSTOWN?
—J.H.

B Y SEPTEMBER 1992, there seemed to be nothing a Met could say that would make New York notice. Fans only wanted the worst team money could buy to get lost for the winter already. But then Vince Coleman uttered the words that are destined to haunt him until the day he takes his tender hamstrings to the great artificial-turf stadium in the sky: "What this field is doing is keeping me out of the Hall of Fame."

I was sitting with Coleman at his locker when he said it, the only reporter in the vicinity. At that moment, I could not have been more astonished if he'd said he'd just murdered Jeff Torborg and told me I could find the body in his office. Covering the Mets for five years had worn down my shock-value quotient—Darryl Strawberry retired the trophy for most controversial and contradictory proclamations in a career before he ever left New York. But this was beyond Darryl. Beyond anything I'd figured to accomplish that day by taking on the most disagreeable Met of them all.

It was September 16, and actually Shea Stadium was the last place I wanted to be.

Bad enough that New York had long since stopped paying attention to the Mets by then, but it was the first day back from a twelve-game road trip. Usually that means an automatic day off or two for a beat writer—long enough to get your bearings and reintroduce yourself to your wife and kids while someone else filled in. I needed a couple of days off later in the week, however, so there I was, cursing the traffic, the Mets, and the newspaper business while bumping along on the Triborough Bridge. In other words, I was in the perfect frame of mind to deal with Coleman by the time I reached Shea.

The idea of confronting Coleman was born of desperation. As had been the case since the Mets had fallen completely out of the pennant race, I needed a story not only for the early edition of the *Post,* to be written before the game even began, but something worthy of a full run. Game stories had become little more than a few paragraphs unless someone hit for the cycle or took a no-hitter into the ninth inning. So the search was on every day for a story that somehow

Torborg, in full profanity himself, told Coleman he was sick of his attitude and not about to allow any player to show that kind of disrespect on the field.

Back and forth it went for a couple of minutes, with Torborg finally telling Coleman he was suspended, turning, and stalking out of the room. Harazin announced the two-game suspension to the media after the game. Torborg, the veins in

---

ttered. Only by now, nothing mattered. e '92 Mets had bored us when the games carry meaning, and now they were put- g a Triple-A lineup on the field every night ile Bobby Bonilla and Dave Magadan and ward Johnson and the rest recovered m injuries. After twelve days on the road, dn't have a single idea.

A phone call from a radio station in St. uis earlier that day made me think of leman, however. While grilling me on the ets for ten minutes, the guy asked about quote he said he'd thought he'd seen or ard from Coleman saying he expected to traded in the wake of his two-game sus- nsion two weeks earlier.

I didn't think much of it right away. It was secret the Mets would try to trade Cole- n after two years of injuries and ill tem- r, but the remaining $5 million he was ed over two years was likely to preclude y such deal. In any case, I debated the a of going to Coleman in the locker room. a journalistic sense, it was like asking to ck Lawrence Taylor in his prime—Cole- n could be that abrasive. It was never sy, and Coleman was especially bitter w about being written out of town by the ys on the beat.

Was it worth the effort? No, I decided. Then I reached the clubhouse, looked around the room at the stories that weren't, and said, What the hell. Coleman looked surprised when I sat down next to him at his locker. He gave me the famous Coleman scowl, but I pretended not to notice. None of the Mets' media had spoken to him since a brief group interview the day he rejoined the team after his suspension, and little did I know he'd decided he wasn't talking to the press.

I asked about the quote the radio guy had mentioned, figuring it was a way to break the ice. Coleman looked suspicious.

"I ain't talked to nobody," he said, turning back to the fan mail he was sorting through.

Uh-oh. Well, I couldn't just walk away, not now. So I asked if he did think he was going to be traded, and that struck a nerve. Coleman lashed out, saying he'd read the stories I'd written speculating about a possible trade. He wasn't as mad about the suggestion of a deal as he was that I'd quoted a couple of scouts anonymously saying that they wondered if Coleman's two years of hamstring injuries had permanently affected his speed and quickness.

•

his neck still bulging, said, "I can't have a player question my authority like that." Coleman, hardly conciliatory, just shrugged when asked if he and Torborg could coexist after the suspension. "It's not like I've gotta sleep with him," Coleman said matter-of-factly.

They did coexist the rest of the season, reaching a cool truce in a two-minute meeting in Torborg's office when

---

WHICH WAY TO COOPERSTOWN?

(continued)

We went back and forth for a few minutes in heated debate about the merit and accuracy of the quotes as well as Coleman's treatment in general by the press. I'd been through this wringer before, and usually if you could ride out Coleman's first wave of anger, he'd talk. Only he seemed to sense my strategy.

"You fuckin' guys are unbelievable," he said. "You write all kinds of shit about me, then you come over expecting me to open up to you."

We'd reached a crossroads. I was about to give up when Jay Horwitz came to the rescue. Coleman apparently had asked him to dig up something to verify his career as a punter at Florida A&M so that he could prove it to Daryl Boston, and at that moment Horwitz brought over an old newspaper clipping detailing Coleman's skill as a college punter. This interrupted our interview, allowed Coleman to verbally abuse Boston a couple of lockers down for doubting him, and brightened his day.

Sensing an opportunity—and having no shame—I asked to see the article and then peppered Coleman with a series of questions about his football experience. By the time we got back to baseball, Coleman was willing to talk. Down deep he'd wanted the chance to express his regret for his confrontation with Torborg, and he launched into what was basically an apology. He said he'd done a lot of thinking, realized he'd let his frustrations over his injuries get to him, and vowed to change.

"I don't want to have to leave this game at some point because people think I'm a bad guy," he said.

At this point, I had a decent story, Coleman talking for the first time about the suspension and all that. *Mission accomplished,* I remember thinking. One day closer to the end of this misery with the '92 Mets. But then Coleman kept talking. Suddenly we were talking about his two years of hamstring injuries and Coleman was admitting he was a much more dangerous player on turf. He blamed what he called a "soft sandy-beach infield" at Shea for his hamstring problems, and then, referring to two years of lost stolen-base figures, he dropped his Hall of Fame bomb.

I can't even be sure what he said next. Alarms were going off in my head. I could

---

•

he returned after the suspension. Mets broadcaster Tim McCarver observes, "The incident on the field with Jeff Torborg was one of the most disgraceful things I've ever seen. He showed about as little respect for a manager as anyone ever could, and he never apologized. If you publicly show up a guy like that, there ought to be a public apology." But Coleman just didn't seem to get it. It was only a week or so later that he

---

ualize the back page, the ridicule Coleman would endure. He was dead serious— re was no doubt about that. He didn't en pause to reflect on what he'd said, but pt rambling on about the soft dirt and sto- bases it had cost him. He even went so as to say that Frank Cashen had torn up infield to make it softer in 1991 after egg Jefferies complained that it was too rd. I just kept looking down at my note- ok, writing as fast as Coleman spoke. I cided that there was no sense theorizing out how absurd the notion was of him, a 2 lifetime hitter whose only major league ll was his speed, someday reaching the ll of Fame. It would only start another ar- ment and end the interview.

Finally, it did end when Bobby Bonilla ke in to kid Coleman, "Hey, you're talk- to the press?" As they exchanged bs, *St. Louis Post-Dispatch* writer Rick mmel came by to talk to Coleman, and I used myself. Somehow Coleman got und to dropping the same Hall of Fame on Hummel, who was equally stunned. anwhile, I hurried upstairs to call the of- , knowing they would want to blow it up the back page. It was tabloid heaven. But v would I write it? I decided I would only

lessen the impact by poking fun at Coleman and, besides, I felt I owed it to him to write the story straight since he'd actually spoken with good intentions.

The reaction was predictable. PAIN IN THE GRASS, the back-page headline read, with the Hall of Fame quote running over a picture of Coleman. Columnists ridiculed Coleman. Even broadcaster Tim McCarver chastised him publicly for the absolute selfishness of it.

I braced for some reaction. Players are quick to claim they've been misquoted or taken out of context when their remarks cause an uproar. But Coleman never said a word to me about the story, never complained to Jay Horwitz. When teammates needled him about it, he laughed and said, "I'm just the whipping boy around here."

For the rest of the season you couldn't watch a TV highlight of Coleman without hearing a voice saying, "and future Hall of Famer Vince Coleman . . ." but an anonymous GM, speaking to Rick Hummel about the story, put it in the best perspective. Noting that you have to be inactive for five years to be eligible for the Hall, the GM said, "Vince only has three more to go."

•

and Daryl Boston began rolling dice in the clubhouse before games for money, twenty-dollar bills strewn on the floor right there by their lockers, in full view of the writers milling about. Such blatant gambling was not only illegal but also forbidden by the same league rules that had applied to Pete Rose.

Coleman didn't seem to know or care. "Come on, six," he shouted, needing to roll a six to win the pot. "C-I-X, six," he howled as he rolled the dice. Writers looked at one another, wondering if their ears had just told a lie. The spelling had to be Coleman's idea of a joke: After all, he did have a phys-ed degree from Florida A&M.

In any case, the craps games went on for a couple of days. One day a couple of other players, including Howard Johnson—who, for all his born-again devotion, still tried to be one of the boys, at least in harmless ways—joined in. This time it caught the attention of hitting instructor Tom McCraw, a wrinkled, wise, well-respected coach, who practically dived into the huddle of players to break up the game. "You guys ought to know better," McCraw said, shaking his head.

SEPTEMBER 14. MONTREAL. EXPOS 7, METS 5.

A HOME RUN MAKES a special sound, one that's different from that of a ground ball or a single, or even the line-drive double. When a baseball hits the bat's sweet spot—approximately three inches from the top of the barrel—it sounds loud and true. Sometimes all you have to do is listen for the contact to know if a ball is on its way over the fence. That's precisely the terror that filled Anthony Young in the ninth inning, hearing what Larry Walker had just done to his best fastball.

The noise Walker's bat made filled up Olympic Stadium as he crushed a two-out, three-run homer off Young, giving the upstart Expos a dramatic, come-from-behind 7–5 win and completing Montreal's three-game sweep of the Mets. Even in the final month of the already-dead season, such a ninth-inning

•

failure crushed the Mets. As Dwight Gooden was to say later, "No matter if you're fifty games out, a game like this can still break your heart." But that wasn't the end of the Mets' crisis. Inside the clubhouse, rookie Jeff Kent decided he would stand up to teammates who'd played a practical joke on him.

Before the game, they'd removed his clothes, filling his locker with an outrageous purple-and-pink pimp's outfit. This was a time-honored hazing ritual, reserved for rookies and newcomers. The Mets had pulled a similar prank on Ryan Thompson the week before in Philadelphia, and Thompson, quickly winning acceptance among the inner-circle Mets, went along with the gag. The kid wore the clothes on the Mets' bus ride to the airport and onto the charter flight to Montreal.

But Kent? He stood in the middle of the clubhouse as the Mets showered and dressed, the sound of Walker's home run still reverberating in their ears, and announced, "Whoever took my clothes, I want them back." In the two weeks since arriving from the Blue Jays, Kent had already established himself as aloof, even bordering on hostile. A reporter who had casually dropped by Kent's locker one day to make small talk noted that he was from Huntington Beach, California, Kevin Elster's hometown.

Kent's face stiffened immediately. "Wrong," he said. "Kevin Elster is from my hometown." Kent: the Met with an attitude. Gerry Hunsicker made it a habit of speaking glowingly about Kent and Thompson, doing his best to cool the still-hot controversy of the Dave Cone trade. But Hunsicker could've never explained away Kent's behavior now, ready to take on his teammates over a practical joke. Even Gregg Jefferies had swallowed the embarrassment back in 1989, wearing enormous green clogs that he then kept as a souvenir. But Kent was so adamant about getting his clothes back, so intent on waiting out the prank, that traveling secretary Bob O'Hara foresaw a more serious crisis. If the Mets delayed getting out of Olympic Stadium, they'd arrive at Montreal's Dorval Airport too late for their charter flight to Chicago. O'Hara took matters into his own hands, hurrying into Jeff Torborg's office and telling the manager, "We've got a problem. They've got Kent's clothes and won't give them back."

Torborg understood the ramifications of rescuing Kent in public; more than once, the manager had been reminded what Davey Johnson's coddling did to Gregg Jefferies's standing in the clubhouse. But Torborg decided it was more important not to be stranded at the airport overnight. Besides, how much worse could it have gotten for Kent, who'd made it clear he wanted no part of the Mets' clubhouse alliance? So Torborg marched into the locker room and shouted, "Give the kid his fuckin' clothes back. It's been a horseshit year, so let's get the fuck out of here."

Just as these profanities left Torborg's lips, the press corps was walking into the clubhouse. The manager was unaware he was being observed, and the beat guys got a true glimpse of Torborg, the baseball man, and not the master of spin control. It was a respectable sight, actually: real anger all over the manager's face, his voice raised, speaking the language athletes understand best. When he did turn around, Torborg saw the seven stunned reporters, but said nothing as he returned to his office. In Torborg's wake the clubhouse had fallen into an embarrassed silence. Kent got his clothes back, having won his small victory. But at what price?

Teammates harassed him throughout the entire bus ride to the airport, on the plane ride from Montreal to Chicago, and all the way to the Westin Hotel in downtown Chicago. "We kept calling him Clark Kent. 'Hey, Clark, where're your clothes?' " one veteran said. "We knew it was making him mad, but who the fuck cared? What he did was weak." Indeed, Kent chose an odd time to make a statement, considering he'd have to live with these same players in 1993 and possibly beyond. The Mets' front office had every intention of handing Kent the keys to second base, which meant he was on his way to replacing Gregg Jefferies as the clubhouse bad boy.

Even Jefferies was mystified by Kent's behavior. Reached

•

in Baltimore, where the Royals were finishing up their own sorry season, Jefferies said, "Wow, I never did that. It's a joke, everyone knows it a joke. It happens to every rookie. You wear the clothes and get it over with. The veterans are watching to see how you react and what you do. If I had any advice, I'd tell Kent to hang in there. But I can't imagine he'll get much support in the clubhouse now."

Traditionally, clubhouse humor can be vicious and crude, so in that sense nothing the Mets did to Kent was out of the ordinary. Actually, they thought they were extending the rookie a welcome mat, but Kent didn't care, not one bit. Even after a full twenty-four hours' meditation on the incident, Kent was still defiant. His first words to reporters were "I will not be taken advantage of," and he further insisted, "I'd gone through this whole thing earlier in the year in Toronto, but these guys wanted to go overboard. I stood up for myself, so maybe these guys will know next time 'we can only go so far with Kent.' I don't mess with them, they don't mess with me."

As badly as Kent overreacted, it was possible to understand his rebellion. After all, he'd just been scooped up and removed from a team that would go on to win the World Series. That alone would cost Kent over $100,000 in postseason revenue. Now he was surrounded by the National League's most notorious underachievers, blowing games in a steady, careless stream. So Kent withdrew deeper and deeper into his private world. Question was, had the Mets inherited a social misfit from the Blue Jays? One member of the Toronto organization, informed of the incident with the Mets, said, "Kent was oblivious about how to get along with teammates, and was alone most of the time. He was the same way with umpires: Even in the first month of the [1991] season [at Double A], he was getting thrown out of games." Incredibly, the Mets seemed to be unaware of Kent's strident nature, or at least glossed it over. "We got ourselves a real red-ass player," VP Gerry Hunsicker said with some pride, employing baseball slang for a no-nonsense, man's man tough guy.

•

But if Kent's red-ass nature meant being hostile to teammates, too . . . well, after a while, the Mets just shrugged and turned their attention elsewhere. Kent slapped on the headphones and spent a full hour at his locker before the game with the Cubs, not speaking to and not visited by anyone. He just listened to his music, alone.

SEPTEMBER 23. ST. LOUIS. METS 3, CARDINALS 2.

THERE WERE NO more than sixteen thousand fans in the stands at Busch Stadium, a desertion of the Cardinals just as severe as that which the Mets had suffered at Shea. This was supposed to be a breakthrough season for Joe Torre and his young Cards team, except they were chewed up and devoured by the Pirates in early September and were now just looking for a fast exit to the off-season. Just like the Mets.

Maybe that's why no one in the ballpark paid much attention in the ninth inning, when Dwight Gooden and Tracy Woodson went one-on-one, both treating the at-bat like it was their own little World Series. There was virtually nothing at stake for the two men. Gooden, especially: He was only 8-13 at the time, no chance of a winning season, no chance of even reaching .500. Yet when the Cardinals had a runner on first base in the ninth inning, Woodson standing at the plate as a pinch hitter, the Mets bullpen suddenly busy, Gooden stood firm.

It was as if an entire season's frustration had been channeled into that one at-bat. There'd been the Florida rape case, the shoulder that took forever to recover, a close call with rotator-cuff inflammation that—even though it wasn't serious—landed Gooden back on the DL. And then there was the season itself, which embarrassed Gooden more than anyone in the clubhouse. One day earlier in September, Gooden had pulled Torborg aside and asked if there was any point in continuing to pitch that season. Doc wondered out loud to his manager: If the shoulder has finally gained back its strength, why

•

keep taking the mound every fifth day? Why not get an early start on an off-season rehab program that would seal off any possibility of reinjury? Gooden was only half serious—and Torborg managed to convince him that the Mets still needed him, even twenty games behind—but the mere thought of Doc sitting out the last two weeks was one more indictment of a bad year.

Certainly, it would've been even worse for the Mets had Gooden not finally found his fastball in September. His recovery conformed to most of the doctors' timetables, which had predicted that it would be approximately a full year after rotator-cuff surgery before he could be expected to throw the high-octane fastball again. Until that point, both Gooden's heater and his usually cheerful exterior had suffered in the aftermath of the Florida rape investigation. He admitted, "It took a couple of months before I was even comfortable around people this year. I mean, I couldn't go out to restaurants without feeling they were looking at me funny."

Yet the crowds at Shea and around the entire National League accepted Gooden as if nothing had happened in Florida. The public seemed overwhelmed by the charges and potential legal ramifications. It was almost too much to digest, the idea of Gooden as a rapist. When the Port St. Lucie police let the case go, fans seemed relieved, almost grateful they wouldn't have to think about it anymore. The equation became simple enough again: When Doc pitched well, he was cheered. When he didn't, he was still cheered. His image remained intact—that of a once-in-a-generation pitcher who, for some reason, still had a hold over New York.

Maybe it was that rookie year, or the magic from that right arm a season later in 1985. Perhaps it was that Doc was the only tangible memory New Yorkers had from the '86 Mets. Howard Johnson had been there, true, but his tenure in New York had been pockmarked with ups and downs and his '92 season had evaporated altogether in a mysterious slump, followed by surgery. And of course Sid Fernandez had played on

•

that mythic team, but as Fernandez finally matured, lost weight, and controlled his temper tantrums, he receded from the public's consciousness. He was no longer eccentric. Sid became normal and, ultimately, boring.

It was Doc who made New York hunger for the golden era at Shea, and it was Doc who suffered right along with the fans. In a private moment that day in St. Louis, Gooden confessed he wouldn't be leaving his Long Island home during the upcoming off-day, just because "I can't face people with the kind of season we're having. At this point, I'm honestly embarrassed to even go shopping or anything." It must've been the same way for the Mets in 1974 and 1975, or the Yankees in 1965. Still, there were irresistible moments, like that one-on-one with Woodson. For one fleeting instant, Doc was the Doctor again, throwing a fastball so mean the best Woodson could do was a comfortable ground ball. Gooden worked free from any further trouble in the inning, and the victory—as empty as it was— belonged to the Mets.

Later, Jeff Torborg said, "The game was Doc's all the way"—meaning Paul Gibson and Lee Guetterman had no chance to intrude on Doc's moment. Gooden nodded appreciatively, and said, "I think the Mets can count on me next year." But the question remained: After two thousand innings, scandal, and surgery, were the Mets asking too much of Doc Gooden?

SEPTEMBER 24. ST. LOUIS. CARDINALS 4, METS 3.

T HE PREGAME Q&A in the manager's office offered nothing in terms of news. With less than two weeks to go in the season, what was left for Jeff Torborg to say? The beat guys would've gladly preempted these meaningless fifteen-minute sessions, except that protocol still dictated at least a cursory visit, and Jay Horwitz was still frantic about having Torborg appear active.

"You gonna need Jeff today?" Horwitz would ask, half-

·

nodding, hoping you'd go along. For some reason, Horwitz thought it'd reflect poorly on him if the media decided there was no point in speaking to Torborg—the last thing the PR man needed was a reverse boycott, the press freezing out the Mets—so out of respect to Jay, the *News*, the *Post*, the *Times*, *Newsday*, and the suburban papers would march sullenly into Torborg's office. Most days, there'd be polite back-and-forth, both Torborg and the reporters knowing it was all so false and pointless. In fact, Torborg had changed considerably as the Mets' season evaporated. He'd dropped his confrontational style, choosing to engage the beat guys in small talk whenever possible. Torborg made eye contact with every reporter who asked a question—even Sexton!—and found time for private interviews, cooperating as fully as possible, understanding there was no winning the war with the papers, at least not in 1992. Torborg even left himself open to being pried for exclusives, and on this day, he made a revealing proclamation: There would be no more afternoon radio spot on WFAN with Mike Francesa and Chris Russo.

Citing time constraints, the manager said he found it increasingly difficult to fulfill his obligations to the station. "I felt like I had to structure my whole day around that three P.M. phone call," Torborg said. That explanation made some sense, but Torborg had also taken more heat than he ever expected over his self-created leaks—like the John Franco bad-elbow disclosure in June—and that had to have contributed to his decision. Torborg himself admitted, "If you talk long enough, you're bound to say something you shouldn't."

For months it astounded veteran reporters how a manager could become so dependent on his own radio show. What was so important about going on air before and after every game? What was the point? How much baseball was there to discuss? Even more puzzling was Torborg's need to appear live, during the middle of the afternoon, still talking about the previous night's game as if the entire city continued to relive it. Maybe it would've made for great radio in September, in the middle of

•

a pennant race. But to hear Torborg drone on, day after day, in July . . . well, even a man who prided himself on speaking without saying anything controversial was running out of fuel.

Finally, it seemed Torborg accepted the New York sports media for the beast that it was: tough, unmanageable, sometimes too loud, sometimes brilliant, but always there. Was Torborg finally ready to move gently with the tide, as Davey Johnson had done so successfully in the eighties? Not entirely: Torborg smiled and said he intended to keep his *postgame* spot on WFAN in 1993.

•

OCTOBER

OCTOBER 4. NEW YORK. PIRATES 2, METS 0.

THE TORTURE, FINALLY, was over. September had felt as if it would last indefinitely. Was there more absolute proof than the '92 Mets that grotesque salaries were ruining baseball in every way—from fans' lack of interest to player indifference? The Mets had begun the year flaunting the highest payroll in baseball and ended it by making major cuts in their minor league development staff, letting at least one coach go at every level of their farm system. It was a sad moment for a franchise that, in the eighties, had taken such pride in rebuilding through its scouting and development. But someone had to pay for the Mets' failures and another fifth-place finish. Attendance had been extraordinarily light in September. The season total came to only 1.7 million, the lowest since 1983 and down by more than 1 million since 1990, the last year Darryl Strawberry played in New York.

Players and writers both had been counting the days, as if September were its own jail term. "Nothing matters, and what if it did," one writer said, stealing from John Mellencamp, as he stood around in the clubhouse, waiting for a story to appear. It was so bad that September's best moment came from *Daily News* sports editor Kevin Whitmer, who headlined a back page of Bobby Bonilla—cartooned in diapers—BABY BO. More than ever, New York wanted the Mets out of its face.

After all, baseball is a dreadful exercise both to play and to watch when it means nothing. All the nuances, the subtleties

•

of strategy and execution that give the game its flavor in a pennant race become irrelevant. Pickoff moves, pitching changes, even pinch hitters seem like so much nonsense designed to turn fans into ballpark hostages. This is especially true in the nineties, when TV-conscious managers and players, as well as television itself, have conspired to make every game a three-hour affair. Managers feel compelled to justify their own growing six-figure salaries and run a game like Tony LaRussa, the patron saint of computer managers.

Torborg was a typical disciple: He overmanaged the Mets from the start, pinch-hitting, pinch-running, double-switching at every opportunity, even, silly as it seemed, in September. Once, when he used three journeyman relievers—Paul Gibson, Jeff Innis, and Lee Guetterman—in the same inning to pitch to a total of five batters, Ed Christine stood up in the press box and yelled at the top of his lungs, "Just let 'em play the fuckin' game, will ya?"

Torborg couldn't hear him, of course, but Christine wouldn't have cared if he did. What was the manager trying to prove, anyway? If anything, the Mets' plight gave Torborg an opportunity now to sit back and evaluate players in every situation, show confidence in them and see what developed. Uh-uh: LaRussa wouldn't do it that way, so Torborg kept making the computer substitutions and kept telling the press how much his team was battling. There was the night Daryl Boston homered and singled in his first two at-bats, only to be pulled for Dave Gallagher—hitting .212 at the time—in the fifth inning because a left-hander was now pitching. This, with the Mets leading by a run in a game against the Cardinals that couldn't have mattered less if it were in March.

Maybe Torborg was still trying to prove he was a victim of circumstance. By now the Mets' hierarchy was hard-selling the injury angle, trying to make the fans believe the lousy baseball they'd watched all summer had been the product of fate and the disabled list. In the daily game notes distributed to the press, a half-page was devoted to the injuries and the fact

•

that the Mets had put more players on the DL in 1992 than any other year in their history. The injuries had indeed gotten out of hand in August and September, but, in truth, the Mets were at least as healthy as, if not healthier than, most of the other teams during the bulk of the season.

No, injuries weren't the cause of the Mets' collapse. They were simply the most feeble offensive team in baseball. They couldn't hit, finishing last in the majors with a .233 batting average, and they couldn't run. Indeed, management badly miscalculated the effect the team's lack of speed and quickness would have. Speed? For much of the year the Mets had threatened to set a major league record for fewest triples in a season; as it was, their total of seventeen was easily the lowest in the NL, thirty shy of the Pirates' league-leading total. Quickness? The absence of young legs was most noticeable on turf: The Mets won only eighteen of fifty-seven games played on turf in '92, and often looked to be moving in slow motion—particularly defensively—compared to their opponents.

What the front office failed to realize, in all the dollars it threw at the Mets, was that they'd assembled an inferior team. More than $44 million couldn't change the Mets' one-dimensional approach to hitting—crush a home run, every time, every swing—and couldn't alter the fact that the Mets simply weren't tough. They rarely made late-inning comebacks, going down quietly time after time. They waited and waited for the dramatic three-run, ninth-inning home run, and when they realized no one was there to hit them, the Mets dried up and died.

No, all the money couldn't bring back the kind of soul that had once made the Mets champions. This team didn't have the personality to thrive in New York, face the press, withstand the booing. If anything, the millionaire Mets became obsessed with their clippings, making them defensive, at times even paranoid. But Harazin, with new budget constrictions and a bunch of players who were virtually untradable because of their salaries, had to talk the talk.

•

Oh, the spin control was slick. Close your eyes, and you could almost drift away with the words. "If not for all the injuries . . . Nobody could have predicted Howard's year . . . It could've been different . . ." Already Harazin was looking ahead, trying to lay the PR groundwork for '93. Meanwhile, no matter how Torborg managed, the Mets kept playing awful baseball, right to the humiliating end. Once again, the Mets couldn't win a single game in a three-game series in Pittsburgh and were forced to swallow the sight of the Pirates clinching the division title against them.

The Mets were no longer capable of feeling pain, but it seemed Torborg had finally gone numb, too. He had taken the Pirates' clinching against his Mets with surprising calm, almost indifference. He conducted his postgame interview standing over the sink in his office bathroom, shaving, his back to reporters. When someone asked how it felt to see the Pirates take what the Mets, many months earlier, thought would be theirs, all you heard was the sound of running water, a razor occasionally tapping against the tile, and then finally "Yeah, it hurts."

Then the stigma of last place had suddenly loomed in the final week of the season. The Phillies had beaten the Mets two straight at Shea to inch to within a single game of fifth place and set up a last-place showdown on September 30, only to make five errors in the game and spare the Mets the ultimate indignity of finishing at the bottom of the East's cesspool.

Now, before the game on this final day of the season, Torborg ran a hand through his hair one last time and admitted that this had been the worst season he'd ever spent in baseball. In the clubhouse players laughed easily and talked of their vacation plans, the burden of the season finally lifted. Upstairs, Harazin looked out over the field from the press level and again proclaimed that it'd be a quiet winter. No major changes, he insisted, knowing it was unlikely that he'd be able to find a new home for Coleman.

Harazin was determined to prove 1992 had been a fluke,

•

a freak, determined to assemble most of the same millionaires in 1993 and show the world the Mets could get it right. Then he went to his private box and watched his ball club lose one final time, with the same blend of ground balls to short and routine fly balls to center that had poisoned the offense all summer. It was the ninetieth loss of the season, a number that left the franchise with no place to hide. It was, as Dave Magadan said, that "the front office spent so much time trying to put together the right kind of clubhouse, they seemed to forget what they were putting on the field."

The glory of the eighties never seemed so distant. Doc Gooden, one of the four Mets remaining who had '86 World Series rings, was still six weeks shy of turning twenty-eight, but he said he felt much older as he shook hands with reporters on this final day. He looked older, too.

It hadn't been so long ago that Gooden's youth, as well as that of Strawberry, Fernandez, HoJo, Cone, Magadan, Dykstra, and the others seemed to promise—even ensure—greatness for the Mets right to the turn of the century. Now, said Gooden, "those days seem like a lifetime ago." What a long, strange trip it'd been. Gooden stood in the locker room, reflecting for a moment. Then he walked out the door, into the off-season, shaking his head.

FIVE WORST METS MEMORIES OF THE EIGHTIES

1. Mike Scioscia's home run in Game Four of the '88 NLCS.
2. Dwight Gooden testing positive for drug use in 1987.
3. Darryl and Keith throwing punches at Picture Day in spring training, 1989.
4. George Foster accusing the Mets of racism in 1986.
5. Bob Ojeda's nearly severed finger in 1988, which probably cost the Mets a World Series appearance.

EPILOGUE

True to his word, Al Harazin hibernated during the winter of 1992–93. Or at least it seemed that way. He made none of the bold moves of the previous year, watching instead as the Yankees dominated the headlines by chasing free agents, making the big trades. Ironically enough, reducing the payroll became a priority for the Mets, the team that had tried to buy its way back into contention a year earlier.

The only major change was the October trade with San Diego that brought All-Star shortstop Tony Fernandez to New York in exchange for right-hander Wally Whitehurst and outfield prospect D. J. Dozier. The deal amounted to a gift from Joe McIlvaine, the former Met executive, who, as GM of the Padres, had been ordered to drastically slash his own payroll.

The Mets, having dumped big money in the David Cone trade, were only too happy to take Fernandez's $2 million salary off McIlvaine's hands. That and the $1.5 million they handed over—out of desperation for a decent number five starter—to thirty-nine-year-old left-hander Frank Tanana represented the two significant additions made for '93.

Otherwise, the Mets, like most teams in baseball, spent the winter tightening their belt, cutting costs wherever possible, widening the considerable gap in salaries between the superstars and the masses. In doing so the Mets set free virtually all veterans who weren't already signed to multiyear contracts: They declined to offer arbitration to potential free agents Wil-

•

lie Randolph, Kevin Bass, Dave Magadan, Daryl Boston, and Lee Guetterman. Then, rather than offer veterans bound to the club the minimum 80 percent of their '92 salaries, as stipulated by baseball's bargaining agreement, the Mets chose not to tender contracts to Kevin Elster, Mackey Sasser, Paul Gibson, and Bill Pecota.

In dismissing nightlifers Boston, Elster, and Sasser, management further cleansed the clubhouse of the spirit of the eighties. As if to make it official, Davey Johnson finally found a baseball job, hired by the Cincinnati Reds as an adviser to GM Jim Bowden. And by January Magadan, Boston, Bass, Sasser, and Pecota had all received guaranteed deals with other clubs, while Elster signed a minor league contract with the Dodgers, earning the chance to prove his shoulder is sound again.

The Mets, meanwhile, will fill their bench more cheaply in '93 with a no-name cast, players like Darren Reed, Jeff McKnight, Tim Bogar, Chico Walker, Dave Gallagher, and free-agent pickup Joe Orsulak. But as different as they will be on the fringes, the '93 Mets will remain constant in their nucleus: As expected, the club found no takers for Vince Coleman, so he's back for a chance at redemption, along with HoJo (at third base again), Bonilla, Murray, Hundley, Gooden, Saberhagen, El Sid, Schourek, Young, and Franco.

Harazin obviously is praying that history can't repeat itself in the form of ninety losses. Is he kidding himself? Comeback years by HoJo, Saberhagen, and Gooden would give the Mets a chance in a weak NL East, but much could depend on the wild cards in the deck, Ryan Thompson and Jeff Kent, the two players acquired for Cone. Both are being counted on as everyday players, and their performance could go a long way in determining both the direction of the Mets in the nineties and the legacy of Harazin's reign.

Was trading Cone one last management blunder in the collapse of the Mets? Or was it the start of another run toward the top? Harazin, who'd said he traded Cone because he

•

thought it would take a five-year contract to sign him, didn't flinch when the right-hander wound up signing a three-year, $18 million deal to return to his native Kansas City.

"I'd still make that trade," Harazin said. "We'll rise or fall with those kids we got. I love that deal."

Of course, the Mets once felt as strongly about acquiring Juan Samuel.

Play ball.

·

ABOUT THE AUTHORS

JOHN HARPER, thirty-seven, recently joined the New York *Daily News*. He covered the Mets from 1988 to 1992 for the *New York Post*, and before that wrote about them as a columnist for the *Morristown* (N.J.) *Daily Record*. He graduated from the University of Bridgeport, where, as a second baseman, he turned more than a few double plays, and he still has the scars to prove it. Harper lives in Cedar Knolls, New Jersey, with his wife, Liz, and their sons, Matt and Christopher.

BOB KLAPISCH, thirty-five, has covered the Mets since 1983 for the *New York Post* and the *Daily News*. He graduated from Columbia University, where, as a varsity pitcher, he once struck out a skinny Yale shortstop named Ron Darling. Klapisch lives in Teaneck, New Jersey, with his wife, Stephanie.